*In*human Rights

*In*human Rights

The Western System and Global Human Rights Abuse

By Winin Pereira

The Other India Press,
Mapusa, Goa, India

The Apex Press,
New York, USA

Third World Network,
Penang, Malaysia

Inhuman Rights: The Western System and Global Human Rights Abuse
By Winin Pereira

First published (1997) by:

The Other India Press
Above Mapusa Clinic,
Mapusa 403 507 Goa, India
Telephone/Fax: 91-832-263305
E-mail: oibs@bom2.vsnl.net.in

in association with:

The Apex Press
Suite 3C, 777 United Nations Plaza,
New York, NY 10017
Telephone/Fax: 800-316-APEX
E-mail: cipany@igc.apc.org

and:

Third World Network,
228 Jalan Macalister,
102500 Penang, Malaysia
E-mail: twn@igc.apc.org

OIP policy regarding environmental compensation:

5% of the list price of this book will be made available
by the Other India Press to meet the costs of raising natural forests
on private and community lands in order to compensate
for the use of tree pulp in paper production.

Distributed in India by:

The Other India Bookstore
Mapusa 403 507 Goa, India.
Telephone: 91-832-263306
Fax: 91-832-263305

India ISBN No: 81-85569-33-9
USA ISBN No: 0-945257-79-1

Printed by Sujit Patwardhan for the Other India Press
at MUDRA, 383, Narayan, Pune 411 030 India.

Publisher's Preface

Many of us will recall that when we were young—even in a city like Bombay (name now changed to "Mumbai")—we avidly read comic books that narrated stories of cowboys and "Red Indians". One piece of education that must have stuck in many people's minds was the repeated observation of several Indian Chiefs in those comics that "the white man speaks with forked tongue."

As the rest of the non-Western world has also now discovered to its discomfiture, that experience has not been limited to Amerindians alone.

The West, as Winin Pereira shows in this book, has indisputably been the greatest abuser of the rights of people everywhere—witness the record of the past 500 years. It continues its relentless assault on the rights of others with even greater determination today through interventionist actions of its powerful financial institutions, war machines, wars, invasions, and a development programme that is threatening to wreck the very fabric of nature and human community across the planet.

Despite this awesome, documented, undisputed, wholly banal record, the West continues to proclaim its championship of human rights, often against the projected and well advertised and allegedly miserable human rights records of Muslim countries, Asians, Chinese, Iranians, Libyans: the list of proclaimed offenders is seemingly endless.

The impression we have of the West's human rights discourse is not just of one forked tongue, but—if one can stretch the imagery—two faces and perhaps six forked tongues. This scenario needs to be roundly exposed. *Inhuman Rights* does just this and does it well. For reasons the author himself briefly explains in the book, it refuses to go further than that.

The normal expectations we have of writers is a detailed analysis of a problem, discussion of remedies, and some options including a possible agenda. Pereira does indicate possible directions and alternatives but does not attempt to present a new "universal" declaration since (he argues) this would be contrary to the establishment of universal justice. There are other compelling reasons as well.

The present human rights debate, the nature of the human rights discourse—the vocabulary used, the categories of thinking relied upon, the legal instruments in force—all these remain dominated and contaminated by the West, by its overt and covert political and economic interests.

The UN Declaration itself, as Pereira shows in this book, is an instrument that enables the West actually to overwhelm the rights of others. There is therefore nothing really "universal" about it. It remains a document that reflects the West, its ethnic concerns, its thinking, its interests. Such thinking may not necessarily be the thinking of intelligent people everywhere. There is no way therefore that the present discourse on human rights can be improved: the entire edifice may have to be sacrificed, beginning with the Universal Declaration on Human Rights itself. The relevant question to ask is whether this Declaration should not now be abrogated—because of its continued complicity in human rights abuse worldwide—in the fiftieth year of its ratification.

This may seem to many an audacious proposal. However, many huge and seemingly gargantuan structures have indeed collapsed without warning in our time and age. We are also witness to the decline and fall of several fake universals. The most outstanding of the latter was the possibility and promise of a universal culture binding diverse peoples in a common unity across the planet.

The intellectuals of several non-Western societies are today convinced that the universal culture proposed during the past fifty years was nothing more than an elaborate westernisation proposal. No compelling reason has been advanced even today which might convince us why the West's ethnic culture—and its thinking on human rights—should become the accepted value of every other culture on the planet. If anything, there are several compelling reasons to argue the reverse: to argue for limiting Western culture entirely in terms of time and space due to several of its features that seem wholly backward. The values that the West propagates today are not merely not universal, they are perverse.

In addition, they are destructive of much that civilisations have held as valid, important and non-negotiable for centuries.

Because of the discovery that the West is in essence a fake universal, there has now developed a vacuum and a search for alternatives to the West-dominated human rights discourse. Such alternatives perhaps cannot be provided by thinkers from the West for it is their collective misfortune that they no longer have any direct experience of alternative conceptions or visions. Many of them in fact are permanently damaged victims of a distorted educational system that gave them the wholly unreal idea that other cultures do not have any human rights concerns at all.

Historically, most non-western cultures have shown a far better understanding of human rights than the West. They do so even today. People everywhere, in fact, have continued to uphold their inalienable rights to their own cosmologies, epistemologies, interpretations of culture *and rights* since they are convinced they contain a greater component of humanity.

China and Malaysia for example are insisting they have a conception of human rights that is different from that of the West. The West and its institutions—including the media—for their part have been insisting these Asian countries have no human rights feelings at all! These Asian proposals advocating different, equally valid, universals must now be seriously considered. Their philosophical underpinnings and legitimation must be examined. People have a *human* right to subscribe to, or uphold, universals that compete with those the West has sought to impose so arrogantly on others. What are these rival universals? Or can there be any universals at all? If scholarly work on these issues was not done for the past fifty years it was solely due to the assumption that the planet was moving towards a global culture with a uniformly valid and applicable system of values. We can now see how nations can be as naive as individuals.

We hope the publication of *Inhuman Rights* will enable scholars to examine these human rights issues with great seriousness, to work towards a perspective that provides new philosophical and conceptual solutions, and to fight as well to grant these adequate political space within the comity of nations.

Claude Alvares
Goa, July 22, 1997 For the Other India Press

Contents

Acknowledgements

I am deeply grateful to Barbara Panvel for her patience in editing the early versions of the manuscript as it developed and her valuable suggestions. Maggie Vicuna deserves special thanks for her invaluable insights, particularly on Women's Rights. Thanks are also due to my numerous friends who have contributed to the work, among them, Susan Dhavle, Lakshmi Menon, Abhay Mehta, and Mangesh Chavan.

I wish to record my heartfelt thanks to Jeremy Seabrook, mentor and kindred spirit. Above all I cannot thank enough, my friend and colleague, Subhash Sule, for his vital assistance, unflagging support and encouragement.

I am grateful to the publishers, Claude Alvares of the Other India Press (and Sam Rao who did the preliminary editing of the manuscript), Ward Morehouse of the Apex Press and Martin Khor, Director, Third World Network, for bringing out the work.

Finally, but not least, I am grateful to members of my family for their continuous encouragement and interest in my work. My sincere thanks to all of them.

Winin Pereira

Introduction

T he West* today triumphantly claims the moral high ground in the global protection of human rights, pointing accusing fingers at every major or even minor misdemeanors committed by other nations. Its overt concern for human rights has been displayed in the ardour with which it promoted the UN Universal Declaration of Human Rights (UN UDHR) and supports recurring UN conferences on the subject.

The very same societies of the West, however, that now so virtuously and vociferously proclaim the need to protect human rights have themselves been constructed on foundations of the most violent abuse of the rights of millions of others.

Though the rights of human beings have been violated from the earliest times by nearly all peoples, the Europeans have been particularly active in the globalisation of such abuse in the last five

---

*The term "West", it must be clearly understood, is not used in a limited geographical sense. In our global society a formidable, entrenched, well organised elite promotes or substantially benefits from installed, imposed Western political, economic, industrial and military systems. This bloc is referred to throughout the book as the "West". It includes the essential collaborators in the Two Thirds World who promote and willingly depend on the Western cultural system with its particular aims, objects and the means used to achieve them. Conspicuous are Western-oriented gentlemen (WOGs) dressed in the insignia of mental servitude: suits and ties, socks and shoes, worn in a tropical climate. Excluded from the term "West" are the powerless in all countries ruthlessly impoverished by these unholy alliances, those living in the geographical West who reject its values and practices and individuals working outside these systems who fight against such exploitation.

hundred years. During the conquest by force, occupation and colonising of most of the non-European globe—the Americas, Australia, India, Africa among other regions—millions of indigenous peoples were tortured, enslaved, starved and killed solely because they possessed lands and other resources that the Europeans coveted. Domination and exploitation could only be carried out by a drastic and extensive denial of the rights of the dominated and exploited, culminating in what is now called the Two Thirds World*. Such exploitation was essential for the launching of the Industrial Revolution which evolved into the system that provides the West's material wealth and power today.

In order to preserve its own credibility, therefore, the West needs to suppress this particular history: the processes which facilitated the construction of the savage and barbarous foundations upon which the enormous structures of affluence and power have been built. The economic growth stated to be essential for the well-being of Western economies and even for the mere maintenance of present levels of wealth, not surprisingly, requires that the Two Thirds World be continued in a state of subjugation. The customs and practices evolved by the West in the early post-Columbus years remain essentially unchanged today.

Proof of this is easily shown: cutting off the West from all its interconnections with the exploitable Two Thirds World would result in a drastic reduction of Western affluence. Hence the West's—almost megalomaniacal—need for the globalisation project, depicted as a sure cure for Two Thirds World poverty, even while it is designed to exploit the latter more extensively and intensively. The rights of an increasing number of people are being abused today in order to quench—if that is at all possible—the West's thirst for the Two Thirds World's resources and remaining meagre wealth. Its current record of human rights abuse—its continuous military, political, economic interventions in various parts of the globe—provokes serious questions about its probity.

Thus there arise dramatic disparities between the West's rhetoric and practice of human rights, its claims to be the champion of human rights and its sustained implementation of programmes that abuse the rights of millions.

---

*Two-Thirds World, from Winin Pereira and Jeremy Seabrook, *Asking the Earth*: "Two-thirds of humanity live in what is commonly misnamed the Third World."

Most attempts to reconcile this mass of contradictions and inconsistencies end in frustration and failure. The only assumption that seems to fit all the facts is that the items in the Western human rights portfolio are all *originally* designed and crafted to enable the West to profit from them.

Western policies regarding human rights are carefully planned and stage-managed hypocrisy. These policies—and the violations that result from them—are not the passing aberrations of a few immoral individuals but official directives, "legally" enacted and implemented over centuries.

The West cannot permit the complete extension of basic human rights to all the people of the world now living—as well as to those to come—since the maintenance, expansion and growth of its system depend upon the systematic denial of such rights. Western society distinguishes itself by its prodigious capacity to forcibly impose, in one way or another, its own distorted, pitiless and limited vision upon the rest of the world. Each of the West's programmes concerning the Two Thirds World can be seen to be dedicated to maintaining or furthering the West's control over this vast part of the globe.

Part of the dramatic transformation of image which a newly virtuous West can now show to the world comes from the fact that it has changed its primary mode of domination. Since physical invasion and exploitation are now less acceptable, new and elaborate processes have been installed for continuing the transfer of wealth from the Two Thirds World to the West. Economic forces are now the West's chosen weapon, being both more diffuse and impalpable in their workings, and less costly than the overt apparatus of military occupation. Further, in order to provide themselves with enduring economic nourishment, Western parasites take good care to limit their exploitation to levels which permit their prey to survive, albeit at extremely marginalised levels of existence.

The structures of injustice through which the West accomplished its earlier subordination of the rest of the world, have not been dismantled; in fact, they are now firmly enshrined in economic "laws". The so-called international institutions, including the UN and its progeny, the International Monetary Fund (IMF), the World Bank (WB) and the World Trade Organisation (WTO), that the West founded and vigorously supports, are merely complex tools created by the West to implement its objectives even while disguising its selfish aims. These institutions act as surrogates for the West, being more effective because they are assumed to be neutral by their unsuspecting and naive victims.

One of these basic instruments is the Universal Declaration of Human Rights (UDHR) adopted by the United Nations on December 10, 1948, an economic weapon that has been camouflaged as a human rights charter. The promulgation of the UDHR—now 50 years old—should have resulted in an obvious reduction in human rights abuses had it been sincerely drawn up to do so; instead, over the last five decades the human rights situation has continued to deteriorate because the scope for such abuse seems to have been carefully built into the very text of the Declaration itself.

The Declaration promotes the right to life while at the same time adding a whole series of rights, essential no doubt, but which are not made contingent on the right to life. It thus permits these "rights" to be wielded as weapons of economic exploitation even though such manipulation leads to the violation of the right to life itself. Further, new rights—such as the right to development—have been added so as to ensure that inhuman economic rights override the original rights listed.

The West can rage self-righteously throughout the world, demanding the implementation of the rights listed in the Declaration, because these rights are mere decoys, giving a superficial appearance of justice, which attracts people to the system. The promotion of these rights does not interfere with the West's pursuit and achievement of its dominant aims.

Thus the West can maintain that it is fostering the right to life even while its economic programmes, imposed in the name of "development", impoverish and kill people. It claims to be spreading democracy, even while it supports tyrants in countries where it has large economic interests. It claims to abhor violence even while it sells arms which incite conflicts around the globe. It promotes the right to food, even while its industrialised agricultural system is unsustainable, and it continues to use food as a weapon for further subjugation. It promotes the right to health even while the effluents of its industries poison people directly and are also responsible for the breakdown of the human immune and reproductive systems. And so it goes: nearly every right that the West claims to promote is matched by actions that violate it.

Direct killing by colonial and other types of conventional conflicts have merely been replaced by equally violent and deadly Western technology and international trade. I G Farben no longer produces the Zyklon B gas which was the main weapon of assembly-line slaughter of human beings in the German concentration camps. But that conglomerate's fissioned descendants, Hoechst, BASF and Bayer, as well as their imitators all over the world, sell equally potent but more subtly acting agents of mass murder: toxic synthetic pesticides, harmful pharmaceuticals, and other hazardous chemicals, many of which are banned or not sold within Western countries themselves. Genocide continues unstoppable. What propelled the Conquistadors and Hitler now drives the TNCs and Western governments.

Arbitrarily assuming authority to define human rights, the West officially champions rights that are carefully selected and sieved so as not to obstruct its material economic and political aims. Included in the West's list are those rights which it feels it can afford to promote: current events of torture, unwarranted imprisonment, and others which do not damage its own hegemony. These human rights issues have proved to be useful levers with which to manipulate other nations. Carefully excluded are distant and delayed violence through economic impoverishment and consequent malnutrition, disease and death.

It is in no way intended to claim here that the abuse of human rights is a monopoly of the West, or even that the West is in these respects "worse" than the rest of the world. What can be asserted is that no other societies have committed such widespread abuse whilst claiming exclusive global championship of human rights.

The Two Thirds World can only "develop" in the Western manner by adopting similarly ruthless and exploitative strategies. However, today not only are there fewer nations to exploit and no new lands to "discover", invade, conquer, colonise and abuse, but those who have been the earlier beneficiaries of such means would be the first to protest that emulative actions are crimes against humanity which must be punished.

The success of the new colonialism is partly due to the cooperation of the elites of the Two Thirds World who, whether coaxed or coerced, offer up their country and its people as sacrificial victims to the great god Mammon. These elites gain or hold on to their power by abusing the rights of their own people. Such

violations are easily visible, for instance, in large industrial development projects, which require the displacement and consequent
impoverishment, suffering and death of millions of people. These
hapless victims then become the "beneficiaries" of trickle down
development.

To avoid the pitfalls and traps that the West has so thoughtfully constructed, it is necessary to work on a more fundamental
basis to human rights than what the UN UDHR provides.

The inclusive right to life is primary and universal: it is the
right to life of every human being now living and of every human
being who will be born for an indefinite number of future
generations, for an indefinite number of millennia. Every human
bring has a right to at least the basic necessities for a reasonably
dignified life; the right to universal justice—intra-generational and
inter-generational equity—follows. The inclusive right to life incorporates all the other sub-rights normally listed separately.
These are the common basic rights that human beings can claim,
whoever they are, wherever they be.

The existing fragmentation of rights not only conceals the
omissions from the existing UN commitments, but also enables
them to be manipulated in ways that cancel each other. Despite
their claims to "universality", they also bear the clear imprint of the
period in which they were formulated—when colonial occupations still existed, in the aftermath of the war against fascism and
the then growing power of the Soviet Union.

Hence, any attempts by the West or the UN to promote
human rights must be looked upon with not a little suspicion and
mistrust. The recent moves to celebrate the fiftieth anniversary of
the founding of the UN by "renewing" it, can only render the
West's dominance more entrenched and improve the efficiency
with which it abuses human rights.

The objective of this book is to expose the real intent behind
the UN declarations on human rights. In particular, an attempt is
made to show how these supposedly international conferences,
with their universal lists of rights, have been co-opted to serve the
purposes of the West's dominant sectors. Possible alternatives are
also indicated, without any attempt to present a new "universal"
declaration, since this would be contrary to the establishment of
universal justice.

CHAPTER 1

A Brief History of Human Rights Violations

Historically, human rights have rarely been honoured in the societies of both East and West. Human rights violations by Eastern "barbarians" and "savages", however, have been often recorded in detailed western-authored histories, while those of the "civilised" West have been usually composed in carefully refined versions. Perhaps a narrative of internal violence, and of territorial theft, racial brutality and rationalised genocide carried out by European "civilising missions to the barbarians" would help redress the balance.

Europe

In the fifteenth century, violence, cruelty and death were common enough in Europe. Johan Huizinga, a historian, noted that the citizens of Mons in Flanders bought a brigand, at far too high a price, for the pleasure of seeing him quartered, "at which the people rejoiced more than if a new holy body had risen from the dead." Huizinga added: "Torture and executions are enjoyed by the spectators like an entertainment at a fair."[1]

From the year 1483, the Holy Inquisition was placed under royal control in Spain. It went "methodically and heartlessly after any variety of heretic or dissenter, reformer or mystic," killing hundreds of thousands by the sword, by torture and by public burning.[1]

Sir Walter Raleigh, a common sea pirate and a favourite of Elizabeth I, had sponsored the first English venture to Virginia in the early seventeenth century. He was, however, detested by Elizabeth's successor, James I, who coveted his enormous ill-gotten wealth. The sentence passed by James I on Raleigh for treason was explicit: "You shall be drawn upon a hurdle through the open streets to the place of execution, there to be hanged and cut down alive, and your body shall be opened, your heart and bowels plucked out, and your privy members cut off, and thrown into the fire before your eyes..."[2]

From 1550 to 1700, between hundred thousand and two hundred thousand people, perhaps 90 per cent of them women, were accused of being witches. Most of them were tortured into confessing, then burned or hanged for the entertainment of the public.[3] In early nineteenth century Britain, more than 200 offences (some of which would be considered trivial today) were punishable by death. Children in Britain learn in their history lessons that stealing a sheep was a hanging matter; a piece of instruction doubtless imparted to demonstrate the progress the British have subsequently made. The gradual invasions and enclosures of the forests and commons in Britain and other parts of Europe by the nobles, which deprived people of their means of support, was a mass abuse of the right to life.

The Occupied Territories

Europe, in the Middle Ages, suffered from shortages of food and other necessities such as fuel and construction wood.[4] There were obvious signs that its population had already exceeded the carrying capacity of its environment, with the spectre of famine continuously haunting it.

While local wars and uprisings vented some of the pressures building up, it was the "discovery" of the Caribbean Islands and the Americas, with their vast resources of land and labour, fields and forests, silver and gold, that allowed the emigration of the surplus citizens of overpopulated Europe to other continents. This provided a major outlet for the combustible energies of people who had nowhere else to go.

Such deliverance required the conquest by force of other peoples, the occupation of their vast territories, their enslavement, their displacement into "reservations" and often their genocidal extermination. In this process racism was endemic, with the rights allowed Europeans denied to the indigenous peoples of occupied territories.

As Clive Ponting remarks: "Many indigenous societies disintegrated under European pressure when they were not deliberately destroyed. The stark truth is that native peoples lost their land, livelihood, independence, culture, health and in most cases their lives. Despite differences in approach the common themes running strongly through European attitudes to the process were a disregard for the native way of life and an overwhelming urge to exploit both the land and the people."[5]

It is being said today that much of the loss of life in the occupied territories was not due to deliberate killing by the invaders but to the inadvertent transfer of deadly pathogens from Europe to populations which had no immunity to them.[6] There are recorded cases, however, where diseases such as smallpox and bubonic plague were deliberately spread through infected blankets.[7] This was an early example of the use of biological warfare.

The most extensive abuse of the right to life, on a scale far exceeding Hitler's appalling holocaust, occurred during these invasions and occupations of most of the non-European world. In the Americas alone, between 70 and 90 million indigenes lost their lives in the last 500 years.[8] This was carried out through multiple modes of genocide, from individual murders to large scale massacres.

When Columbus "wanted to capture the recalcitrant Kaseke Caonabo, whom he described as 'the principal king of the island', he dispatched a commander who gave the Taino leader some polished steel handcuffs and leg irons and persuaded him to wear them, just as, he said, did the great King of Spain; once shackled, Caonabo was dragged away from his village and led back to Isabela, thrown in jail, and then shipped to Castile—dying *en route*."[9]

In March 1495, the Spaniards claimed they encountered more than one hundred thousand Indians. With no provocation, they mowed down dozens with point-blank volleys, loosed their dogs of war trained to rip open the bellies of the "enemy", skewered many of the frightened fleeing Indians on their swords and pikes, and captured the rest, who were also later butchered.[9]

This process proceeded apace with multiplying invasions, expanding occupations and later the colonisation of heavily populated lands that simply could not be cleared of people.

While the Spanish invaders were mainly interested in gold, the English occupiers wanted land to own and cultivate, a resource which was only available to the nobility within their own national boundaries.

One may consider the view that since the Europeans did not hold each other's territories within Europe sacred, it was "normal" that they invaded lands outside Europe. However, while Europeans admitted that fighting each other was wrong—there were even attempts at making peace between opponents—no sign of guilt was visible in those who conquered and brutally killed the inhabitants of lands outside Europe. There is little sign of regret and repentance for such actions today either, since that would require reparations and the return of the lands to their original owners.

The arbitrary declaration of one's right to occupy someone else's native land provided the primary foundation of the non-European white-controlled nations in existence today, in the Americas, in Australia and elsewhere. The human rights of millions of indigenous peoples have since 1500 AD been subordinated to the right of Europeans to conquer and occupy.

However, the right to live in the region in which one was born was considered so fundamental that it was universally acknowledged even before it was formally defined. Ingenious and elaborate attempts to rationalise Europe's attempts at undermining it had to be made for maintaining double standards.

Thomas More who was prepared to die because he thought the dictates of his conscience had priority over his king's orders, found soothing reasons for the violence associated with the American occupations. More's *Utopia*, first published in 1516, was based on the "newly discovered" lands of America. Using the Utopians as a mouthpiece for European thought, he wrote that "if the inhabitants of that land will not dwell with them to be ordered by their (the invaders') laws, then they drive them out of those bounds which they have limited and appointed out for themselves. And if they resist and rebel, then they make war against them. For they count this the most just cause of war, when any people holdeth a piece of ground void and vacant to no good nor profitable use..."[10]

This fiction became enshrined in "principles" which British colonists—initially in New England—cited when they wished to justify their usurping the lands of the existing Natives.[11] "As for the Natives in New England, they inclose noe Land, neither have any setled habytation, nor any tame Cattell to improve the Land by, and soe have noe other but a Naturall Right to those Countries, soe as if we leave them sufficient for their use, we may lawfully take the rest, there being more than enough for them and us."[12]

"The lawfulness of removing out of England into parts of America," it was claimed in 1622, was derived from the fact that "our land is full ... (and) their land is empty...(T)heir land is spacious and void..." The same writer alleged that the Natives "do but run over the grass, as do also the foxes and wild beasts. They are not industrious, neither have (they) art, science, skill or faculty to use either the land or the commodities of it..."[13]

As a matter of fact, indigenous Americans had cultivated and improved their land for centuries. Although not demarcated by fences, walls and trenches, they reserved land for differing purposes and had well-defined tribal boundaries.[14]

When displacing indigenous peoples from their lands, the British declared: "As much Land as a Man Tills, Plants, Improves, Cultivates, and can use the Product of, so much is his Property. He by his Labour does, as it were, inclose it from the Common."[15]

Such high principles were and are not, of course, acceptable within Europe or the European-occupied territories today. Peasants in early Europe for instance could not occupy the lands of the nobles by claiming that those lands were "empty"; Hitler's demands for *lebensraum* were forcibly rejected; at present, potential non-white immigrants, by a symmetrical historical reversal of the rights of Europeans to occupy the territory of others at will, are determinedly kept out of Euro-America.

Since it was not considered right and just to appropriate land from equals, it was first necessary to inferiorise and down grade the indigenous peoples in the scale of being. Politicians, plantation owners, scientists and academicians fabricated ingenious and diverse arguments for considering the original inhabitants as lesser mortals: they claimed they were uncivilised, ignorant, intellectually inferior, lazy, racially subordinate and so on.

Displacement and genocide could then become legitimate. One A K Newman spoke for many whites when he observed that "taking all things into consideration, the disappearance of the race is scarcely subject for much regret. They are dying out in a quick, easy way, and are being supplanted by a superior race."[16] In the mid-nineteenth century, a writer claimed that "all other races ... must bow and fade" before "the great work of subjugation and conquest to be achieved by the Anglo-Saxon race."[17]

Genocide was enthusiastically endorsed by, among many others, several US Presidents. Andrew Jackson urged American troops to root out Natives from their "dens" and kill women and their "whelps."[18] Thomas Jefferson claimed that the US government was obliged "now to pursue them (the indigenes) to extermination, or drive them to new seats beyond our reach." In his much-acclaimed first inaugural address, delivered in 1802, he foresaw the US as a "rising nation, spread over a wide and fruitful land, traversing all the seas with the rich productions of their industry, engaged in commerce with nations who feel power and forget right, advancing rapidly to destinies beyond the reach of the mortal eye..."[19]

President Monroe called for helping the American Natives "to surmount all their prejudices in favour of the soil of their nativity", so that "we become in reality their benefactors" by "transferring them west." When consent was not given, they were forcibly removed. Consciences were eased further by the legal doctrine devised by none other than Chief Justice John Marshall: "Discovery gave an exclusive right to extinguish the Indian right of occupancy, either by purchase or by conquest....[T]hat law which regulates and ought to regulate in general, the relations between the conqueror and conquered was incapable of application to...the tribes of Indians,...fierce savages whose occupation was war, and whose subsistence was drawn chiefly from the forest."[20]

Theodore Roosevelt stated that the extermination of the American Natives was inevitable when "a masterful people...finds itself face to face with the weaker and wholly alien race which holds a coveted prize in its feeble grasp."[21]

The land of the Americas, with its forests and other resources, formed the foundation of the US and resulted in it becoming the most militarily dominant nation on earth, wielding a power that allows it deliberately to trample on the rights of others today.

In Australia, where the aboriginal population was decimated by mass murder, the invading Europeans misused Darwin's theories to claim that "to the Aryan...belong the destinies of the future....The survival of the fittest means that might—wisely used—is right. And thus we invoke and remorselessly fulfill the inexorable law of natural selection when exterminating the inferior Australian."[22]

Such arrogance, remarkably similar to Hitler's, still persists in the West, with its claims to being the "most developed" region on earth, having the right to impose its "civilisation" on the world and to punish those who venture to disagree.

The West considers the Nazi atrocities a rare aberration in its history. In the recent "celebrations" over the end of the 1939-1944 war in Europe, the question was often asked: Can it happen again? However, Hitler's actions were merely an inferior version, a weakened legacy, within European boundaries of what had been accomplished so much more efficiently in the previous centuries in nearly all non-European territories in the world.

The US has never stopped killing the American indigenes, directly or indirectly, within the US as well as through its surrogates in the rest of the continent.[23] As long as invaders occupy a country, the rights of the original inhabitants are abused, even though the occupation may have commenced hundreds of years ago.

These monstrous violations of human rights were merely the prelude to the effective globalisation of human rights abuse. Throughout the West's post-Colombian history, the rights of millions of indigenous peoples, of West African slaves, plantation workers and colonised peoples in general, have remained subordinated to the allegedly superior right of the West to "develop", that is, to conquer and deprive others of their rights.

The Colonies

By the nineteenth century the plague of colonialism had spread. The non-European world was soon carved up between the Portuguese, the Spanish, the Dutch, the English, the French, the Belgians and the Germans.

The invasion, domination and economic exploitation of these colonies could not have been carried out without the abuse of practically all the specific rights later sanctimoniously catalogued in the UN UDHR. The human beings in the territories concerned were not considered worthy of possessing any rights.

The British claimed that they denied sovereignty to Indians in their own land for purely unselfish reasons, for "India's good." It was Britain's "duty" to hold Indians in bondage and rule over them without their consent in spite of their insistent protests against such unwelcome benevolence. While Britain approved of the Indians' aspiration to be free and to rule themselves, the latter were unfortunately inferior people, ignorant, only partly civilised, who really did not know what was good for them, at least not as much as their superior British masters did. Therefore, they had to be dealt with like children. Britain did benefit greatly from Indian revenues, markets and raw materials, but this was a just reward for bearing the "white man's burden". A British writer ironically commented: "It is unfortunate that the people of India are so steeped in barbarism that they do not appreciate what a blessing it is to be killed by civilised foreigners rather than by one another."[24]

Some Englishmen at least were proud of their abuse of human rights. In 1899, for instance, a senior British bureaucrat explained colonial policy thus: "In every part of the world, where British interests, are at stake, I am in favour of advancing and upholding these interests, even at the cost of annexation and at the risk of war. The only qualification I admit is that the country we desire to annex, or take under our protection, the claims we choose to assert and the cause we desire to espouse, should be calculated to confer a tangible advantage upon the British Empire."[25]

Britain claimed to be a model democracy at the same time that it vigorously denied the right to self-government to the peoples of the countries which it had forcibly occupied or colonised in the process of extending and maintaining its "great" empire. While individual kings and rulers were easily overcome in open warfare, it was more difficult for the British to "conquer" the Adivasis (tribals), since their egalitarian communities had no highly visible leader who could be bribed, overthrown or replaced. They were particularly annoyed by the nomadic tribes who would not be coaxed to occupy taxable "settlements". In 1871 therefore, the British enacted the Criminal Tribes Act which declared about 200 nomadic tribes "criminal" and compelled their members to report to the nearest police station every day. The Settlement Act of 1924 went further, caging them in concentration camps surrounded by barbed wire fences.[26] Those who disobeyed or escaped were hunted like the wild beasts in their forests.

The British claimed their system of justice was superior to the Indian system, even though British judges were mostly unaware— or did not care about—the cultural basis of the latter. Many of their actions, however, would have been categorised as abuses of the rights laid down later in the UN Declaration of 1948.

The famed British system of justice in India favoured persons of European origin against Indians. In an article in *The Empire Review* of February 1919, Justice Beaman of the Bombay High Court candidly declared: "Every reform, every large measure, all important administrative changes should be referred to one standard and one standard only, the interests of England."[27]

The leading features of the Rowlatt Acts, operative in India from 1919 on, were: the arrest without warrant of any suspected person and detention without trial for an indefinite duration of time. The trials were conducted in secret, and the proceedings not made public. The accused were kept ignorant of the names of their accusers or of the witnesses against them, and were denied the right of defending themselves with the help of lawyers. No witnesses were allowed for the defence of the accused. The right of appeal was denied. Anyone associating with ex-political offenders could be arrested. Even so, these draconian laws were deemed insufficiently severe and were strengthened in 1932. Judge Rowlatt was honoured and rewarded with the insignia of Knight Commander of the Star of India.[28]

A C Mozumdar wrote in *The Indian World* of February-March 1909 that British-administered courts seemed usually to "value Indian lives at from fifty to a hundred rupees (from £5 to £10, at that time) each."[29] Europeans who killed Indians were usually punished with a negligible fine (a few pounds at most), rarely with a few months imprisonment.[30] In one case, an Englishman kicked an Indian, rupturing his spleen, which resulted in his death. He was ordered to pay a fine of Rs 50 only.[31] In 1920, Motilal Nehru, the father of Jawaharlal Nehru (India's first Prime Minister), who had practised law for 30 years, wrote: "During the last 150 years every Indian who has met with death at the hands of a European has either had an enlarged spleen or his death has turned out to be the result of pure 'accident'. There has not been a single case, so far as I am aware, of murder pure and simple."[32]

The honour of Indian women was held equally cheap when compared to that of European women. An Indian was sentenced

to twenty years imprisonment for attempting to rape an English-
woman, while in the same province an Englishman who gagged
and raped an Indian girl of eighteen was acquitted, with no
punishment at all.[31] Women and children were raped and violated
in tea plantations, on board steamers, in railway carriages and
stations, around military encampments. They had no access to
legal redress. The helpless victims either died or, preferring death
to dishonour, committed suicide.[32]

Millions of Indians lost their lives in the continuous wars that
the British fought against them for nearly two centuries. At least a
hundred thousand were killed in the first war of Indian independence in 1857. Employing the ingenuity for which they were so
famous, the British developed new methods of torture and execution. Indian soldiers accused of being mutineers were tied to the
mouths of cannons on Mumbai's Esplanade maidan. The cannons
were then fired and the spectacle of the mutineers' heads, torsos,
and limbs flying in all directions was considered entertainment of
a high order.

Equally, millions of Indians were drafted into the 1914-1918
war effort to help the British. With Britain winning, many Indians
expected freedom or at least a relaxation of its exploitative and
vicious hold on them. To the contrary, increasingly harsh laws
were enacted to discourage rising demands for independence.

In April 1919, just about seventy-five years ago, General Dyer
ordered his soldiers to shoot at a peaceful gathering of between
fifteen to twenty thousand men, women and children, assembled
in Jallianwala Bagh in Punjab to protest against repressive legislation. The people were shut up in a walled-in garden from which it
was almost impossible to escape as the soldiers occupied the only
exit. Hundreds were killed and over a thousand wounded.[33]

The British declared martial law in several districts as the
people of Punjab rose in revolt. Innocent people were stripped
naked and flogged while tied to special stands set up in the most
frequented streets. Many of them died. Attendance at schools was
made compulsory with thousands of students forced to walk up to
twenty-five kilometres to attend. They were forced to salute the
Union Jack and sing "God Save The King."

In Lahore, when a public notice was torn down by an
unknown person, all the students of a medical college were
compelled to walk twenty-five kilometres a day in the hot sun,

every day for three weeks. Men were made to draw lines on the earth with their noses. For eight days all the people living in one of the streets of Amritsar were compelled to crawl on their bellies "like worms." There were hundreds of merciless public whippings, some of the victims being school boys. Sentences of death and transportation for life or long terms of imprisonment were pronounced on over 500 persons; later, however, a Revision Court reduced or annulled some of these.

General Dyer, the "hero" of the affair, claimed praise for his shocking deeds on the ground that by it he had "saved India."[34] Dyer was mildly censured, not because he ordered firing on an unarmed assembly of men, women and children, but because he fired without first giving warning, and because he continued the firing too long. When his case came up before the British House of Lords a large majority refused to express any form of disapproval of what he had done. He was generally praised as a patriot and a hero and was presented "with a jewelled sword and a purse of $150,000."[35]

Various policies of the British contributed also to the deterioration of health. Among them were the enclosure of forests which deprived people in the neighbourhood of nutritious wild foods, medicines, and manures for their crops: their very right to life. Wheat was exported from India by the British even while famines raged.

Salt was essential for those who subsisted on a vegetarian diet. Before the East India Company rule, salt could be produced freely, for trade or private use. The Company first imposed a tax on the salt trade; later it made salt a monopoly and increased its price. Claude Alvares gives revealing figures of the enormous revenue that accrued: "By 1844, the cost of producing salt was one anna per maund, but the tax on it was two rupees (32 annas). In 1883, one W S Blunt recorded in his diary: 'The police are empowered to enter houses night or day and, on their accusation of there being a measure of earth salt in it, the owner of the house may be fined fifteen rupees, or imprisoned for a month....The cattle are dying for want of it, and the people are suffering seriously...'" Blunt observes that a kind of leprosy had already begun to prevail along the coast, but the government continued to collect all the salt found. Alvares continues: "In 1883, the salt revenue netted £6 million for the British. In 1930, the salt revenue netted the same authority £25 million, out of the £800 million being (annually) taken out of the country."[36]

Most of the British felt no guilt for what they had done in their colonies and saw no reason why they should not continue to rule them. Winston Churchill, in 1914, reminded his cabinet colleagues that "we have got all we want in territory, but our claim to be left in unmolested enjoyment of vast and splendid possessions, mainly acquired by violence, largely maintained by force, often seems less reasonable to others than to us."[37]

When the US, itself a colonisation of Native lands, occupied Hawaii and the Philippines, its argument was, if Britain could do it, why shouldn't we? The US at one time even contemplated appropriating a "good fat slice of China" for itself.[38]

The Industrial Revolution

The wealth of the West is claimed to be a consequence of the hard work and sheer intelligence that culminated in the Industrial Revolution. But this Revolution could not have developed as it did without enormous abuse of human rights.

The British cotton textile industry, which formed the foundation of the Revolution, required the violent displacement or killing of indigenous peoples in the Caribbean and the Americas for the land on which cotton could be cultivated. Native Americans first supplied the cheap slave labour in the cotton plantations. When this supply was exhausted by diverse forms of genocide, it was replaced by the capture, transportation and enslavement of millions of Africans.

Workers to run the textile mills in Britain were available at low wages from the vast pool of the impoverished created by the system of enclosures. Later, British hand spinners and weavers, displaced by the new "efficient" machines, added to the pool. Such labour kept the cost of machine manufactures low enough to compete with handmade articles.

Gold and silver from the Americas provided the capital for investment in all stages of the developing industry. A vital prerequisite was the piracy of Indian dyeing technology. The Revolution required the economic and cultural subjugation of consumers and the forcible elimination of competition to enable the British to sell their inferior textiles in the mass markets of conquered India. This, in turn, resulted in the disemployment of millions of Indian hand spinners and weavers, with colossal accompanying country-wide suffering and death. Britain's "dedication" to the free market may be seen in the vigour with which it barred Indian textiles from its own country and the violence with which it imposed Manchester cloth upon India. The British textile industry would not have been "successful" without relying on every one of these human rights abuses.[39]

The multiplication of mass production industries required vast quantities of coal and later, oil and gas for energizing their machines. The rights of future generations to nonrenewable resources and a clean environment were irreparably destroyed, even as the Industrial Revolution was in its infancy.

With the further spread of industrialisation, the efforts of workers to secure an adequate livelihood increased. The Combination Acts at the turn of the eighteenth century forbade workers to organise in trade unions. It took half of the nineteenth century before the workers learned the rules of the industrial game, and another half century before they knew how to apply them effectively to their own ends. The poor, the unemployed, the sick were considered to be feckless, lazy, and morally depraved because they did not work. As a monument to British humanitarianism, the Poor Law of 1834 enabled the establishing of workhouses in which a form of domestic slavery was legalised, with all indigents above the tender age of three forced to perform hard labour.[40] The ruling elite showed little enough mercy to its own people. It is scarcely to be expected that it would exhibit a greater degree of compassion for others elsewhere in the world.

The resources of the occupied territories, so necessary for many of the industrial products manufactured in the West, were obtained at ridiculously low prices fixed by the colonial masters. This was—and still remains—a major means of transferring the wealth of the occupied territories to the West.

Wars

Wars are an extreme form of violence, which cause injury and deny the right to life of people *en masse*. War is also a violation of the right to sovereignty, often used to keep uncooperative regions under control.

As nations "ascended" historically, the invention and use of new arms technologies resulted in an increase in the distance and area over which violence and murder could be practised, igniting more widespread conflagrations. In addition there was a rise in the rapidity with which these gruesome tasks were carried out. It was the early development of firearms that enabled the Europeans to invade, subdue and colonise indigenous peoples around the globe: the latter were armed with less sophisticated weapons.

Swords and spears required hand to hand fighting; arrows and firearms distanced fighting. Napoleon in his 1799 war against Egypt set lines a hundred yards from the enemy because this was the maximum distance at which a musket ball could be effective. At the time of the American civil war, rifles could be used up to 400 yards. The 1914-1918 European war (it was by no means a world war), brought out the use of airplanes and of chemical weapons, which caused horribly painful death. Today, the use of nuclear arms and ICBMs could induce global extinction.

It is strange, therefore, that at the beginning of the twentieth century, international regulations were drawn up which allowed the legal denial of human rights to people on a large scale. Of course, at that time the wars were mainly in the European colonies, where human beings, leave alone their rights, did not count. However, the regulations were soon required to be implemented in the 1914-1918 war.

The 1907 Hague Regulation on War permitted destruction and killing with some defined but usually unpractised constraints. Acts of violence, for instance, which were not necessary to further the declared aim of war were prohibited. Violence which caused disproportionate suffering to soldiers and civilians when compared with corresponding military gains achieved was forbidden. In other words, the conduct of warfare ought to maximise the benefit-cost ratio, where the benefit was the declared aim of the war and the cost referred to the subject of violence, that is, life and property. The regulation also prohibited attacks on civilian undefended buildings, towns and ports.[41]

Inspite of such rules, the number of military casualties during the 1914-1918 war has been estimated at 8.4 million on both sides with 21 million combatants wounded. Further advances in war technology raised these figures to 35-60 million deaths, military and civilian, during the war of 1939-1944.[42]

The aims for which wars could be fought were left undefined, whereas that definition should have been the principal object of such international regulations which ostensibly sought the avoidance of war. But there never was any intention to eliminate war. How else would new colonial territories be won from indigenous peoples or wrested from other imperial powers?

When the Iraqis revolted against British domination in 1919, the RAF Middle East Command requested authorisation from Winston Churchill, the then Secretary of State at the War Office, to use chemical weapons "against recalcitrant Arabs as experiment." Churchill sanctioned the use, dismissing objections: "I do not understand this squeamishness about the use of gas...I am strongly in favour of using poisoned gas against uncivilised tribes." Chemical weapons, he added, were merely "the application of Western science to modern warfare."[43] The British prevented the 1932 Disarmament Conference from banning bombardment of civilians, with Lloyd George observing: "We insisted on reserving the right to bomb niggers."[44]

It was Churchill, not Hitler, who proclaimed the doctrine of "total war", not only against enemy armies but civilians although attacks on the latter were prohibited by the Geneva Protocol of 1925. While this was a shocking departure from rules of "gentlemanly war etiquette" in Europe, it was a routine operation in the colonies and other occupied countries.

"Total war" allowed for the bombing of Dresden, where it was the loss of ancient monuments and art treasures that were given more attention than the deaths of approximately 135,000 inhabitants of that city.[45] It permitted blockades against the enemy, with no relief even for allies in the resistance movements. In the autumn of 1941, the Allied blockade of Greece led to severe famine. At its height, people died at the rate of over 1,500 a day.[46]

"Total war" allowed the massacres of Hiroshima and Nagasaki where the US holds the world record for the instantaneous mass abuse of the right to life. In a few seconds, on August 6 and 9, 1945, around 150,000 people, old and young, men, women and children were vapourised or charred to unrecognisable corpses. Further hundreds of thousands would have preferred instant death to the prolonged agony from horrendous radiation burns. More have been psychologically and genetically affected, perhaps for generations. The speaker of the US House of Representatives,

Newt Gingrich, recently declared that the dropping of the nuclear bombs was an event which "will make Americans proud."[47]

The Americans, while claiming that the Japanese were barbaric in their treatment of prisoners of war and civilians in occupied territories, were not above barbarism themselves. An article in *The Atlantic Monthly* is explicit: "We shot prisoners in cold blood, wiped out hospitals, strafed lifeboats, killed or mistreated enemy civilians, finished off the enemy wounded, tossed the dying into a hole with the dead, and in the Pacific boiled the flesh off enemy skulls to make table ornaments for sweethearts, or carved their bones into letter openers."[48]

On the other hand, the punishments dealt out to those who were unfortunate enough to be defeated were determined, not by the extent of their violations of human rights, but purely by the level of their utility to the victors. The aim was to use the erstwhile enemy's knowledge and personnel to strengthen US military-industrial sectors, with amnesty for those who could contribute to them. Werner von Braun, a member of the Nazi SS, was responsible for developing and producing the V2 missiles which killed thousands in Britain, yet he was unconditionally absolved of war crimes because he agreed to work for the missile programme in the US. Von Braun was named one of the hundred most "important Americans of the 20th century" by *Life* magazine in 1990.[49]

The Japanese emperor, as head of the nation, was responsible for the war. But he was not charged with war crimes and was allowed to continue to enjoy his position so that civil stability could be maintained and the economic exploitation of Japan undertaken undisturbed.

Japanese doctors carried out shocking experiments on Chinese civilians in the 1930s. One of them recently revealed that he dissected a live man, from chest to stomach, without anesthetic. The "patient" who underwent this vivisection had been deliberately infected with plague so that the "researcher" could look at the internal effects of the infection. The ultimate aim of the research was to develop bombs to start outbreaks of plague. This was only a small part of a vast project to produce weapons of biological warfare, including those that could spread anthrax, cholera and other pathogens. The US granted immunity from war crimes prosecution to the doctors and gave them stipends in exchange for their research data.[50]

The United Nations Organisation

The turmoil created by the first European war of 1914-1918 led to an attempt by the victors to keep tighter control of the global situation through the formation of the League of Nations. Among other provisions, the League gave its members an aura of legality for retaining existing colonies and acquiring new mandated territories, at the same time controlling rival imperialist nations so as to permit more efficient colonisation. The League institutionalised global colonialism.

The League did not include the protection of human rights in its charter apart from a vague call to member states for the "just treatment of the native inhabitants of territories under their control."[51] Justice in those days of frenetic imperialism, was loosely applied and, naturally, did not include independence for the colonies.

The Atlantic Charter of 1942 spelled out the objectives of the second European war as defined by Churchill and Roosevelt. Its preface maintained that a "complete victory over their enemies is essential to decent life, liberty, independence and religious freedom, and to preserve human rights and justice, in their own land as well as in other lands."[52]

At the Yalta Conference in 1945 it was agreed, among other things, that the new agency would include a trusteeship system that would succeed the League of Nations mandates, thus ensuring the continuation of colonialism in a new format.[53]

The term "United Nations" was first used during the second European war to denote the nations allied against Germany, Italy and Japan. Although now usually seen as the champion of human rights, the UN itself institutionalised their major abuse. The constitution of the organisation is far from democratic, with a supreme Security Council of just fourteen members, five of whom are permanent members with the right to veto any resolution. Veto power has been liberally used to defend the particular interests of the five, especially when they themselves were major abusers of the rights of millions of others.

The only qualification of the five privileged members is that they fought—and won—a war. Today, with Japan and Germany— identified as "enemies" in the original UN Charter—being considered for membership of the Security Council, it is clear that it is economic (and not only military) power which is a necessary qualification.

Given that these five members now control most of the nations of the world, the UN Organisation is surely the most undemocratic institution that has ever existed on the planet. "Some would even argue," says Chandra Muzaffar, "that with the end of the Cold War and the demise of bipolar politics, it is just one military superpower which controls the Security Council and the UN. The dominance of that superpower over global political processes implies a form of authoritarianism in international relations which has no precedent in history."[53] Accordingly, he says, the UN "plays an ever bigger role in perpetuating the existing global system with all its injustices and iniquities. The UN Security Council has, in fact, become a tool of the centres of power in the North, manipulated every now and then to legitimize their illegitimate activities in international politics."[54]

Weaker countries are excluded from the Security Council on specious grounds although these should be represented in a body that claims to be democratically reducing global injustice. The Clinton administration has said that the issue of India's permanent membership of the Security Council will depend on its "improved relations with Pakistan and settlement of the Kashmir issue." Which would be fine provided the US applied the principle equitably to all the Security Council members, including itself. The US did not relinquish its membership of the Security Council when it had poor relations with both the USSR and communist China during the cold war period. When China had an extremely bad relationship with its neighbours—the USSR and Taiwan—the US made special efforts to make China a permanent member of the Security Council in 1971 in place of Taiwan.[55]

Even the General Assembly has become a tool of the US, with several members succumbing to bribes and threats. The UN has now become an institution where there is no longer any genuine democracy: only the rights of the US and its allies prevail.[56] It is the supreme instrument for freezing existing concentrations of power.

The Charter of the United Nations which came into force on October 24, 1945, was signed by fifty-one nations. The primary stated objective of the UN was the maintenance of international peace and security, thus effectively denying the colonised the right to fight for their independence.[57] Again, although the first article of the Charter declared that the organisation was based on the equal rights and self-determination of peoples, no efforts were made to give the colonies their freedom.[58]

This hypocrisy was repeated several times over as if the injustice would simply go away by this process. The General Assembly recognized the right of peoples and nations to self-determination "as a fundamental human right" in resolution 421 D (V) adopted on 4th December 1950. On 14 December 1960 the General Assembly solemnly proclaimed "the necessity of bringing to a speedy and unconditional end colonialism in all its forms and manifestations." It then adopted the Declaration on the Granting of Independence to Colonial Countries and Peoples. This Declaration states that the "subjection of peoples to alien subjugation, domination and exploitation constitutes a denial of fundamental human rights, is contrary to the Charter of the United Nations and is an impediment to the promotion of world peace and co-operation." A Special Committee on Decolonization was established whose main task was to monitor the implementation of the Declaration.[59] While this contributed to the liberation of Namibia in 1990, it did little else.

It has to be conceded that the UN is ashamed of some of its past actions. In celebration of its fiftieth anniversary, the UN has published a commemorative volume entitled "Vision of Hope", listing its achievements but carefully omitting the more embarrassing references. Among those missing are the fact that the Soviet bloc, Saudi Arabia and South Africa had abstained from voting when the UN UDHR was adopted in December 1948, and the exclusion of the Dalai Lama's participation in the 1993 UN Human Rights Conference in Vienna.[60]

The West continues to make strenuous efforts to retain its stranglehold on the UN, ensuring that it is not given a "Third World tilt." The fact that the latter constitute a majority of the UN's members is irrelevant in this "democratic" institution. No matter what the intentions of the original members were, they have been co-opted to support the Western system, even if it is to their own disadvantage.

With such an heritage, the uncharacteristic attempts of the UN to promote human rights during the last few decades can be looked at with not a little suspicion.

CHAPTER 2

The Universal Declaration of Human Rights

References to human rights today, by activists and governments equally, usually relate to those defined in the Universal Declaration of Human Rights, adopted by the UN General Assembly in December 1948 [See Appendix I]. This Declaration originally comprised thirty Articles, but a large number of UN resolutions have since been added to the document.

The intentions of the UN Assembly in drafting the Declaration appear to be impeccable. The preamble expresses considerable concern: "Whereas recognition of the inherent dignity and of the equal and inalienable rights of all members of the human family is the foundation of freedom, justice and peace in the world....Now, therefore, the General Assembly proclaims this Universal Declaration of Human Rights as a common standard of achievement for all peoples and nations, to the end that every individual and every organ of society, keeping this Declaration constantly in mind, shall strive by teaching and education to promote respect for these rights and freedoms and by progressive measures, national and international, to secure their universal and effective recognition and observance, both among the peoples of Member States themselves and among peoples of territories under their jurisdiction."

A declaration of such noble intentions should have served as a sharp turning point in the history of human rights, with an immediately visible improvement in their implementation. But no such sea change occurred. The question that arises, therefore, is: Does the UN UDHR reveal a genuine concern for human rights or is it an instrument carefully designed for furthering the West's global ambitions?

As stated earlier, a close scrutiny of the Declaration leads to the conclusion that it has been carefully crafted to serve the ulterior purposes of leaving the West free to promote and consolidate its economic and cultural hegemony over the rest of the World, even while appearing to honour the human rights listed in the document. This explains the increasing human rights abuse after the Declaration came into effect.

Several of the Articles in this noble Declaration could be interpreted as exonerating past and present human rights abuse by the West, while others appear to foster those institutions through which it continues to exploit the Two Thirds World. Contradictions in the text of the Declarations occur as the West attempts to conceal its real intentions, while at the same time giving the appearance of being the most ardent advocate of the rights of all human beings.

The Declaration itself is a badly drafted document; the rights are listed at random, and many of the Articles are repetitious or implicit in other Articles specified. The fundamental human right being the right to life, rights such as those to health, education and others, should follow naturally from its upholding and observance. Considering such rights as distinct and separate, however, enables the West to apply the relevant Articles to specific Western subsystems even when these operate directly against the right to life. For instance, the right to health is effectively restricted to the promotion of the allopathic system of curative medicine, thus displacing health-enhancing and lower cost traditional systems.

Among the rights enumerated, those most emphasised in practice are the rights to life (within a narrow definition), liberty and security of person and those relating to torture or cruel, inhuman or degrading treatment or punishment. [Articles 3 and 5] These abuses of human rights, even with limited meaning, are not negligible: arbitrary arrest and imprisonment of individuals because of their political or religious beliefs, detention without trial, extrajudicial executions, torture of prisoners, harassment of dissidents, the more recent "disappearances", and so on, are real violations. However, even such rights are only reluctantly conceded by most States, and often after bitter and bloody fights by activists, whose efforts are usually reduced to ensuring the full implementation of this small set.

The upholding of these particular rights can, with impunity, be the concern of Western governments since they are interpreted in a strictly qualified manner, and relate to practices generally implemented in dealings with their own nationals, apart, of course, from those they choose to label terrorists and extremists. "Friendly"—economically subservient—regimes are also generously exempted from even such tenuous observance of human rights. The deliberately limited UDHR perspective frequently makes it necessary for the UN to focus on specific topics and conjure up another subset of rights, when pressures in that particular area can no longer be contained. Thus the rights of indigenous peoples, the rights of children and the rights of women, are given special attention when all such rights would follow naturally from the implementation of the basic right to life. By ensuring that the right to life is splintered, it becomes necessary to enumerate and legalise each specific sub-right before the system deigns to acknowledge it.

While worthy conferences and declarations catalogue family rights, economic forces are being fostered to erode them. A whole new set of inhuman economic rights has been promoted as taking precedence over even those limited rights listed in the UN UDHR.

The following chapters examine in detail the rights so selectively conceded by the West. They throw some light on the real extent of human rights abuse perpetrated or condoned by it and reveal the internal and external contradictions arising from such definitions, when the main Western aim is to maintain and increase its affluence and power.

CHAPTER 3

The Right to Life

E veryone has the right to life, liberty and security of person." [UDHR, Article 3]

    Article 3 presents an appearance of an inalienable right but its fragmentation either allows it to be annulled or produces spaces into which the West can import its own for-profit institutions for exploitation.

    Whatever the Declaration may state at present, the right to life is interpreted in a purely negative manner as a right not to be killed by a criminal or maniac, or if killed, to have the murderer punished. The state need not strive to keep its citizens alive.

    Interpreted comprehensively, this Article should exclude any activity by individuals, governments or international institutions, which reduces or threatens to reduce a person's access to essential sustenance and, therefore, diminishes her or his life span or its quality. Economic impoverishment usually results in malnutrition or starvation which is a threat to health, and therefore an abuse of the right to life.

    Article 25, therefore, unnecessarily states: "Everyone has the right to a standard of living adequate for the health and well-being of himself and his family, including food, clothing, housing and medical care and necessary social services, and the right to security in the event of unemployment..."

    What this conveys is that the right to life does not automatically imply a right to health, well-being, food and so on. That is, even if people are ill, malnourished and miserable, their right to life is deemed to be satisfied.

A just interpretation of the right to life requires that all human beings living today and those who will be born in an indefinite number of future generations, have their basic needs satisfied so that their life is not diminished, in duration or quality.

The right to security cannot be limited to the payment of subsistence welfare during unemployment—as it has been, but increasingly is ceasing to be, in practice, in the West—but must include freedom from indirect threats from toxic pollution, global climatic change, and even the WTO's adverse effects on self-reliance in agriculture and food.

Recognition of the inclusive right to life would imply that the State will so organise itself as to ensure that each and every citizen receives adequate supplies of food and other basic necessities in a healthy environment and that people live and grow in dignity. Allowing people to die of neglect is as abusive as direct murder. The right to work, the right to housing and other rights follow, and those who are unable to work due to physical disability, old age and lack of job opportunities, should still have access to food and other basic entitlements.

Moreover, the failure to meet basic needs is not seen as a direct abuse of the right to life, because it is assumed that the needs of the poorest will be met by the right to "trickle down development". But the imposition of this type of development in the "developing" countries serves merely to transfer the already meagre resources of the masses to an affluent few, within the country or outside it, making the situation of the impoverished even worse.

Genocide is the most practised abuse of the right to life. Article II of the UN Convention on the Prevention and Punishment of the Crime of Genocide, also adopted in 1948, defines genocide as "any of the following acts committed with intent to destroy, in whole or in part, a national, ethnical, racial, or religious group, as such: (a) Killing members of the group; (b) Causing serious bodily or mental harm to members of the group; (c) Deliberately inflicting on the group conditions of life calculated to bring about its physical destruction in whole or in part;..."

Many of the activities of the Western system come within this definition, though the intent is rarely so starkly stated. Mass murders and genocide by deprivation are practices which have continued with increasing intensity towards the end of the 20th century. Killing goes on all the time, in the fields of farmers (through synthetic pesticides), in the factories (through worker exposure to pollution) and in homes (through the policies of the free market economy). The deaths often occur at places remote from the centres of origin of the abuse (the Washington offices of the World Bank, the vehicles and industries which "manufacture" atmospheric and oceanic pollution), and far into the future (carcinogenic and mutagenic effects, climatic change and so on).

No ceremony, however, attends the dying hours of dispossessed people, hungry children and sick adults, whose lives are circumscribed or cut short by poverty, insufficiency and lack of livelihood. The real rites take place in Western celebrations of affluence based on the sacrifice of impoverished victims to the great god Mammon.

Article IV of the UN Convention on Genocide however does state that "Persons committing genocide...shall be punished, whether they are constitutionally responsible rulers, public officials, or private individuals." But the narrow interpretation of genocide ensures that the West gets away with its mass murder.

Violence

"No one shall be subject to torture or to cruel, inhuman or degrading treatment or punishment." [UDHR, Article 5]

Physical or mental violence often results in premature death and hence is a major abuse of the right to life. However, concern about violence is usually limited to the immediate physical, conspicuous and overt, and no doubt horrifying violence that one reads about and sees daily: international battles, police brutality, minority conflicts, rape and abuse of children. But torture and cruel, inhuman or degrading treatment are not limited to such cases. As in the right to life, the notion of what constitutes violence is limited in the UN UDHR and it needs to be extended.

The violence of the State or its minions is often directed against people who are fighting for rights which are denied them because they hinder the expansion of the Western system. [See Appendix II, for a case study.] Violence is used against people who claim a right to live in their ancestral lands, against slum dwellers who claim a right to barely survive in the streets of cities, against rural communities who claim a right to govern themselves, and so on. Unless these rights are seen to be fundamental, violence will continue until the people concerned are subdued.

There is also random violence, direct and indirect, generated as a result of increasing social inequality in Western societies. In the US, a country that boasts about the liberty of its citizens, the right to bear arms is seen as a constitutional right by a large number of US citizens. This constitutional right was originally established to give white US citizens the right to shoot indigenous people in their invasive "self-defence". Today, they claim that arms are required to defend themselves against their fellow-citizens, leading to a mild but pervasive and escalating civil war. In a country of 260 million people, there are at least 150 million guns in circulation. Guns are used in one million crimes of which 15,000 each year are homicides. More Americans die annually in such shootings than were killed in combat at the height of the Vietnam war.[1]

Gandhi defined violence in a wide sense: causing any sort of harm, physical or mental. Violence can be committed personally, it can be instigated or aided, or it can be condoned by observing it without protest. Participating in or benefiting from a harmful practice is violence.[2]

Any threat to human dignity or peace of mind not only constitutes mental torture but also adds to physical stress. "Human rights", as Chandra Muzaffar says, "interpreted mainly in terms of political and civil rights will not satisfy the quest of the poor for human dignity and social justice."[3]

Mental violence occurs in assumptions of superiority by "higher" castes or classes over the "lower", by the formally "educated" over the "uneducated", by "experts" over "lay persons". Such violence may be overt or implied, but it is omnipresent in the hierarchies and stratifications of wealth and power which also characterize the "advanced" societies of the West.

Mental violence is often caused by everyday treatment of women, and the mentally or physically handicapped, as if they were less than normal beings. Human dignity requires that all people be treated as equal human beings, even though they have unequal mental and physical abilities. Otherwise, as Raymond Williams noted: "Such inequality, in any of its forms, in practice rejects, de-personalises, degrades in grading, other human beings.

On such practice a structure of cruelty, exploitation, and the crippling of human energy is easily raised."[4]

The anguish caused to people when they are excluded from making some useful contribution to the work of society is a form of intense mental torture. Mental violence is also produced by the loss of creativity which passive entertainment produces and the enclosure of technological and other areas of activity by modern machinery.

Considerable distant and delayed violence is perpetrated by Western and local power holders. Much more widespread and subtle is the violence committed by most people who live "within" the Western development system, by using its products and depending on it for a living. Violence is embedded and inherent in the objects and services of the Western system, but because most of these originate far away from consumers in space and time, consumers can be kept in ignorance of their harmful content. Almost every product in use involves hurting others. An examination of the industrial and commercial processes, from mining and manufacture to their sale and use, reveals their violent interconnections.[5]

Furthermore, the increasing separation of producers from consumers within the "integrated" global economic system only institutionalises the ignorance of the privileged of the sufferings and exploitation of those who provide them with their daily necessities. And this "absolves" them of any responsibility for the lives which are damaged by their heedless purchases in the marketplace.

Such violence can be more damaging than immediate physical violence, but since it is an integral, essential part of the Western system, it is not mentioned in the UN UDHR as a violation of human rights.

CHAPTER 4

Democratic Rights

---

*E*veryone has the right to take part in the government of his country,
directly or through freely chosen representatives."

"*The will of the people shall be the basis of the authority of government;
this will shall be expressed in periodic and genuine elections...*" (UDHR,
Articles 21 [1] and 21 [3])

The West has never ceased to assert that democracy is the
supreme prerequisite for the protection of human rights. Yet the
whole of Western society has been built on the violation of the right
of peoples to self-determination. Even today, democracies are
used as conduits for imposing Western economic policies. In the
West itself, the existing democratic system itself does not meet the
requirements of Article 21 (1).

The History of Democracy

Western civilisation claims to derive its basic concepts of
democracy from the Greeks who developed them in the early fifth
century BC. The word "democracy" stems from the Greek term for
"government by the people". However, it was never "government
by all the people". Greek men had the wealth and leisure to discuss
and deliberate on democracy only because of the widespread use
of slaves and women to provide them with sustenance and care.
Their strict hierarchy put free men at the top of the human
pyramid, over women and children, with slaves at the bottom. In
Athens, around 430 BC, the number of slaves is estimated to have
been nearly half the total population.[1]

In England, the Magna Carta is claimed to be the single greatest step taken from monarchy towards democracy. Yet its main consequence was that a few barons obtained from the king the right to oppress their own "subjects".

In the embryonic English Parliaments the nobles and the gentry—the small landowners—reserved to themselves the right to vote. The first threat to these ruling powers came from the newly rich mercantile adventurers, initially encouraged and funded by their monarchs, who colonised, plundered and looted the non-English world at will. They asserted that their wealth gave them a right to enter parliament, which the ruling class reluctantly conceded, thus absorbing the threat. That pattern of absorption and neutralisation of threats, of conceding power without giving it up, has been the secret of survival of the British and other ruling classes till today.

As profits from colonialism and the Industrial Revolution rose, this time the manufacturing middle class which emerged in the early industrial era began to pose a more significant threat. They were initially despised by the traditional landed interests but when the latter perceived their prodigious capacity for getting rich, they judiciously conceded the franchise to them, even selling them their daughters in marriage.

The Reform Bill, passed in 1832, extended the franchise to householders above a certain income level, the middle class and even a few artisans. But the reform also focussed on manipulating constituencies. Thus it became more representative of the manufac-turing interests, while the great bulk of people were still excluded.

In 1868, the Second Reform bill extended the franchise to include more of the better off artisans and householders in the cities. It was the growing power of labour that prompted this reform, but it also occurred during the long high summer of Victorian prosperity from 1851 to 1873, the peak of colonial expansionism and exactions from India and elsewhere. Eventually the working class became the beneficiaries of colonialism and industrialisation and they demanded a greater say, using their power of strikes to get their own vote.

The ruling classes, however, had begun to make concessions to the working class even before this happened. They passed legislation to limit the hours of work and to restrict the employ-ment of young children and they initiated workmen's compensation Acts for fatalities or injuries at work. Later, in the 1906 reforming administration of the liberals, arrived the first old age pension and the rudiments of social security. The strategy to attach an alienated working class to the system was clear. It was to be no different from the processes by which the industrial entrepreneurial middle class had been earlier incorporated, through a series of concessions, ameliorations and reforms. In this way, they hoped to demonstrate to a once refractory and mutinous working class the wisdom and unalterability of the economic system in which they lived.

Suffrage was grudgingly and belatedly entrusted to all only after they had been economically entrapped within the system, that is, when voters could be bought by the increasing consumer items provided in Britain made possible by the transfer of cash and commodities from India and the other colonies. The satisfied lower and middle classes could then be depended upon to support the existing power structures and could be safely given the right to vote. Many still needed to be persistently blackmailed by the possessing classes into not throwing the existing arrangements of society into chaos by deselecting those who ruled. Even then, women received the franchise only in 1921.

In the US, initially, "democracy" was reserved for the European invaders only, with the indigenous peoples being altogether excluded from voting. Also barred from the franchise were the slaves, the blacks, women, the non-property owning "lower" classes—all those in fact whom the rulers needed to exploit for their own enrichment.

In 1787, James Madison, the leading framer of the US constitution, observed that in England "if elections were open to all classes of people, the property of landed proprietors would be insecure." To ward off such injustice, he added, "our government ought to ensure the permanent interests of the country against innovation", establishing various devices, so "as to protect the minority of the opulent against the majority." That is the first principle of government, he stressed, to prevent these "communists" from "plundering the rich."[2]

In 1857, seventy years after the American Constitution was accepted, and sixty-six years after the promulgation of the Bill of Rights, the US Supreme Court observed that "the Constitution did not apply to the blacks as they were considered to be an inferior race." It was only with the Civil Rights Act of 1957 that blacks in the US finally achieved the right to equal status with the whites.[3]

Foreshadowings of Hitler's desire for racial purity were also apparent. H H Goddard, director of research at the Vineland Training School for Feeble-Minded Girls and Boys in New Jersey, devised a hierarchy which put at the bottom of the heap, criminals, alcoholics and prostitutes, and even the "ne'er-do-wells", all clubbed together as morons not capable of making an informed choice and hence not permitted to vote. The toiling workers came next as the merely dull: "The people who are doing the drudgery are, as a rule, in their proper places." They must be told exactly what to do, they must be followers not leaders. "At the top are the intelligent men who rule by right and have a right to live in comfort." Democracy, Goddard argued, "means that the people rule by selecting the wisest, most intelligent and most human to tell them what to do to be happy. Thus Democracy is a method for arriving at a truly benevolent aristocracy."[4]

Although the colonies were being freed from the late 1940s, several of them followed the Western way of democracy rather than returning to their traditional community-based systems, many of which were more just. Democracy was the preferred choice because it had been well dinned into them that it was the most equitable system of governance in existence.

Democracies in the ex-colonies were also the choice of the West because such regimes could be more easily manipulated when compared with those of a nationalist leader with traditional tastes. Control was necessary in order to ensure that the ex-colonies would continue to be sources of cheap raw materials and sinks for the West's expensive industrial products. The new leaders were therefore encouraged to retain the structures and institutions of their colonial past, though it was precisely these which had so terribly impoverished them. They were induced to look to the industrial world for their inspiration in developmental terms.

Tyranny of the Majority

In a representative democracy, those who do not have representatives or whose representatives do not get elected, for all practical purposes lose their right to be represented. "Everyone", therefore, does not include unrepresented minorities, making Article 21 self-contradictory.

The larger the nation, the greater the chance of the rights of individuals being violated. By widening the electoral constituency, the will of minorities in a particular area can be diluted allowing the will of, for instance, tribals or environmentally affected people to be "democratically" ignored.

By its very nature, majoritarian tyranny occurs in all representative democracies. The claim that the greatest good of the greatest number overrides the good of minorities enables those who rule to smother the will of any minority which does not willingly accede to their demands. The violation of human rights is guaranteed in the representative democratic system. The spectacular example of a disfranchised minority in the West now is the poor. Since these constitute a minority of the people—albeit a significant one—they can vote as they wish, but this will not disturb what has come to be known as the "electoral process", which now means trivial disputes between representatives of the possessing classes—exactly as it was before the franchise was ever conceded to the masses.

Today's industrial projects defend their trampling of the rights of people they displace, disemploy and pollute by claiming that it is the democratically determined will of the majority. Such democracy claims to balance the profit, comfort and convenience of one group against the loss of human rights of another, an obviously unjust endeavour.

The consequences of the blind tyranny of majorities may be seen in such intractable situations as the North of Ireland, the plight of ethnic minorities in Europe, the fate of the original inhabitants, blacks and recent immigrants in the "great democracy" of the USA. Majority rule has been misused by France when it encouraged ethnic French to settle in Polynesia, claimed to be a French Overseas Territory, not an old-fashioned colony. France now holds elections with universal suffrage, assured of the status quo.

Private Corporate Tyrannies

Though apparently conferring power on all citizens, the representative democratic system merely transfers real power—

and wealth—from the individual and the small community to a minute group of the elected. The latter are comprised mainly of industrialists who use that power for promoting a hyperconsumptive society required for minting profits.

In Europe, the 1950s marked the beginnings of the society of mass consumption of "consumer durables"—washing machines, refrigerators, vacuum cleaners, TVs, cars and other gadgets. Many of these offered convenience and relief from household drudgery, particularly to women, but it occurred to few people that there could be anything wrong with such a benign development.

These products, however, had a purpose other than their ostensible function: they helped to lure people into a system which created ever new desires. The progress of consumerism since that time has been one of deepening penetration of human life by marketed products, services, and entertainment, all requiring ever higher expenditures. What has occurred is the colonising of society by the market, the conquest of daily life by purchased commodities and services. This has set up a profound dependency in the peoples of the West upon a continuation of constantly enhanced income so that they may buy back from the market everything that was expropriated from them and enclosed by it. Food, for instance, which could be earlier obtained directly from the farmer or the corner shopkeeper, has now to be transported over long distances—often from other countries—and elaborately processed and packaged, before being sold in supermarkets, adding (monetary) value at each stage, even while it may become appreciably poorer in nutrients in the process.

The extension of the consumer society has deeply influenced people's attitude to democracy. Far from contesting the legitimacy of the wealth-making processes, all the political parties vie with each other in their promise to make it all work even better. People have become so accustomed to the existing order that any politician who offered a radical change would be instantly marginalised.

People's participation is, therefore, limited to electing "freely chosen representatives" who have been painstakingly preselected by those who already possess power and money. Such selection, earlier carried out by restricting the franchise, is now regulated by the costs of standing for election.

The trend can be seen in the US where for the 1992 presidential election the primaries alone cost over $175 million. As

Senator Barbara Mikulski noted, the US has the best Congress money can buy.[5]

The politicians are largely drawn from that section of society which directly or indirectly benefits from the extension of consumerism. The majority of the people elected as conservative politicians all over the Western world are industrialists, landowners, large scale farmers, builders, traders, and lawyers, with a few token members from the "working classes". The Trilateral Commission in the US stated that those not connected with these groups were undermining "democracy" by attempting to enter the arena of democratic politics instead of keeping to their "function" as "spectators", leaving their betters to run the show.[6]

The shadow boxing of individual contestants in the West is largely influenced by the compliant communications media. Much of the election expenditure goes for TV exposure and other publicity purposes. In fact, the quality of a candidate's public relations specialists plays a decisive part in her/his winning the election. The media serve to disseminate the views of politicians and "experts", all members in good standing of the power elite. The experts include compliant economists who constantly provide dire warnings that the economic system will collapse if the particular interests of their favourite parties are not served.

From this follows the next step: those who are good actors, who can convince their audience that they are sincere even while concealing the meanest of motives, who can recite the ghostwritten lines that please the people and who have a good TV presence, are those who win. Knowledge of the country's problems, the intelligence to work out just solutions and moral probity, play little, if any, part in winning such elections.

Such democratic systems are designed to translate the apparent "will of the people" into the will of the most powerful group in the region, allowing power-holding elites to continue to be elected as "representatives" of the people. As a consequence, the State is naturally the main actor in abusing its own citizens' human rights.

The manipulation of electorates perhaps reached its apogee of cynicism with the reelection of Boris Yeltsin in Russia in 1996; the image of a discredited, unpopular and moribund leader was skilfully repackaged by a cohort of American "experts", so that he was rapidly transformed into a dynamic and charismatic figure.

The whole process was revealed to have been a dance of death led by foreign corporate image-makers, a sophisticated conspiracy against the Russian people.[7]

Those finally elected are controlled by party policies, themselves determined by the powerful lobbies of narrow industrial and farming sectors—pharmaceuticals, tobacco, alcohol, vehicles, the oil industry, the defence industry, and so on, in which their constituents have a vested interest. It is the market which controls the government, not the other way about. The politicians are often reminded that the business of the government of the United States is business.

Over time, real power has long deserted or suborned the legislatures and taken up its abode in the boardrooms of TNCs, banks and other great financial centres of the world. This requires the dedicated undermining of any attempt to maintain true democracy, accomplished by transferring power even from a subservient government to, what Chomsky calls, "private tyrannies, which are unaccountable, unregulated, totalitarian in their internal structure, international in scale." Adds Chomsky: "These are recent forms of totalitarianism and they are crucially free from the threat of popular participation that is kind of a lingering danger in parliamentary systems."[2] Indeed, "participation" has been the real victim of these processes; the purpose of voters being simply to mark a piece of paper once every four or five years. It is scarcely surprising that less than half the electorate in the US decides to use its choiceless vote in any presidential consultation.

Racist conspiracy exists between the elite, industry and politicians. The "Yankee Patricians", a subgroup of the White Anglo-Saxon Protestants (WASPs), "still retain a firm grip on the US social order. They are prominent in the headquarters of large corporations, banks, insurance companies, law offices, and educational, cultural, and philanthropic institutions."[8] The last is not a sign of their charitable disposition but merely another means of extending control.

The president of the WB is nominated by the president of the US, the current incumbent being James Wolfensohn, president and chief executive officer of James D Wolfensohn, Inc. of New York, a large private banking firm.[9] It is not surprising, therefore, that a major concern of the World Bank is the protection and promotion of the interests of Western banks.

However, there is little need for active conspiracy. Industrialists, politicians and the affluent consumers, all have convergent interests. All the powerful are satisfied when the powerless are exploited.

The power elites can also be non-nationals, further emphasising the farce of democracy. TNCs regard themselves as supra-national entities, free to break laws of individual nations within whose territories they operate.

A director of Nestle made a generally applicable admission: "It will not be possible to regard us as purely Swiss, or purely multinational, namely belonging to the whole world, if there could be such a thing. We are probably something in between, a race apart. In a word, we hold a special nationality, 'Nestle nationality'."[10]

The influence of corporate America over the political process is further strengthened through the "revolving door" device: the movement of high-ranking persons, particularly cabinet staff, to jobs in the industrial complex and back again as the government switches between Democratic and Republican regimes.

The Bechtel Group, founded by Warren Bechtel, now the largest construction firm in the US, is known for the enormous power it wields in the US government. Warren Bechtel entered into partnership with John McCone during the 1939 war. The company constructed about 750 Liberty ships, among other war-related items, making huge profits.[11] It then began developing the oil reserves of Saudi Arabia. To this end, Warren Bechtel's son, Steve Bechtel, cultivated a cozy relationship with King Ibn Saud's son, Prince Faisal, who recommended Bechtel to his father.

To obtain the contract to build a pipeline from Saudi Arabia to the Mediterranean, Bechtel agreed not to employ Jews and arranged for a loan from the US Export-Import Bank.[12]

In the early 1950s, McCone left Bechtel to join the US government, later becoming chairperson of the Atomic Energy Commission (AEC). With McCone's help, Bechtel advanced in the commercial nuclear power business, designing or building about 40 per cent of the nuclear plants, licensed or under construction, in the US by the end of the 1970s.[13]

When McCone became head of the CIA, he used Bechtel's vast contacts in the Middle East for gathering information and the company itself, as a cover for CIA agents. Bechtel, in turn, used the same techniques as the CIA in its business activities and availed itself of the CIA's "intelligence" to its own advantage.[12]

With the collapse of the Nixon administration, George Schultz (Treasury Secretary), Caspar Weinberger (former Secretary of Health, Education and Welfare), Richard Helms (CIA director), Robert L Hollingsworth (AEC general manager) and several other Nixon appointees were taken on by Bechtel at several times their government salaries.

Bechtel was accused of violating the 1977 Foreign Corrupt Practices Act by bribing South Korean officials in order to obtain nuclear power plant construction contracts.[13] At that time, George Schultz was vice-chairman of the Bechtel Group board and was responsible for its internal auditing division; Casper Weinberger was Bechtel's top legal advisor, a vice-president and a director of the company. Both were in positions to know about the alleged bribes.

When Ronald Reagan was elected US president in 1980, the "revolving door" allowed Weinberger and Schultz to return to government in cabinet posts. Several other Bechtel executives were also given high government positions controlling national as well as international US policy.

The most influential lobbies are often run by ex-politicians thus ensuring mutually gratifying back-scratching. Henry Kissinger, former Secretary of State, was worth about $30 million in 1992, thanks to Kissinger Associates which lobbies for over thirty international companies. In 1992, two former members of the firm were key administration figures: Brent Scowcroft, National Security Adviser, and Larry Eagleburger, Deputy Secretary of State.[14]

That politicians in democracies can be bought by lobbyists is no longer doubted. In the UK, for instance, it has been suggested that concerned scientific organisations should start lobbying British MPs because grants to universities and other scientific research establishments have been drastically reduced of late. Simon Wolff wrote recently in the *New Scientist*: "They have to start paying MPs. It doesn't matter what political colour these individuals are so long as they have a chance of election. And if and when elected the bought MPs continue to be paid a healthy whack (as 'consultant' or 'adviser') only so long as they exert suitable pressure within the corridors of power."[15]

Disillusionment

People are becoming increasingly aware of their loss of power. In 1994, a poll showed that 82 per cent of the US population believed that the government is run for the benefit of a few special interests and not for the people at large; 83 per cent thought that the economic system is "inherently unfair."[16]

Such decay in confidence in the system serves the purposes of the corporate tyrannies, since the victims see no hope within the democratic system and simply refuse to go through the farce of voting. As stated earlier, under 40 per cent of the electorate in the US participate in elections.[16]

Democracy is being promoted as the only system that can provide justice, tyrannical dictatorships being portrayed as the sole alternatives. The failure of the only other major system of governance—the socialist USSR—that had pretensions to a different ordering and prioritising of human needs, is taken as confirmation that the Western democratic system is part of natural law. The Soviet collapse is used by the US to reinforce its claim that it is its manifest destiny to rule the world, even as the earlier overthrow of the native populations "proved" that the white race had a god-given right to the land.

Democracy—far from being a system which provides justice for all—has proved pliable enough to be extensively manipulated by institutionalised deceit for the organised management of impotence. The promotion of democracy, as the rule of the people, has become an exercise in deep global deception, an excellent tool for not-so-subtle exploitation. It is this system which has been sanctified and is being imposed on all other nations, in order that the West may perpetuate its injustice. There is no possibility of changing such systems of democracy from within.

The idea of democracy as the supreme political organisation to which human beings can aspire has been so thoroughly internalised that no search for an alternative even seems necessary. This is its ultimate success. It seems that the will of the people has become mysteriously congruent once more with the will of the powerful; and the world is prepared for a new kind of feudalism in which a diminished and acquiescent technopeasantry acknowledges its subservience and insignificance in the presence of those whose destiny it is to rule over it.

The Continuing Colonies

"Everyone is entitled to all the rights and freedoms set forth in this Declaration, without distinction of any kind such as race, colour, sex, language, religion, political and other opinion, national or social origin, property, birth or status. Furthermore, no distinction shall be made on the basis of the political, jurisdictional or international status of the country or territory to which a person belongs, whether it be independent, trust, non-self-governing or under any other limitation of sovereignty." (UDHR, Article 2)

The use of democracy by a few as a means to a profitable end must lead to enormous inconsistencies between the West's rhetoric and practice, none more glaring than its need to hold fast to its colonies even while claiming to be a champion of democracy. If "everyone is entitled to all the rights and freedoms", then there cannot be people in trusteeship or non-self-governing territories or territories with limitations of sovereignty. The Article also contradicts other listed rights, particularly the right to a nationality (Article 15 [1]), the "right to take part in the government of his country, directly or through freely chosen representatives" and "The will of the people shall be the basis of the authority of the government." (Articles 21 [1] and [3]).

The words used are simply meaningless and are expressed merely to give a pretense of apparent concern for justice. The only conclusion one can reach from such obvious nonsense is that it was never intended that "everyone" is entitled to all human rights. The profitable occupation of the West's colonies, therefore, can continue uninhibited. The entitlements of indigenous people in Canada, the USA, the rest of America, Australia and, in fact, wherever they exist, can be blithely ignored. Minority ethnic groups within practically all national entities are also denied such freedoms.

To ensure that there could be no punishment for their horrendous past colonial violations of human rights, the imperialist nations bestowed on themselves an unconditional, anticipatory absolution for all their past and future colonial transgressions. Article 11 (2) states: "No one shall be held guilty of any penal offence on account of any act or omission which did not constitute a penal offence, under national or international law, at the time when it was committed."

This is a vital element in the West's determined attempt to rewrite its own past. The erasure of memory is a necessary condition for the clean slate upon which its brave new version of human rights is to be inscribed.

It has often been said, and repeated now *ad nauseam* on the occasion of the fiftieth anniversary of the end of the 1939-44 war, that children should not be expected to bear the burden of guilt for their forefathers' misdeeds. However, this guilt must persist so long as those children benefit from those crimes, even if they were perpetrated 500 or more years ago. It will also endure as long as the children of those who were originally denied their rights are still suffering their consequences.

Further, at the time the UN Declaration was composed, the main "enemy" of the West was the Soviet Union with its imputed expansionist policies, competing with the West's equally ambitious aims. The preamble to the Declaration can be seen as advice to the Soviet peoples to rebel "against tyranny and oppression", if their human rights were not "protected by the rule of law." That this was directed at the communist regimes alone is evident from the last paragraph of the preamble which states that the (listed) rights have to be recognised and observed "both among the peoples of Member States themselves and among peoples of territories under their jurisdiction." They were not, of course, applicable to the colonies under Western "jurisdiction."

The occupation of Native lands by the Europeans continues uninhibited today in Diego Garcia, New Caledonia, the Amazon region, the Caribbean area, Hong Kong and above all in the immense, but apparently invisible, occupied territories, the US, Canada, Australia and New Zealand. The US in addition to its mainland, occupies such remote lands as the Virgin Islands, the UN Trust Territories of the Pacific Islands, Hawai'i and several pieces of other people's territories.

Britain's far flung island colonies, euphemistically called Dependent Territories, continue to be sources of exploitable natural resources. Their populations range from a few thousand down to a mere fifty.[17]

Diego Garcia is a small island which is part of the Great Chagos Bank, a pristine atoll in the Indian Ocean. It rightfully belongs to Mauritius but the atoll is occupied by the British who have, without consulting Mauritius, leased it to the US for fifty years. In 1970, about 1,200 natives—the Ilois community—were forcibly evicted from their homeland and dumped in Mauritius. Britain paid Mauritius $1.43 million to take care of them, just enough it appears, to house and maintain them in the slums of Port Louis.[18] The US built up a huge communications and military base on the island to "protect its interests in the area"—its interests taking priority over the rights of the Ilois.

Ascension Island, where the British have spent billions of pounds on "defence" installations, is in the mid-Atlantic just south of the equator. It provided the essential stopover for the RAF during Britain's war over the Falklands.

After being forced to grant independence to most of its colonies, Britain sanctimoniously demanded that democracy be the norm in the new nations. Hong Kong is an excellent example of just this sort of hypocrisy. The first—indirect—elections to the Hong Kong Legislative Assembly were held only in 1986 after the agreement between the UK and China for ending UK sovereignty on July 1, 1997 was ratified. Yet the territory's governor, Chris Patten, virtuously orated in 1993: "Britain must stand up for democracy in Hong Kong....What we are talking about is putting in place for the 1995 elections, the last ones under British sovereignty, electoral arrangements that are clean and decent and straightforward—election arrangements which won't guarantee a rubber-stamp legislative council."[19] The people of Hong Kong, after being ruled autocratically for nearly a century, have much to be thankful for in this deathbed repentance. But the main aim of this cynical playacting seems to have been a petulantly childish wish to tweak the tail of the Chinese dragon. To top it all, the British prime minister had the audacity to attack China's human rights record.[20]

That the record of China itself has involved systematic abuse of human rights does not redeem the record of Britain or the other Western powers. China invaded Tibet in 1949 and a mass uprising that failed ten years later forced the Dalai Lama to flee to India. Since then Lhasa has witnessed several massacres such as that which occurred in Tiananmen Square, claiming thousands of lives. Chinese immigrants and troops have been pouring into Tibet in an apparently successful attempt to destroy Tibetan culture and its Buddhist religion. These events have been studiously ignored by all the major world powers as well as by the UN.

The US: Champion of Democracy?

The pious defence by the US of the right to democracy is largely negated by its calculated use of democratic rights as a device to dominate other countries for its own economic advantage. This is demonstrated by the ease with which it disposes of those democratic regimes which become a hindrance to its hegemonic ambitions, replacing them with totalitarian or tyrannical ones which can be manipulated to sell their country cheaply for money deposited in Swiss banks. Chomsky observes that the US has "compiled an impressive record of aggression, international terrorism, slaughter, torture, chemical and bacteriological warfare, human rights abuses of every imaginable variety."[21]

In the year of the adoption of the Declaration on Human Rights, even while democracy was being formally promoted as a basic human right, the US State Department assigned a subsidiary role to each region of the Two Thirds World. The US would take charge of South America and the Middle East, the latter with the temporary help of Britain. Africa was to be exploited for the reconstruction of Europe, and Southeast Asia would "fulfill its major function as a source of raw materials" for Japan and Western Europe.[22] Later, Carter's South America advisor explained that the US was willing to let other nations "act independently, except when doing so would affect US interests adversely"; the US has never wanted "to control them", as long as developments did not "get out of control."[22]

This "Reagan Doctrine", as it was then called, "states the case for the moral superiority of democratic institutions." Yet a senior State Department official revealed: "We debated whether we had the right to dictate the form of another country's government. The bottom line was yes, that some rights are more fundamental than the right of nations to nonintervention, like the rights of individual people."[23] The "individual people" were limited to US citizens, and democratic regimes were tolerated only as long as they did not "get out of control."

Less than five years after the adoption of the UN Declaration, Britain and France invaded Egypt and the US replaced Iran's democratically elected prime minister, Mossadegh, with the Shah monarchy, later known for its horrifying human rights record. All this was done for the sake of maintaining the West's trade routes and sources of oil. And the West, human rights notwithstanding, unashamedly continues to pursue such policies.

The West accepts and supports particular tyrannies so long as the countries concerned cooperate in offering themselves as prey for its parasitical needs. To help its partners, the US maintains a well-known training school in Fort Benning, the US Army's School of the Americas, which has trained mainly South and Central American dictators—and their police and armies—in carrying out terrorist activities. Over 60,000 persons have been taught "to make war against their own people, to subvert the truth, silence poets, domesticate unruly visionaries, muzzle activist clergy, hinder trade unionism, hush the voices of dissidence and discontent, neutralise the poor, the hungry, the dispossessed, extinguish common dreams, irrigate fields of plenty with the tears of a captive society, and transform paladins and protesters into submissive vassals." Panamanian President Jorge Illueca called the School, "the biggest base for destabilisation in Latin America." Among its successful alumni have been the region's most despicable tyrants: Omar Torrijos of Panama, Guillermo Rodriguez of Ecuador and Juan Velasco Alvarado of Peru—all of whom overthrew constitutionally elected civilian governments. To disguise its activities, the School now claims to be teaching human rights.[24]

Numerous examples can be given of violation of the sovereignty of other nations by the US when it suits its own purposes. The point to emphasize is that a superpower democracy is self-contradictory.

Chile

Salvador Allende was elected president of Chile in 1970 in democratic elections. He improved Chile's human rights record, using a socialist rather than a capitalist model. The US feared that Chile's success would tempt other nations to follow its example, thus getting out of US control. It decided to remove Allende, with the help of the CIA, by making "the economy scream."[25] The US Ambassador explained his strategy: that the US would "do all within our power to condemn Chile and the Chileans to the utmost deprivation and poverty..."[26] Allende was assassinated in 1973 by a military force under General Augusto Pinochet. US TNCs such as ITT were involved in the overthrow of the Allende Government.

In 1974, Pinochet was acclaimed a success by the US because his policies established a free market economy which permitted the US to exploit Chile's valuable resources. Following this, the proportion of the population that fell below the poverty line increased from twenty to 44 per cent by 1987. Health care expenditure was reduced to half of what it was earlier, with an explosive growth in poverty-related diseases. Consumption dropped 30 per cent below 1973 levels for the poorest, but increased by 15 per cent for the richest. Education at the university level was no longer free, but restricted to the rich.[25]

Guatemala

Juan Arevalo and his successor, Jacobo Arbenz, the heads of Guatemala, introduced extensive social reforms between 1945 and 1954. Social groups, unions, peasants, and political parties were able to organise themselves without fear of repression or murder.[27] However, land reform, the organisation of trade unions and other socially just moves, did not suit the interests of US TNCs in Guatemala, in particular that of the United Fruit Company. Using psychological warfare and terrorist operations, a tiny mercenary army, headed by Colonel Armas, ousted Arbenz and installed an autocratic regime in 1954.[28] CIA documents revealed that Liberacion, a front organisation for the military, was set up and armed under orders from CIA director Allen Dulles, brother of Secretary of State John Foster Dulles. Both had been lawyers for United Fruit, some of whose property had been earlier expropriated (with compensation).[29]

Armas, after coming to power returned the Arbenz-expropriated lands and permitted plantation owners to cut down wages by about 30 per cent.[30] Since that time, under US tutelage, no economic and social reforms have been carried out, democracy has been stifled, and state terror institutionalised. Political murder and large scale repression have been reintroduced. With the emergence of a small guerrilla movement in the early 1960s, the US trained the Guatemalan army in counterinsurgency techniques.[27]

Several human rights organisations documented the forcible relocation of hundreds of thousands of farmers and villagers into camps, accompanied by the government's widespread killing, tending to genocide, of peasants including women and children.[31]

Yet Ronald Reagan informed Congress that the US would provide more arms "to reinforce the improvement in the human rights situation following the 1982 coup" that installed Rios Montt, the man responsible for the killing.[32]

All this was not an aberration of a senile president, but had the active support of even the higher academic institutions. General Hector Gramajo was rewarded for his contributions to mass murder in the Guatemalan highlands with a fellowship to Harvard's John F Kennedy School of Government. This was "the State Department's way of grooming Gramajo" for the job of the next president.[33]

In an interview he gave to the *Harvard International Review*, Gramajo explained his "70-30 per cent civil affairs programme", used during the 1980s "to control people or organisations who disagreed with the government." He boasted: "We have created a more humanitarian, less costly strategy, to be more compatible with the democratic system. We instituted civil affairs (in 1982) which provides development for 70 per cent of the population, while we kill 30 per cent. Before, the strategy was to kill 100 per cent." This he explained is a "more sophisticated means" than the previous crude assumption that you must "kill everyone to complete the job" of controlling dissent.

Former CIA director William Colby sent Gramajo a copy of his memoirs with the inscription: "To a colleague in the effort to find a strategy of counterinsurgency with decency and democracy."[34]

The Bush administration, in a show of anger over the killing of an American, cut off military aid to Guatemala in 1990, but secretly allowed the CIA to send millions of dollars to the military government to make up for the loss.[35] On the other hand, an American woman's Guatemalan husband was allegedly murdered by a Guatemalan colonel who was in the payroll of the CIA. It took her over three years to get the government to investigate the incident.[30]

The killings naturally continue. The Guatemalan Army deliberately executed 11 Indian peasants in October 1995, according to a report released by a United Nations team. Members of a military patrol "seriously violated human rights" by firing on the peasants, including women and children.[36]

Panama

Since 1856 there have been sixteen invasions and military interventions by the US in the Panama region, the latest occurring on 21 December 1989. President Bush claimed that this attack was necessary to save American lives since Panamanian troops were threatening US civilians and military personnel in the country, to protect traffic through the Panama Canal, to restore democracy to Panama although the country had been ruled by the military since 1968, to stop drug trafficking and to bring General Manuel Noriega to justice. What the US government failed to mention was that Noriega spent twenty years on the CIA payroll and received his training in the US.[29]

Further, in 1991, the Independent Commission of Inquiry, headed by former US Attorney General Ramsey Clark, published a report which tells a very different story. According to the report, the US, in 1977, signed treaties which affirmed that the Panama Canal would be turned over completely to Panama by the year 2000 and that the fourteen US bases in Panama would be returned to Panamanian control. Accordingly, in January 1990, a Panamanian was appointed to oversee the administration of the Canal. For five years before the invasion, the US had been demanding the renegotiation of the 1977 treaty, to continue its hold on the Canal. Further, Admiral John Poindexter (of Iran-Contragate fame) had demanded repeatedly that Nicaraguan Contra forces be based in Panama. The US had also insisted that Panama end its economic and political cooperation with Nicaragua and Cuba. Noriega refused all the US demands.[37]

The US invasion of Panama left 20,000 homeless and about 1000 dead. The US installed a government with Guillermo Endara as the president. Most Panamanians are black or Indian, as well as poor. Endara's revered mentor is Arnulfo Arias, who admired the Nazis and advocated white supremacy for Panama.[38] The Independent Commission discovered a chart giving out the names of US State Department and Pentagon officials in Panama who were in charge of every ministry in the new Panamanian government.[37]

According to the Council on Hemispheric Affairs, the proportion of Panamanian poor has risen from 33 per cent of the 2.3 million population before the invasion to 50 per cent today.[39] Since the invasion, Panamanian administration of the canal was stopped and three US military bases which had been returned to Panama were taken back by the US.[37]

The claim of the US that the purpose of the invasion was to stop the drug trade is belied by the fact that Endara was the Secretary of the directors of Interbanco, a bank known for laundering Colombian drug money.[39]

Nicaragua

The US openly supported the undemocratic and violently brutal Somoza regime in Nicaragua which killed about 60,000 of its own people. When it was overthrown by the more democratic FSLN (the Sandinistas) in 1979, the US provided the Contras with arms to slaughter Nicaraguan peasants and practically declared war against that small nation, even to the extent of mining its harbours. In 1986 the US was condemned by the World Court of Justice for crimes and violations committed by the CIA and Contras against the State and people of Nicaragua. Ordered to pay billions in compensation, the US ignored the decision and continued its illegal activities until the US Contra War ended in 1990. By then Nicaragua's infrastructure had been destroyed and an estimated 35,000 civilians had been killed.[29] The invasion of Panama took place just weeks before elections in Nicaragua, sending a threatening message to Nicaraguan electors about what could happen if they voted for the Sandinistas.

El Salvador

In the 12-year war conducted by the US-supported regime in El Salvador against its own people, tens of thousands were killed, wounded or driven into exile. Both Reagan and Bush supported the death squads and the strategy of mass terrorism. In December 1981, in six remote villages, perhaps 750 people were killed by a Salvadoran unit led by an American-trained colonel. The massacre of nearly the entire village populations was thorough: men first, women next, children and babies last, by bullets, knives, bayonets and hanging. Young girls were spared only till they became victims of rape. The next day Reagan certified to Congress, as American law required him to do if aid to El Salvador was to continue, that El Salvador's government was "making a significant effort to comply with internationally recognised human rights."[40]

The Dominican Republic

Juan Bosch, the first democratically elected president of the Dominican Republic in over thirty years, instituted land reforms and mass education, attacked corruption, and improved the general human rights situation. These policies threatened powerful internal vested interests. Bosch's overthrow by the military after just nine months in office had at least the tacit support of the United States. Two years later, the Johnson administration invaded the Dominican Republic to make sure that Bosch did not resume power.[41]

Vietnam

After the defeat of the Japanese in 1945, Vietnam attempted to free itself from its colonial bondage under France. In a long and violent war, the French were ignominiously defeated in 1954. Thereafter, the Geneva Accord established a partition of Vietnam at the 17th parallel, pending reunification through elections within two years. The US pledged not to obstruct these arrangements but it quickly undermined the agreement by its military support for the Diem regime in the south. The US worked desperately to prevent elections, which would have almost certainly led to a unified Vietnam under Viet Minh rule. Diem proved unable to control the situation so the US invaded the country in 1965.[42] The rhetoric used to justify its invasion was that the US had a duty to look beyond its purely national interests to serve all mankind—a new white man's burden.

The United Nations did not ever condemn the US intervention nor did it investigate or denounce the crimes committed in the course of US military operations.[43] The air and ground attacks of the US forces devastated Vietnam as well as parts of neighbouring Laos, Cambodia and Thailand.[42] For the US allies, in particular Japan and South Korea, the profitable war led to their economic "take-off".[43]

Civilian casualties were regarded as unavoidable side effects of "a job that had to be done", requiring no moral questions to be raised.[44] In 1968, American soldiers launched an attack on the My Lai complex of villages, claimed to be harbouring members of the Vietnamese National Liberation Front (NLF). The Americans encountered no resistance whatsoever and no sign of NLF activity but still murdered almost everyone they found: 504 people, including 182 women and 173 children (fifty-six of them babies).[45] In the massacre at nearby My Khe ninety civilians were reported killed. Proceedings against the officer in charge were dismissed on the grounds that this was merely a normal operation in which a village was destroyed and its population murdered.[46] The death toll in the whole of Indochina was about four million.[47]

The war brought out the racism in the Western cupboard. The US media, particularly TV, presented events as a battle between the US forces of good and Hanoi's forces of evil. The former were depicted as "brave men", "the greatest men in the world", "heroes", exuding competence, humanity, and high morale as they fought against "Communist aggression" in the "battle for democracy", who "win hearts and minds" by caring for sick and injured civilians after a village "was burned and blasted to death."[48] The North Vietnamese and Vietcong were portrayed as "savage", "brutal", "murderous", "fanatical", "suicidal", "halfcrazed", mere vermin in areas that were "Communist infested" or "Vietcong infested", and thus had to be cleansed by the American liberators.[49] Most of these epithets were remarkably similar to those used by the European invaders in their wars against the Native Americans. More media attention was given to the 57,000 Americans who were killed than to the two million Vietnamese.[50]

The Vietnamese environment was totally devastated through chemical warfare, specially with the use of an herbicide, Agent Orange. The resulting massive defoliation laid waste some two million hectares of forest and farmland.[51] The highly toxic Agent Orange possibly led to the high rate of stillbirths and an increase in birth defects. While the US chemical companies that manufactured Agent Orange paid about $180 million in compensation to US soldiers who were victims of the herbicide, the Vietnamese who suffered much more and are still suffering from it have received nothing.[52]

In the early years of the war, it was taken for granted that the US would certainly win, not only because the US was more powerful but also because it was presumed that right was clearly on the US side.[49] When the war was lost, in petulant revenge the US refused reparations, aid and trade. President Carter asserted that the US owed Vietnam no debt and had no responsibility to render it any assistance because "the destruction was mutual."[53]

While the US lost the war in Vietnam in 1975, it finally won it in 1995. The Vietnamese have now been happily brought into the global capitalist family, with all the sacrifices of the millions who suffered and died being in vain. The successful economic weapon used by the US was the embargo.

Cambodia

Before the fall of Cambodia to Pol Pot and his Khmer Rouge, the US bombed Cambodian territory mercilessly, with numerous casualties going unrecorded. Pol Pot was termed a villain worse than Hitler, and the atrocities committed during his regime were described in all their gory detail. But after Pol Pot's ouster by the Vietnamese, the United States flip-flopped to support Pol Pot.[54] The West even approved of the Khmer Rouge's occupation of Cambodia's seat at the UN, despite the genocide which the regime had unleashed while it was in power.[55]

Indonesia

The US supported Indonesia because it welcomed Western investment, even when it invaded East Timor in 1976, with large scale massacres of its natives.[54] Indonesia annexed the country, an act not officially recognised by the United Nations.[56] The US is mainly responsible for supporting Indonesia in its continuing occupation and slaughter.

Iraq

Back in the 1890s, much of imperial Britain's power in the Middle East resulted from its hold on Kuwait, which had a good harbour and was an important port on the overland trade route. Britain used Kuwait as a base from which it could control piracy, the slave trade, and foreign influence in the region. Although Kuwait was under Turkish domination, Britain claimed in 1897 that it had "never acknowledged Kuwait to be under Turkish protection", and that Turkey had not "effectively maintained" its sovereignty over Kuwait, reasons remarkably similar to those used earlier by Europeans when occupying North America. It was only after territories were annexed by such outrageous means, that international law formulated by the European powers, was invoked to sanctify the conquests. A semblance of justice was maintained by Britain installing a local sheikh as a puppet ruler.[57]

Middle East oil had been under British, Dutch and German control since 1912 when the Turkish Petroleum Company was given the concession to prospect for oil in the then Ottoman provinces of Baghdad and Mosul. However, in the war of 1914-18, Turkey made the fatal error of joining the side which lost. On November 1914, British troops landed at Shatt al-Arab to protect the oil installations at Abadan. In March 1917 the British captured Baghdad, taking Mosul in the next year. In April 1920 the League of Nations awarded Britain the mandate for Iraq; the Iraqis ineffectually revolted against the British mandate in July 1920. Till the revolution of 1958, Iraq remained under British influence. Kuwait, although belonging to this region, officially became a British protectorate and remained so till 1961 when it was given its independence.[58] This manipulation of Kuwait's status formed the basis of Iraq's later occupation of the territory.

Middle East oil later went under the control of US petroleum companies, with the oil fields and refineries nominally owned and operated by the Arabs. But with the oil reserves of the US being rapidly depleted, and with the ever imminent possibility of Islamic fundamentalists overthrowing US-oriented regimes, the US thought it wise to make its control firmer by maintaining a military presence in the region.

Subsequent events reveal the meticulous planning which goes into the manipulation of human rights to serve the West's material interests.

In 1980, President Carter, in his State of the Union Address, asserted that any attempt by an outside power to gain control over the Persian Gulf region would be considered an assault on the vital interests of the US.[58] In February 1992, a secret Pentagon paper on Defense Planning Guidance for budgetary policy till the year 2000, stated that in the Middle East "our overall objective is to remain the predominant outside power in the region and preserve US and Western access to the region's oil."[59] The US military establishment planned the invasion of the Arabian area eighteen months prior to the actual start of the Gulf War.

This occupation of the Arabian region by the US is comparable to the manner in which Britain "conquered" the numerous Indian independent states. It egged on a particular state to start hostilities with its neighbours, suggested that it needed help from the British, and then occupied both states.

Iraq had informed the US about its intention to invade Kuwait if talks on long-standing disputes did not succeed. The US ambassador to Iraq, April Glaspie, told Saddam Hussein: "We have no opinion on the Arab-Arab conflicts, like your border disagreement with Kuwait." This gave the clear impression that the US would not interfere if Iraq did invade Kuwait.[60] Yet when Iraq entered Kuwait, the US pretended to be surprised and shocked.

The West raised its bloodied hands in horror at such wanton wickedness, claiming in effect a hereditary monopoly on major human rights abuse. The West now preaches that others should not occupy their neighbour's lands though the European occupation of the continents of America, Australia and several other land masses were the largest, most violent occupations in history. In doing this it parades the virtue of the sinner who no longer has need for the benefits of the vice. It appears that the claim to permanent occupation overrides the basic rights of indigenous peoples, a remarkable moral mutation which turns vices over a certain magnitude into admirable, but not to be emulated, virtues.

Saddam Hussein had been maintained in power by the West for years, in spite of his enormous human rights violations. After Iraq's invasion, the US and the UN showed a sudden concern for human rights in Iraq, even while condoning similar abuses in neighbouring Turkey, its trusted NATO ally. Chandra Muzaffar put it bluntly: "While the UN...has demonstrated in no uncertain terms its concern for the human rights of the Kurds of Iraq, it has given very little attention to the brutal suppression of the Kurds of Turkey."[61] More recently, the Turkish army invaded the Kurdish areas and openly slaughtered the Kurds. Turkey has clearly stated that it intends to keep its forces in this area indefinitely.[62] The US and the UN have raised no objections.

Though Saddam showed no intention of doing so, the US convinced Saudi Arabia that the invasion of its territory was imminent. The US claimed that satellite images revealed a huge Iraqi force ready to attack. This was an essential deception required to persuade Saudi Arabia and other Islamic countries to permit infidel forces to enter into their territories to "protect" them.

Employing the UN as a puppet to serve their own purposes, the US and its allies persuaded a majority of the members of the Security Council to vote for the war resolution No 678, which was not supported by any article of the UN charter. The persuasion was supported by bribery, blackmail and threats.[63]

The Soviet Union was bought with $4 billion from the Gulf States and by US promises to review its policies on food aid and agricultural credit. The US restored diplomatic relations with China and arranged for its first World Bank loan since the Tiananmen Square massacre. Turkey was bribed with $8 billion military aid, a promise of admission to the European Community, a greater market for its products in the US, and a licence to persecute Turkish Kurds. Egyptian debts of more that $14 billion were written off by the World Bank. Syria's President Hafez Assad, till then labelled by the US as one of the "sponsors of terrorism", was given Washington's go-ahead to wipe out all opposition to his occupation of Lebanon, helped by $1 billion worth of arms. Iran had been denied WB loans since the 1979 Islamic revolution; a WB loan of $250 million was approved the day before the US launched its ground attack against Iraq.[63] The ease with which the disbursal of WB and IMF loans was stopped or permitted reveals the close control the US has on these so-called independent international institutions.

Britain had broken off ties with Iran because of the death sentence imposed by it on Salman Rushdie, a British citizen. Britain restored relations with no change in Iran's position, apparently on the moral principle that the enemy of my enemy is my friend.

Afraid that the question of its violations would be raised in the UN, the US bribed Zaire, the president of the council, by writing off its military debts. Zaire obligingly refused requests from Cuba, Yemen and India to convene the Security Council, even though it had no power to do so under the UN Charter.[63]

Those countries which opposed the US position were duly punished: US aid to Yemen was stopped, it began to have problems with the WB and 80,000 Yemenis were expelled from Saudi Arabia. Zambia suddenly had difficulty obtaining IMF loans, and Sudan, though in the grip of a famine, was denied a shipment of food aid.[63]

Resolution No 678 was passed, confirming the cracks in the credibility of the UN as a neutral international institution. The manipulation of the UN was further evident in the insistence of the

US on the quick implementation of this Resolution even while numerous UN resolutions under which Israel was commanded to vacate its much more extensive and long-standing occupations of the territory of Palestine, Lebanon, Syria and Jordan were not carried out.

The UN resolution authorised its member states to use "all necessary means" to force Iraq to withdraw from Kuwait.[64] The member states modestly transferred this collective responsibility to the US alone. This permitted the US, under the cover of implementing the resolution, to carry out large scale crimes against humanity, the bombing of civilian women and children, hospitals and schools, historical and religious monuments despite these people and places being protected by international laws of armed conflict, the Geneva Conventions of 1864 and 1906 and the Hague Conventions of 1899 and 1907.[65] Pentagon officials later acknowledged that the 43-day air attacks on Iraq's infrastructure and civilian installations were designed to make recovery from the war extremely difficult without foreign assistance.

About 150,000 Iraqi civilians and 170,000 under-five children were killed during and immediately after the attacks. In addition, around 1.8 million people were forced to leave their homes. Iraq's urban, agricultural and industrial infrastructure was substantially destroyed, resulting in malnutrition, starvation and epidemics of typhus, cholera, polio, meningitis, hepatitis and others diseases.[66]

The civilian casualties were called collateral damage, unfortunate accidents of war, though the Western media actually gloated in such death and destruction. Describing the first air attack on Baghdad, John Holliman of CNN elatedly exclaimed that it was "like the fireworks finale on the Fourth of July at the base of the Washington Monument."[67] Time magazine reported that Baghdad was "lit up like a Christmas tree."[68]

The underlying racism still rampant in the US was again brought out in the terminology used in the Gulf war; the US Marines began the ground war by storming "Indian" country at "High Noon."[69]

The foresight of building a military base on Diego Garcia was amply demonstrated when the B-52 strategic bombers stationed there pounded much of Iraq back into the Middle Ages with extraordinary precision. These bombers dropped 26,000 tonnes of bombs, 40 per cent of the entire tonnage unloaded on Iraq during the war. It was a lesson for all within range of the base—including India—to behave themselves as the US wanted them to.

After the war ended, UN Security Resolution 687 demanded, among other things, the elimination of chemical and other weapons of mass destruction and related research facilities in Iraq, constituting a violation of Iraq's national sovereignty. Such a demand should have been extended to every member of the UN. The US today still maintains a stock of the nerve gas, Sarin, sufficient to kill every single person, and much of animal life too, in the world.

During the war, the rights of nationals of several Two Thirds World countries were affected as thousands of expatriate workers lost their jobs and oil supplies became uncertain. High-technology warfare damaged the environment and threatened life in places at and near the scene of battle, as well as far beyond the war zone. The Gulf War demonstrated the wide variety and intensity of these harmful ecological effects. On the battleground, thousands of tanks and heavy vehicles crushed the fragile desert ecological systems, some of which may take decades to recover. Tens of thousands of tonnes of high explosives compounded the damage. The massive fires that resulted from bombing oil refineries and storage tanks, and only later from Iraq's ignition of gushing crude oil at wellheads, polluted the atmosphere for thousands of kilometres across Asia. The considerable oil spills from damaged shipping and broken pipelines contaminated the ocean and shores all along the Gulf.[70] Uranium-tipped missiles and shells have probably resulted in what is called the Gulf War syndrome.

The subsequent embargo imposed by the UN, under US orders, on trade with Iraq greatly increased mortality in Iraq, particularly among children. The embargo forms part of the total war policy where civilian human rights are not allowed to enter the picture at all.

The US has profited greatly from the reconstruction programme, thus boosting its own economy. Since "liberation", Kuwait has spent about $50 billion on repairing its infrastructure alone, most of it carried out by US companies. Saudi Arabia still owes the US about $15 billion for the "aid" provided by the US in occupying its country. It has therefore requested the US not to lift the embargo on Iraq since the price of oil would drop when Iraq returns to the world market.[71]

The US claims that it was essential to remove Saddam because he is a dictator. The Saudi Arabian government is noted for its absolute autocracy, King Fahd claiming that "the democratic system...does not suit us in the region."[72] Yet not a whispered word sullies its reputation since the US is dependent on that regime for its oil. Ramsey Clark has observed: "The industrial countries' unquenchable thirst for Middle East oil...has always been antagonistic to democracy and human rights throughout the Arab world."[73]

Having got Iraq completely under its control, the US has now returned to Iran, the only major oil producer left in the region which is not under US domination. Claiming that Iran was promoting global terrorism, it imposed trade sanctions on the country in March 1995. But the sanctions have made little difference to Iran's oil trade, forcing the US to threaten Iran with more curbs on trade.

CHAPTER 5

The Right to Development

From the late 1940s, colonies vigorously demanded—and were reluctantly given—their independence, an independence which the colonial powers resisted with all their force, branding all freedom fighters "terrorists" or puppets of communism. The stories of Malaya, Algeria, Kenya, and of Zimbabwe demonstrate the desperation of the imperial powers to hang on to the resources of others.

However, the elites of these colonies were nearly all educated and trained in the West. Many thus became willing prey for their erstwhile colonisers, with the result that the new structures of power remained essentially subservient to the West. There was also considerable Western pressure. Ithiel Pool, a political scientist at the Massachusetts Institute of Technology (MIT), has observed that throughout the Two Thirds World "it is clear that order depends on somehow compelling newly mobilised strata to return to a measure of passivity and defeatism."[1] The violation of the rights of the people of the Two Thirds World by the West, therefore, did not stop with the achievement of political freedom, but was continued through economic means.

The economic subjugation of the globe was official US policy at least as far back as August 1949. A US National Security Council policy statement on Asia asserted that the US must find ways of "exerting economic pressures" on countries that do not accept their role as suppliers of "strategic commodities and other basic materials."[2]

Human rights issues have been used as a potent tool by the West to achieve such control by the simple expedient of claiming that development, in the Western path alone, is a fundamental human right. In the last few years there has been desperate hyperactivity by the UN, with one conference after another, ostensibly promoting human rights, while supporting Western development.

The Vienna conference of 1993 openly affirmed what was already implicit in the 1948 UN UDHR, that the West's promotion of human rights would be used primarily as a means of imposing its own developmental model on the rest of the world. Paragraph 5 reads: "Democracy, development and respect for human rights and fundamental freedoms are interdependent and mutually reinforcing. The international community should support strengthening and promoting democracy, development and respect for human rights and fundamental freedoms in the entire world."[3]

These assertions are stated as if they were fundamental axioms when they are not based on any facts. All the evidence points to the contrary—that development is to the economic advantage of the West and not to that of protecting human rights.

It is further claimed that the West's own special system, restricted to the free market ideology, is globally valid. This has been ingeniously expressed in Article 28 of the UDHR: "Everyone is entitled to a social and international order in which the rights and freedoms set forth in this Declaration can be fully realised."

A universal order implies that differing local orders are an abuse of human rights. The free market economy, merely the creed of one social and economic system, is the "international order" which the West seeks to universalise as if it were a "law of nature". This, it then claims, gives it the right to impose inhuman development policies which violate people's rights, even those specifically listed in the UN Declaration. If the West's targets suffer and perish for economic reasons, this is seen as an unfortunate but essential consequence of the supremacy of its economic rights as a natural outcome of conformity with the unique "international order".

With the general acceptance by the dominated of tight and explicit linkage between human rights and development, the West no longer needs the ghoulish apparatus of repression which distinguished so much of its not-so-distant past. The Western policy of choice today is economic warfare, its starved victims being less gory and repulsive than those of mutilation and violent death.

Physical occupation is replaced by control of global agriculture, industry and trade. This is easily accomplished through the apparently reasonable persuasion of UN organisations and the more coercive policies of the West's moneylending and trading institutions: the IMF, WB and GATT. Disguised as international organisations with the interests of every unfortunate human being at heart, these institutions are controlled by a coterie of Western industrialists and their governments who manage the world economy and politics for their own profit.

Just as the British defended their colonial occupation by declaring that they were in India mainly for India's good, so too do the WB, IMF and WTO proclaim today that their interest is purely altruistic. Together they have resumed the "white man's burden", imposing conditionalities and structural adjustment programmes (SAPs) purely for India's good. They thereby convey, not too subtly, that the Indian government is too backward and obtuse to manage its own economy.

This is but another illustration of how traditional colonial racism merges seamlessly with its modernised successor, the procession of experts, professionals, advisers and consultants who stream out of the Western academic institutions to bring the backward and superstitious inhabitants of the Two Thirds World into the pure light of the economic reason of the West. Unfortunately there is a transition period, they sorrowfully reveal, when the poor will get poorer as liberalisation leads to increasing unemployment and malnutrition. They gently imply, though, that it is so much more civilised to die of SAPs than of plain old poverty.

The economic methods, instruments and institutions formulated by the West serve the same purposes of domination, coercion, torture and exploitation that the earlier overt colonial occupations, killings, slavery and forced trade did. Today the West uses these institutional surrogates to make the economies of those nations it wishes to control "scream", in order to force them into their West-designated places. Moreover, if particular nations refuse to accept the West's economic system, force is used to subdue or destabilise them. Acceptance is ensured by subjecting them to trade sanctions, embargoes, or revolutions and other measures plotted and executed by such undemocratic, unaccountable agents as the CIA and its equivalents in other countries.

The inhuman right to free markets subsumes and sometimes snuffs out all other rights. The free market turns out to be freedom for TNCs to invade and occupy other countries and enslave their people to work for them, freedom to retain the Two Thirds World countries as sources of cheap raw materials, dumps for toxic wastes and, most important, recipients of their destructive hyperconsumptive culture which binds the whole system together and allows it to proceed unquestioned. The rights to life, security, freedom, sovereignty, food, health, employment and several others are all subordinate to the West's "economic" rights.

Moreover, the much touted free market economy is neither free, nor is it a market, and it certainly is not economic. It isn't free because it prioritises the whims of the rich over the necessities of the poor; it isn't a market, because although capital moves more freely around the world, and goods fairly freely—subject only to the ingenious barriers which the WTO erects against the imports of certain Two Thirds World goods into the West—the freedom of movement for labour is severely limited. And it is scarcely economic, when the whole system depends upon passing costs on to others, costs that would cause the system's collapse if they were internalised.

New lands can still be openly occupied by the West through its demands for access to large tracts for free trade zones, TNC factories, industrialised agriculture and the inevitable golf courses for the top personnel of these corporations and institutions who bear the considerable burden of administering the profitable exploitation of the natives. Economic wars can be vigorously pursued even in times of so-called peace.

The negation of national sovereignty is essential to the accomplishment of the West's universal order, since nations cannot be permitted to stray from the straight and narrow path of liberalisation to the detriment of Western economies. The Indian Finance Minister submitted to the IMF/WB team in New Delhi, a summary of the 1992 budget provisions eight months prior to their presentation in Parliament, thereby ensuring that the former's recommendations were in place.[4]

The WTO came into operation on the first of January, 1995. Aware that the Indian parliament would not pass the damaging amendments to the existing patent laws required for entry into the WTO, the government promulgated Presidential ordinances bringing the changes into force, bypassing the legislatures of the "largest democracy in the world".

The WTO's rules "legally" take away the right of nations to control their own industry, agriculture and trade—thus preventing them from implementing even their own social programmes. Laws on patents are modified to satisfy the WTO's (read TNC's) requirements, rather than those of local health and other essential needs, with neither the electors nor the elected having any say in the matter. Trade sanctions are automatically authorised if the country does not change its laws when told to do so by a WTO dispute panel.

The Agreement on Sanitary and Phytosanitary Standards covers food safety and applies both to import regulations and to domestic standards. Levels of harmful chemicals in food can no longer be set by conditions prevailing in individual countries. Nations cannot protect their citizens' rights to health by insisting on toxin levels below those set by the WTO and the Codex Alimentarius committee, which is governed by TNCs.

The local elite, necessarily obedient to the will of the West, make the laws that allow such "democratic" overruling of the human rights of their own fellow-citizens. The term "national interest" is most often used when the interests of the elected do not coincide with those of the electors. "National interests"—unjust as they are—have now been totally subordinated to "international interests": the profits of TNCs. With local governments controlled by the tyranny of the international market place, this makes a hollow mockery of the individual's democratic rights and the sovereignty of individual nations. The current rhetoric about "economic integration" leads everywhere to local social disintegration; this demonstrates the supremacy accorded to the rights of the Western economic system over mere human beings and their poor ragged and flouted rights.

There is overwhelming evidence that SAPs cause drastic declines in the earnings of the already impoverished. After the imposition of SAPs, incomes dropped by about 15 per cent on average in most of South America and 30 per cent in sub-Saharan Africa during the 1980s. In the poorest forty-two countries, expenditure on health fell by over 50 per cent and on education by 25 per cent.[5] Opposition to such obviously impoverishing policies has occurred in nearly all countries where SAPs have been imposed.

The debacle in Mexico is an example of the necessary failure that must result from such Western policies. The much-acclaimed North American Free Trade Association (NAFTA) had provisions remarkably similar to those of the common variety of SAPs. Mexico had to abandon foreign exchange restrictions, open its borders to US products and allow US manufacturers to set up factories, taking advantage of the lower labour costs, lack of strict workplace safety and pollution controls to reduce the prices of their products so as to compete on the world markets.

As expected, the foreign exchange deficit increased rapidly leading to a loss of confidence in the Mexican economy and a panic flight of foreign exchange so large that the economy collapsed. The problem was "solved" through the benevolence of the US which arranged for a $38 billion dollar loan to the Mexican government, to be used primarily to rescue US investors.

Further, Mexico had to pledge all the proceeds of the sale of Mexican oil towards repayment of US loans. Mexico was also compelled to allow US companies to do oil exploration in the Gulf of Mexico, previously restricted to Mexican companies only.

This US "solution" saved US investors in Mexico while putting the Mexican nation deeper into debt and making its people poorer. In the past year, the peso's devaluation and the austerity measures imposed by the Mexican government as conditions for the loans, have cost the country more than 1.6 million jobs. The purchasing power of the average wage has been reduced to less than 50 per cent. More than one of every three Mexican businesses have failed and another third are currently on the verge of bank-ruptcy.[6]

The Chiapas rebellion was a natural result of this extensive impoverishment. The perverse influence of US banks was revealed when Chase Manhattan Inc. prepared a memo which recommended that Mexico needed to eliminate the Chiapas. Within two weeks, the Mexican government began a vicious campaign to achieve this goal.[7]

These situations merely preview, in fast-forward mode, the utter disregard for human rights that must result from the paths of development along which the countries of the Two Thirds World are being led by diktats of IMF, WB and WTO. Western development is the development of poverty.

The insistence on repayment of World Bank loans by Two Thirds World countries is another innovative form of human rights abuse. The West demands its pound of flesh, literally, with millions driven to starvation. The UNICEF estimates that around 650,000 children die in the Two Thirds World each year because of international debt alone.[8]

Village moneylenders and traders are rightly condemned for their exploitation of those subjected to their strained mercies. But while each of these impoverishes a few dozens at most, the international institutions turn entire populations into bonded labourers to supply the cheap raw materials and products the West requires to maintain its nonnegotiable standard of living.

The West impoverished the Two Thirds World by its colonial extractions of enormous quantities of capital, raw materials and labour surplus, which far exceed in value the paltry sums the Two Thirds World now owes as debt. If the colonial drain of capital had not taken place, these countries would not now be prostrating themselves before foreign lenders as supplicants for the return (that too, as loans) of a minuscule portion of their expropriated wealth. In fact, the Western countries would be in no position to lend, since their affluence is a direct result of earlier exploitation.

The Two Thirds World debt should therefore be adjusted against colonial credits. It is often said that such reparations cannot be demanded because it all happened so long ago. This is not true. In the Indian context, for example, the extractions continued right up to the days of Independence, less than fifty years ago.

Resource and Environmental Rights

Rights to natural resources and a clean environment should automatically accrue from the right to life, but the right to "develop" is given precedence. "Development" is taken to mean an ever-higher level of consumption of material products, requiring increasing quantities of resources. Present methods of exploitation depend on seducing victims with the virtual carrot that similar levels of affluence would be achieved by all, if only the West's painful prescriptions were bravely swallowed. The credulity of the elites of the Two Thirds World in endorsing these chimerical fantasies, it must be presumed, is the more readily won by the handsome rewards and handouts they receive.

Such hyperconsumption of the kind that is promised can never be equitably "enjoyed" by all the people of the earth because of constraints in supply. If all human beings are born equal in rights (Article 1), then all people now living on the globe and all who will be born in the future have an equal right to the earth's resources. Each person is thus constrained to limit her or his own consumption to a minimum in order to ensure the rights of others. Hyperconsumption by a small section of the global population deprives others of their rights. This is particularly serious when the destruction caused by hyperconsumption is irreversible as in the case of the exhaustion of particular resources like fossil fuels and of the loss of animal and plant species. These constitute one of the major, yet rarely mentioned, abuses of human rights today, with the latter also violating the rights of other living creatures. This is an abuse that is perpetrated by nearly all citizens in the West and those in the Two Thirds World who imitate the consumption patterns of the West.

Numerous natural resources are being overused by the West today, often taken from the Two Thirds World, while the latter are blamed for the resulting environmental damage. The poor of the Two Thirds World, especially tribals, are blamed by the hyperconsumers for the destruction of forests but they take merely what has been their time-immemorial right for their own minimal basic needs. The chief culprits of forest destruction are the remote urban furniture and building industries and assorted mass manufacturers of trivial non-necessities.

Further, the Western industrial system was able to develop only because of its high use of fossil fuels, since no renewable sources could and can provide the huge amounts of energy required for mass production, transport and other services.

The total known global reserves of oil in 1992 were about 1000 billion barrels.[9] The global consumption of oil was about 24 billion barrels a year in 1992. Global oil reserves will, therefore, last another forty years or so. This assumes that the consumption rate will not change, but an increase of just 3 per cent per year will exhaust reserves in about twenty-five years. Natural gas will last a little longer and coal perhaps a century or so.

Of the known global oil reserves, Saudi Arabia alone has 25.6 per cent, with Kuwait 9.3 per cent and Abu Dhabi 9.2 per cent. The Gulf War enabled the US physically and economically to capture all these reserves. Iraq has 9.9 per cent which is why the US is trying so hard to overthrow Saddam Hussein. The US also needs to turn Iran, which has 9.2 per cent, into an enemy in order to control its oil too. After Mexico's engineered collapse, its 5.1 per cent is now firmly in the grip of the US, while Venezuela's 6.2 per cent was economically captured years ago. The US now has about 58 per cent of the world reserves, including its own, under its control.

North African oil reserves have been generously allocated to Southern Europe, Russia's to the rest of Europe, and Malaysia's and Indonesia's to Japan. The rest of the world can fight over the minimal balance.

Of course, new reserves will be discovered, but each will cost more in money as well as in energy terms. An increase in cost will reduce the number of people who can use this sort of energy directly or as manufactured products. Ultimately, the costs will become too high for particular industries to survive. Although oil provides only around 30 per cent of global energy consumption, there are industrial sectors which are almost totally dependent on it.

The most vulnerable will probably be the transportation system, the loss of which will bring nearly all industrial and agricultural production in the West to a halt.

Because people are being made utterly dependent on fossil fuels they will be left helpless when fuel prices increase or supplies run out, unless drastically reduced consumption permits renewable sources to be adequate. If no such alternatives are prepared, and it turns out to be a cold turkey de-addiction process there will be immense suffering and trauma. The therapy has therefore to begin long before the lights go out.

One reason why the general public are not informed about such an impending threat is that mainstream economics sees the production of scarcity as a good thing, forcing prices and profits to rise.

The West also claims that new technologies will produce fuels which will replace depleting fossil resources. If this were so easy why, one may ask, are the problems being left for future generations to solve, and why did the US find it necessary to spend billions of dollars during and after the Gulf War to maintain its hold on Middle East oil?

The mining and production of fossil fuels as well as their conversion into electricity lead to further human rights abuse. Original populations have to be moved out by force from ancestral lands to make way for coal mines, oil and gas wells, generating plants and waste dumps. More displacement occurs in the case of hydroelectric power plants because of the huge areas covered by the reservoirs.

The pollution produced by thermal generator plants affects crops, and therefore the food supply in the surrounding areas. While only coal-fired generators may produce excessive quantities of sulphur oxides and nitrogen oxides, which yield acid rain, coal as well as oil and gas powered stations discharge carbon dioxide which causes global climatic change. Bert Bolin, President of the Intergovernmental Panel on Climate Change has asserted that "a major change in the climatic system is practically irreversible", even at current emission levels.[10]

Some consequences of changes in climate could be devastating. Most of the people inhabiting the low-lying islands of the globe are likely to be driven out of their lands by rising sea levels. They will become victims of an environmental genocide engendered by a few hyperconsumptive individuals insisting on their rights to comfort. Instead of attempting to eliminate the cause, environmental economists claim such phenomena can be the source of enormous new avenues of profit. They also "prove" that people value their lives less than they value their comforts. It may seem strange that people can value comforts when they are no longer alive but the economists cleverly balance the comforts of one small set of people against the lives of another large set. These economists also put high values on the lives of Westerners, compared to those of people in the Two Thirds World, just as the British did in their systems of "justice" in India.

Since the energy produced is so tainted with human rights abuse, those who use that energy are also, unwittingly or not, guilty of human rights abuse.

Other types of pollution need to be externalised until they can be turned into sources of future profits. The ban on the use of ozone depleting CFCs and allied compounds was only promoted after Du Pont and ICI were able to manufacture replacements which could be sold at even higher prices. Even these replacements are to be phased out soon since they, too, deplete the ozone layer, though to a smaller extent. The replacements for the replacements will naturally be priced even higher. And then there are the new markets for sun protection creams, for the detection and treatment of skin cancer, and so on.

The West cannot maintain its level of affluence, let alone increase it, without the continued use of these essential "ingredients" of human rights abuse to be found in each and every product and service of the Western industrial system. Moreover, it may not be possible to cure the Western system as a whole since unsustainability is built into it. As Arnold Toynbee observed, "any species that overdraws its renewable resources, or exhausts its irreplaceable resources condemns itself to extinction."[11]

The Trade in Human Rights

To extend the theatre of its Two Thirds World extortion, the West now brazenly uses the issue of human rights itself as an instrument for the control of trade, principally to prise open the economies of those countries upon which it needs to prey. However, the West needs to be particularly selective in choosing the virtues it wishes to so righteously define and defend, in order to avoid revealing the fragility of its own reputation.

Since its interest in human rights violations in the Two Thirds World does not arise from concern for the sufferings of the human beings involved but from a need to ensure access to their markets, such selectivity cannot always operate. The West publicly condemns the human rights abuses of those Two Thirds World countries whose policies differ from its own, while others guilty of equally sinister or worse violations are ignored.

Early in 1993, President Clinton issued an executive order requiring China to make "overall significant progress" in complying with a long list of human rights demands within a year, or lose Most Favoured Nation (MFN) status. China refused, claiming that the US violated the rights of its own citizens—the Natives, the Blacks and other minority groups—and so had no business telling others what to do. US manufacturers, worried about losing access to such a huge and profitable market for their products, pressurised Clinton not to remove China's MFN status. To solve the dilemma, the US has officially decided to separate human rights issues from trade policy.

The hypocrisy however continued. In January 1995, the US claimed it saw no improvement in China's human rights record and warned that long-term improvement in Sino-US relations would depend on improvement in China's human rights record. Secretary of State Warren Christopher, however, confirmed in December 1995, that the US relationship with China would continue to focus on improving trade, with no prospect of linking commerce to human rights.[12] US investment in and trade with China continues to increase. Coca Cola and cigarettes are traded in for the rights of those killed in the Tiananmen Square massacres and the continuing genocide in Tibet.

In February 1995, the US State Department accused Russia of a string of human rights violations, including the overuse of force in breakaway Chechnya, dismal prison conditions and police beatings. Yet the US condones all these because Russia is a vast potential market.

Prompted by economic considerations, Canada says it does not make sense any more for it to refuse trade with countries having a bad human rights record. Ottawa would not "risk trade by taking a tougher line on human rights violations by China in Tibet, Indonesia in East Timor, or Russia in Chechnya."[13] Other Western countries may not have been so explicit, but they follow the same line.

The Trade in Aid

The West has impoverished the Two Thirds World by its colonial extractions of wealth, a tiny part of which is now, with well publicised benevolence, handed out as aid.

Even in this gesture, the West exhibits its continued culture of imperialism since most aid is given conditionally with much of the amount donated rapidly transferred back to the donor, to be profitably recycled as more aid. This "charity" is also proving irksome and therefore reasons have to be found to make it more selective. So Western governments are now using trade as a criterion for aid.

Lynda Chalker, Overseas Development Minister of the UK, stated in August 1991 that Britain's aid to the Two Thirds World would hereafter be dependent upon the particular country's human rights record and on sound economic policies. The first condition refers properly to the response of the target State to its dissident citizens but the second is a code for economic policies that can only aggravate the condition of the poorest citizens of the target nation.

Douglas Hurd, Britain's ex-foreign minister, submitted a proposal to the European Commission with a view to influencing the joint European aid policy. This was a plea for cutting aid to those Third World countries who do not conform to democratic norms and do not respect human rights.[14]

But during its own colonial rule, Britain frequently made the claim that India's affairs were solely "domestic concerns of Great Britain", and should, therefore, be left to Britain alone; any suggestion from other countries concerning them, or criticism of the manner in which they were managed, was impertinent and wrong.[15]

The Trade in Poverty

The Social Summit in Copenhagen (March 6 to 12, 1995) was an attempt by the West to legitimise its massive and systematic abuse of human rights and simultaneously to transfer blame for such abuse to the victims.

The Summit was a strategic offensive to disassociate Western policies from the poverty that those very policies continuously create. The Summit was a grand opera of blaring brass and tinkling cymbals, composed and orchestrated by the major Western powers to drown out the increasing cries—too loud to be ignored any longer—of the impoverished all over the Two-Thirds World.

The Summit, the West emphatically declared, would solve the problem of poverty. It attempted to accomplish this laudable objective through some lavish expenditure: the Danish Government spent $30 million merely for organising the event. Hotels and other enterprises earned $35 million from the conference, much less than what these unfortunates had expected to make.

About 4,500 representatives of NGOs attended the Summit, with each spending thousands of dollars, all of it in foreign exchange earned by their respective countries through internal impoverishment.[16] Not one cent went to the poor.

Only one of the heads of State had the courage to point out that the emperor had no clothes. President Bakili Muluzi of Malawi refused to attend the Summit. He said the trip would have cost his delegation at least £125,000 and he said he would rather spend that amount on poverty alleviation at home.[16]

The Report of the Summit is a document of more than a hundred pages, seemingly designed to deter readers, with a plethora of repetitive statements, each a jumble of differing objectives clubbed together for no rhyme or reason. There are declarations, principles, goals, a list of ten commitments, and finally a programme of action—which till now has not succeeded in producing any discernible sign of movement.

The Report admits that urgent action needs to be initiated "taking into account that the major cause of the continued deterioration of the global environment is the unsustainable pattern of consumption and production, particularly in industrialized countries, which is a matter of grave concern, aggravating poverty and imbalances."[17] The US immediately objected to these revelations of the West's own injustice, insisting that the opening sentence from paragraph 4.3 of Agenda 21 be inserted: "Poverty and environmental degradation are closely interrelated."[18] It is well known that the UNCED Conference at Rio in 1992 which produced Agenda 21 was dominated by the US TNC lobby.

While claiming that it is necessary to correct structural causes, any attempt to do so would require the total rejection of the West's own industrial-economic system. Instead of admitting that poverty is a necessary consequence of "the expansion of prosperity for some", it is treated as an unfortunate fallout of Western programmes, requiring no modification or elimination of, for instance, the SAPS that directly cause it.

This cover-up of the real causes of impoverishment is frequently repeated in various distorted forms in the Report. "Globalisation, which is a consequence of increased human mobility, enhanced communications, greatly increased trade and capital flows, and technological developments, opens new opportunities for sustained economic growth and development of the world economy, particularly in developing countries."[19] Globalisation in fact has been enforced by the West and has caused and continues to cause the "development" of an elite few at the cost of the impoverished many.

The coupling of democracy with development is reiterated almost as if it were an unquestionable dogma in the Report: "We are convinced that democracy and transparent and accountable governance and administration in all sectors of society are indispensable foundations for the realization of social and people-centred sustainable development."[20] Similarly coupled are human rights and development, the signatories undertaking to "Reaffirm and promote all human rights, which are universal, indivisible, interdependent and interrelated, including the right to development as a universal and inalienable right and an integral part of fundamental human rights..."[21] These solemn pronouncements are made even while Western development requires the abuse of nearly all the other rights.

It is also claimed in the Report that "equitable social development that recognizes empowering the poor to utilize environmental resources sustainably, is a necessary foundation for sustainable development."[22] Translated, in the light of current practice, this means that the poor are to be left to find their own solutions to the problems created by the imposition of the Western system of globalisation. They cannot be empowered to reject globalisation, however. In other words, the impoverished should put up with their misery and internalise it or shut up.

That the signatories to the Report have absolutely no intention of implementing even some of the commitments listed, is confirmed by their claim to "Reaffirm the right of self-determination of all peoples, in particular of peoples under colonial or other forms of alien domination or foreign occupation..."[23] Not one of the occupying countries—which include Britain, the US and France—has taken even a micro step to move out of their existing colonies.

The Ten Commitments, which form the basis for launching a "global drive for social development", mainly reiterate Western commitment to continue the processes of exploitation through the UN, WB, IMF and WTO, while claiming these will alleviate poverty.

The burden of finding solutions to the problems of poverty has been gratuitously laid on Two Thirds World governments who are urged "to intervene in markets, to the extent necessary, to prevent or counteract market failure, promote stability and long-term investment, ensure fair competition and ethical conduct, and harmonize economic and social development, including the development and implementation of appropriate programmes that would entitle and enable people living in poverty and the disadvantaged, especially women, to participate fully and

productively in the economy and society."[24] The privatisation
policy of the Western system creates the problems while national
governments are supposed to solve them, even as the WTO
prohibits just this sort of intervention. And "stability" means
security for the upper classes and TNCs in order that each may
freely carry out their vulgar fractions of exploitation.

Commitment 1 (k) states the signatories will "Strive to ensure
that international agreements relating to trade, investment, technology, debt and official development assistance are implemented
in a manner that promotes social development."[25] This in fact
ensures that all signatories toe the Western line and in particular
that the enormous debt of the Two Thirds World will have to be
paid even if it means the total impoverishment of the debtor nation.

The Report presents an appearance of universal benevolence
even while the policies on its agenda are wholly malicious. In a UN
meeting to finalise the draft programme of action, India demanded
the inclusion of exhaustive rights to food, shelter, work, education,
health and information. The US led the rich countries' resistance to
demands for such rights, all of which have been guaranteed by the
original UN UDHR.[26]

The Western system of wealth creation is, in the main, a
transfer of assets from the impoverished to the affluent, even
within the "developed" countries themselves. The economic
indicators of enhanced GNP, of rising disposable incomes, of
general prosperity must, therefore, go hand in hand with social
breakdown. Many of those who have been dropped out of the
system are thereby driven to crime. Some indications of this are:
the US now has a higher percentage of its population in prison than
any other country, with 1.1 million "criminals", mostly black, in
the American gulag.[27] A half of US marriages end in divorce, and
one in three people in the US now lives alone. In Britain, the
distribution of income has now regressed so that it is almost
exactly as it was one hundred years ago.

Chomsky sees this dissolution of Western society today as
similar to that in Europe after the Black Death. He enumerates the
signs: fear, anger, hostility, cynicism, religious fanaticism, and so
on.[28] There is a resulting proliferation of cults which promise
instant salvation from all these confusing burdens.

The same processes of disintegration, of social dissolution,
occur in all "developed" countries, although the forms of that

breakdown may vary from culture to culture. Japan's high suicide rate is a different type of "tribute" exacted from human beings by the wealth creating processes. Corporate Japanese males are subject to intolerable pressures which make them bonded labourers of their companies. With their families being semi-strangers to them, they need, among other things, the synthetic consolations arising from the abuse of the bodies of a quarter million sex-workers from the Philippines alone.

The privileged now routinely use the wealth accruing from human rights abuse to further violate the human rights of the impoverished. Sex tourism, which has led to a flourishing trade in women and children in Thailand, the Philippines and Sri Lanka, offers those who can afford it the opportunity to satisfy their desires exploiting the bodies of the most defenceless people on earth. To facilitate this, young women are now routinely trafficked from Yunnan in China, from Burma and the villages of northern Thailand into the brothels of Bangkok, where they become yet another commodity to enhance the freedom of choice which the global market now graciously offers.

Corruption has permeated the whole system, with the majority of its "beneficiaries" prepared to underwrite any degree of cruelty, barbarism and crime committed against the poor of the earth in the interests of maintaining their addiction to high consumption life-styles. Even the potential victims of the affluent system within the West are themselves unwilling to change things because of their utter dependency on the system. Living under the constant terror of losing the crumbs from the tables of conspicuous hyperconsumption, they can no longer even imagine a life without all that has become "indispensable" to them. In this way, even the people of the West live in a state of terror and chronic insecurity, and are blackmailed into accepting whatever horrors may attend their abusive life-style. Levels of stress, anxiety, fear, isolation and emotional breakdown suggest that even the human rights of the beneficiaries of the unjust system are being undermined at source, as it were.

The Trade in Violence

Any activity that promotes war should naturally be considered a violation of human rights. Yet the sale of arms, essential for conducting wars, is considered normal commercial business. When moral objections are raised, it is justified by one state asserting that if it did not sell arms to a particular customer, another would do so. Or, that once the arms are sold, what the buyer does with them is not the responsibility of the seller. It is claimed that the most terribly destructive weapons are only intended for defence.

Arms sales are essential for the maintenance of Western affluence. The power of the five permanent members of the UN Security Council is revealed by the extent of their control over the international arms trade. These five account for 85 per cent of global arms exports, with the US alone responsible for 40 per cent.[29]

The West promoted an image of the socialist USSR as a major enemy, thus successfully engendering an enormously profitable arms race. With the cold war over, the West gloats that no nation now exists which can attack the West. However, the US economy is suffering from the resulting decline in arms manufacture. The US therefore needs to actively invent new enemies which could be targeted by its old and new weapons. While the fundamentalist Islamic countries have been the first choice for this human rights prize, plans are being made to include many other nations as well.

The Clinton administration announced in February 1995 a new conventional arms transfer policy, brazenly stating that the United States "continues to view transfers of conventional arms as a legitimate instrument of US foreign policy." Arms sales will be linked to the human rights, terrorism and nuclear proliferation record of the recipient.[30] The manner of the linkage is not specified.

The West gave $56 billion as "aid" to the Two Thirds World, $36 billion of which went back as payments for arms alone.[31] More will flow back for the purchase of ammunition, spare parts and continuously needed replacements.

Half of US military aid for the western hemisphere goes to Colombia, the region's biggest human rights violator.[32] In fact, most of the aid given by the US goes to countries which are major abusers of human rights.

Scientists and technologists, the cream of the educated elite, have contributed much to the technology of weapons. Their amazing ingenuity produced the gadgets which ensured US victory in the Gulf War. Computerised technology enabled the US to carry out a war in the air for several days without endangering its ground forces. The enemy became an impersonal distant blip on a radar screen, a blemish to be targeted and eliminated, with no rights whatsoever. Computers and "smart bombs" could not be programmed to distinguish soldiers from innocent civilians, so the 1907 Hague regulations on war, restricting targets to military personnel alone, were blithely abandoned in order to use the technology developed.

The US defence department was delighted because their intricate and expensive weapons systems were tested and proved convincingly successful. The Gulf war turned out to be a live sales exhibition, shown on prime time TV, for US arms—from Patriot missiles to Stealth bombers carrying smart bombs—vividly displaying the efficiency with which thousands could be instantly killed.

The industrial military machine claims that though its requirement of funds for "defence" is high, civilian benefits result from the development of machines of mass destruction. But such supposedly benign spin-offs cannot compensate for the human rights abuse arising from the use of the arms themselves. In particular, there is no evidence of any "peace dividend" as a result of the end of the cold war.

Among the alleged spin-offs are the electronics technologies that made possible small computers and the satellite communications systems, both of which have contributed to the spread of Western high-consumption culture. The development of military jet fighters and bombers led to civilian jet transport, which in turn has made possible the expansion of the global control by TNCs, environmentally destructive tourism, the transfer of essential, perishable food from the Two Thirds World to the rich countries, pollution of the stratosphere and other malignant "benefits". These major "advances" in Western technology would not have been possible without the military system bearing the research and development costs.

A closer connection between military and civilian use of new technology is revealed in the development of chemical and biological weapons (CBW). Many of the extremely environmentally harmful pesticides in use today are descendants of the nerve gases that were developed for chemical warfare in the 1939-1944 war and later.

Efforts at providing international safeguards against CBW began in 1925, culminating in the 1969 Geneva Protocol, which the

UN requested all member States to ratify. Among the big powers, only the US initially desisted from doing so, though it later announced its renunciation of production, stockpiling and use of biological weapons. The US, however, did not include anti-plant agents in its renunciation, arguing that such agents were not intended to be covered by the Protocol.

Many nations, however, had demanded a comprehensive ban which included every type of chemical and biological weapon without exception. In December 1969, the UN discussed just such a comprehensive ban, which was opposed by the US, Australia, and Portugal. Thirty-six countries, most of them US allies, abstained.

To avoid embarrassing situations like this, the US, while dutifully signing international agreements, retains an in-built mechanism which it claims unfortunately prevents it from implementing their provisions. The US, when it signs an international convention, does it in a way which makes it "non-self-executing". This means the agreement or convention does not apply unless enabling legislation is democratically passed by the signatory's legislature. Such legislation is never passed in the US if it encroaches even marginally on the corporate right to exploit. The US also only ratifies UN agreements subject to many explicit "reservations", and it has innovated treaty practice by lodging a considerable number of "understandings" and "declarations", thus holding itself above the internationally agreed upon code of human rights.[33]

Finally, the production and use of bacteriological and toxic weapons was banned by the Convention of 1972. Yet research and testing continues to this day, with many binary techniques (which mix two relatively harmless chemicals to produce the toxin only when required) having been developed after signing the agreements.[34] Such activities are not held to be a breach of the Convention because the work was ostensibly being done to test defences— for example, vaccines—against weapons that might be used by an enemy. The hypocrisy of this claim is obvious from the fact that the number of potential biological agents which can be developed becomes extremely large, particularly with the use of genetic engineering.

The US has been much praised for its magnanimity in unilaterally giving up the production of chemical weapons. There could be two reasons for this apparently altruistic behaviour. The Gulf war has shown that its high-technology "conventional" weapons are sufficient to destroy completely any country that dares defy US interests. There is also the fact that there is no need for the development of chemicals for the specific declared use as weapons. This is because the US has a whole arsenal of "weapons" that it manufactures openly and even uses regularly. These are the highly toxic herbicides and pesticides, dozens of which are capable of incapacitating people in seconds or killing them outright by mere contact or inhalation. Herbicides could also be effective in destroying whole crops, hence the insistence by the US on excluding anti-plant agents from CBW agreements. New "civilian" biotechnological products will add to the arsenal.

While the policy of choice of the West is economic warfare, it is also prepared to use its military might where it feels the former is ineffective. This unspoken blackmail underlies all its "negotiations", all its deliberations and consultations in the conclaves of the world. The stark choice available to the Two Thirds World is to accept economic warfare or risk military action. Brian Beedham writing in *The Economist*, gives this advice to Western powers: "Take care to mark on the map all the exploding countries, surly religio-historical culture-zones and chip-on-shoulder dictatorships around the globe that can still cause military trouble for the democracies..." Beedham was frank in explaining that the democracies "will want to make sure *that they can keep on getting the raw materials their economies need*." [Emphasis added].[35] Note the use of the word "democracies" to signify the West and the West alone.

Beedham gloats over the possibility that the world will "break into two parts." The West's part will be an archipelago of comfortable civility, the people outside will be suffering awful things. They will, however, need to be kept minimally alive in order to supply the low-cost commodities that the West's comfort is dependent on.

Although a democracy, he puts India "near the top of the list for explosiveness." An Indian alliance with China would be taken by the West as a serious threat to its own interests, and would, presumably be cause enough for initiating a high-technology war. Another justification for war would be a bid by China for leadership of the countries that oppose American-European-Japanese hegemony—dominance evidently being considered the sole prerogative of the US and its allies.

As Beedham explains: "A decision by China to try to make itself a power in the world would also mess things up considerably. At the very least, it would *end the attempt to use the United Nations as an instrument of the new world order.*" [Emphasis added] He clarifies: "The United Nations can be peace-keeper—or peace-maker—only when those with the power to say YES or NO agree on the desirability of putting a UN label on their common will." The near total control that the West has over the UN frees the former to openly declare the exploitative utility of the UN.

To take care of situations that cannot be economically controlled, the West's soldiers must prepare to fight in more distant places. While not stated by Beedham, this would require the continued possession of military bases—perhaps in colonies—all over the world. Detailed plans are being worked out for the strategic placement of expeditionary forces, fighters, ground-attack aircraft, global-reach bombers, large transport aircraft, sea transport, and other military attack forces. Technology will be so far advanced that "a corporal may press a button that kills the enemy's commander."

What queers the pitch and makes things a bit hazardous for the West is that the West has sold arms to dozens of countries all over the world. "On one count twenty-three countries currently have 1,000 or more tanks apiece. More than one of these countries is in a position to do something the democracies would think they ought to stop." Hence the need to keep control of the "world rules".

The US is attempting to correct this earlier error by persuading nations to accept its armed forces on their soil, instead of selling them arms. By portraying Iran and Iraq as security threats, the US is trying to persuade Saudi Arabia to accept a further 60,000 US troops in its country.

The West sees hope in its ability to retain control since "the military gap between the advanced economies and the vast majority of Asian and African countries is still widening." Racism again surfaces in that no threat is seen from the white countries, who regard themselves as the sure custodians of universal and enduring values, which makes it impossible for them to act in any dishonourable manner whatsoever.

The strategy is not to let the Two Thirds World catch up. Pressure has been put on India not to proceed with its space programmes, missile development and deployment, though India should without prompting reduce its defence expenditures. So-phisticated fighters will not be sold, so the West can be sure that its bombers do not face too much opposition.

In the case of nuclear armaments, the war chicken has come home to roost. The danger lies, Beedham asserts without noticing the irony, in "foolish Western businessmen, unemployed ex-Soviet scientists", using the free enterprise system to sell their nuclear expertise and technology.

Conspiracy is proposed if not already in action. The work has to be done by countries which have discovered by experience that their aims will be broadly similar, and that they can work together in putting those views into practice. These are to be strictly limited to the US, Canada, Europe, and any other solid democracies that care to apply—Sweden, Austria, Finland, Switzerland, and Japan for nonmilitary operations.[35] All these are white, except for the honorary whites, the Japanese, so nominated by Apartheid South Africa years ago.

The US is to be considered the first among equals "by having more nuclear arms and hi-tech kit than anybody else." The main purpose of the alliance is to police the world. Its global aim would be to enhance the "military efficiency of democracy", "enabling the democracies to defend their interests." The military efficiency of democracy, naturally, has nothing to do with democracy at all; it is a euphemism for the violent maintenance of privilege.

Military warfare is messy with a large number of dead bodies to prove that human rights are being obviously abused. This stigma is proposed to be removed by the use of nonlethal weapons. Janet and Chris Morris, research directors of the US Global Strategy Council and acclaimed defence consultants, state US aims plainly: "Without relinquishing our massive force capability or damaging our national strength, the United States can now announce and demonstrate to the world a new national policy of Nonlethality....By so doing, we can take the moral high ground internationally and manage global change so that our far flung interests are pro-tected."[36]

They continue: "America's vision of Nonlethality will stimu-late, nurture, and protect economic growth worldwide as we make the transition to a free and open international economic system. It will help all civilised nations shape the geopolitics of the future and guide the growth of embryonic nation-states towards democratisation."[37] Patent breaches of human rights, notwithstanding.

Among the nonlethal weapons the kinder, gentler Morrises propose to use are lasers. They benignly state that "eyes struck directly by lasers will be damaged according to the power of the laser or optics."[38] The impression given is that the eyes are disembodied, there being no mention of human beings permanently blinded.

However, the review conference of the 1980s Treaty on Conventional Weapons held in October 1995 in Vienna prohibited the use of lasers specifically designed to blind people permanently. The protocol also requires signatory states to take all possible precautions to minimise such damage as a result of the use of other laser systems.[39] But the scientists who are dedicated to inventing and developing such weapons will merely shift their attention to other "advanced" technologies which are not yet banned.

The German Nazis justified their war conduct in terms of the right of the Aryan race to rule and dominate lesser breeds. The same racial arrogance underlies the present-day attitude of nuclear weapon nations, who claim that only they have the moral capacity to use such weapons judiciously or to inhibit those countries which, due their infantile inability to control themselves, need to be watched over by those of greater maturity and wisdom. Such nuclear terrorism is compatible with the spirit of Auschwitz and Buchenwald.

The superior moral capacity of nuclear states was recently exhibited when, immediately after the indefinite extension of the NPT was signed, China and France announced the resumption of tests. France has now conducted several tests in the Mururoa region of the Pacific. Some islanders, Greenpeace and other environmental organisations have protested strongly against these tests, which were only possible because of France's colonial occupation of the islands. Strangely, no member of the UN Organisation has challenged France's claim to hold on to its colonies, though France and its friends signed the Copenhagen Social Summit resolutions agreeing to eliminate colonialism. France has dodged this by designating the islands as French Overseas Territories over which it possesses a military *droit de seigneur*.

On the fiftieth anniversary of the allied victory in Europe, apologies by the heirs of those who initiated the aggression are being freely given. But such repentance is hollow. The culture which saw the death of others as unimportant and which rated self-interest as supreme when those crimes were committed is still alive and reigning. The same German companies that made up I G Farben, which produced Zyklon B for the gas chambers and which used women from the concentration camps as experimental animals, today traffick in drugs that are banned in their own country and in toxic pesticides which injure the health of millions. Others use thousands of women in the Two Thirds World as guinea pigs to test their new birth control vaccines and devices. The descendants of those who destroyed the American native peoples appear to think nothing of introducing institutions and policies which destroy now the peoples of the Two Thirds World.

However, the hidden culture of violence is recoiling upon the US itself, seen for instance in the ultra right's bombing in Oklahoma. This incident uncovered the underlying racism in the US as well as elsewhere. Without any supporting evidence, it was instantly assumed that Islamic fundamentalists were responsible. Although white right-wingers were ultimately charged in the case, members of Congress, exploiting public fear and anxiety, proposed a repressive anti-terrorism bill that would establish new courts which would be allowed to use secret evidence to deport non-citizens suspected of terrorist activity and limit those condemned to death to one appeal in federal courts.[40]

There is a very noticeable division within the West itself as individual nations compete to retain their slice of the unjust consumption cake: the US vs Japan, the US vs China and even the US vs Europe. The future scenario could be one with vastly increased numbers of such economic conflicts, as the US fully intends to pursue its policy of global economic control, with the use of old-fashioned military force where necessary. The February 1992 secret Pentagon paper on Defense Planning Guidance also stated that the US must hold "global power" and a monopoly of force.[41]

It is worth remembering that the US escaped from the 1929 Great Depression only when the 1939-44 War allowed enormous growth in production of expendable arms and ammunition and other military material. With Western economies spiralling into a recession, will another global military adventure be conjured up if the West loses its economic wars?

CHAPTER 6

The Rights to Food and Health

*E veryone has the right to a standard of living adequate for the health
and well-being of himself and his family, including food, clothing,
housing and medical care and necessary social services, and the right to
security in the event of unemployment, sickness, disability, widowhood,
old age or other lack of livelihood in circumstances beyond his control."*
(UDHR, Article 25 [1])

The "right" to Western-style development is a major instrument which the West uses to subvert several of the other rights
listed in the UN UDHR, in order to facilitate further exploitation.

The right to life naturally encompasses the right to an adequate food supply and a right to health and housing, yet the
Declaration separates them from the right to life, while joining
them with several other rights. The rights stemming from the right
to life are thereby diminished in importance, thus permitting them
to be abused with impunity even though they directly infringe on
the primary right to life.

The Right to Food

The right to food can be violated in several ways. For
instance, by reducing food security through the promotion of high-
risk, unsustainable agriculture, by depriving people of the food
already being produced, by reducing the purchasing power of the
people, by denutrifying food by means of industrial processing,
and many others.

Although security is mentioned in this Article, it evidently
does not apply to food security, even though any reduction of the

food security of an individual, community or nation is a violation of the right to food, and hence to life. Food security requires the elimination of all factors which reduce sustainability. No agricultural, industrial or economic practice should have a potential for diminishing food production now and in the foreseeable future.

Food security requires self-reliance in food production. Threats to self-reliance in food are not as obvious as those to military security, but are far more damaging, which is why the erosion of food security takes such a high priority in the West's agenda of domination.

Most nations or regions were self-sufficient in their food needs before the unwelcome advent of their own particular colonial powers; they had to be, otherwise they would not have survived. The destruction of self-sufficing agriculture was a necessary condition for the production of cash crops to satisfy the needs of the metropolitan countries, which had already far exceeded their own environmental carrying capacity. This had naturally a diminishing effect on food production and consumption in the occupied territories.

G F Keatinge, Director of Agriculture, Bombay Presidency, wrote in 1913: "The old self-sufficing agriculture by which each tract, each village and each holding supplied its own needs is now largely a thing of the past....The Bombay Presidency draws much of its food supply from outside, while it exports large quantities of cotton and oilseeds. Its agriculture has become commercialised."[1]

The French forced the African nations they controlled to replace the cultivation of traditional food crops by groundnut, which they required since they had no large local source of edible oil. This cultivation pattern persists today, requiring the continuous import of food, even in the absence of drought.

Western agriculture is itself unsustainable. It is claimed that the green revolution, with its high yielding varieties (HYVs) is the main factor which has allowed an increase in food production, without which there would be extensive famines in the world. But this particular system of agriculture is dependent on the use of synthetic fertilisers and pesticides produced from mineral oil and natural gas, and on the use of fossil fuels for powering tractors, irrigation pumps and transport. Moreover, it has recently been discovered that the HYVs have a much reduced ability to store micronutrients like Vitamin A, iron, zinc and others. The loss of these essential nutrients to populations subsisting mainly on HYV cereals not only causes direct ill health but also has a major damaging impact on the immune system. While food production grew, an increasingly large number of people have suffered from extensive malnutrition and its consequences.[2]

The traditional agricultural systems, not dependent on these factors, survived for millennia till they were displaced by this transitory "modernisation".[3]

A change in the climate and the depletion of the stratospheric ozone layer could cause major reductions in food production, since the extremely narrow genetic base from which high-yielding varieties are derived could result in widespread crop losses. The high susceptibility of the new varieties to pest attacks is another factor contributing to insecurity. At the same time, the creativity which produced the tens of thousands of different traditional crop varieties adapted to numerous ecological niches is being destroyed by TNC producers of special seeds.

While the West claims that the available land and other resources will be inadequate to provide food for rising populations, it encourages the use of food in a most inefficient manner: many grains directly edible by humans are now being redirected to cattle, pigs and poultry to obtain expensive milk, meat and eggs. India at present grows sufficient food to provide all its people with adequate basic nourishment, yet about one third of the population living below the poverty line do not get sufficient to eat. The godowns are overflowing, but the people cannot afford to buy the stored food. The grain merely goes to maintain a population of rats and other pests, including the population of synthetic fertiliser and pesticide manufacturers.

While the UN Declaration lists the right to food as one of the human rights, the West uses an artificially created need for imported food as a weapon to coerce the Two Thirds World to allow itself to be further exploited.

The principles are simple: the US, Canada and Australia are major exporters of food, not surprisingly, since the vast lands that the Europeans overran long ago and still occupy make surplus food production easy. Prices are kept low by subsidies as well as by drawing down environmental capital such as soil fertility and ground water. A demand for imported food has to be therefore

created, by forcing target nations to switch over from self-suffi-
ciency to large-scale deficiency.

Here, too, supposedly neutral international institutions have
served Western interests. The FAO, for instance, ably helped to
create further dependency under its UN mandate to feed the large
populations of the Two Thirds World, by providing information
about market trends and agricultural statistics through its Industry Cooperative Programme. The FAO actually functions as an
agent for the TNCs in the Two Thirds World.[4]

In the 1970s, the US even considered the use of food aid in
cases of natural disaster as a means of gaining influence over the
individual unfortunate country. A former US Secretary of Agriculture, Earl Butz, starkly declared that "Food is a weapon."[5] In an
article published in the November 1975 issue of *Food Policy*,
William Schneider of the Hudson Institute, argued that food
should be used as a tool of economic warfare.[6]

In the 1970s, the fear was there would be global cooling rather
than warming, since another ice age was due. Such a global
catastrophe was anticipated with unabashed glee: "In a cooler and
therefore hungrier world, the US' near monopoly position as food
exporter...could give the US a measure of power it had never had
before....In bad years when the US could not meet the demand for
food of most would-be importers, Washington would acquire
virtual life and death power over the fate of the multitudes of the
needy. Without indulging in blackmail in any sense, the US would
gain extraordinary political and economic influence. For, not only
the poor LDCs, but also the major powers would be at least
partially dependent on food imports from the US."[7]

Today the US probably looks upon global warming and its
effect on crops with equal anticipation of increased power. However, since climatic change has proved to be too slow for Western
purposes, other means have been instituted to serve the same goal.

The West's claim to the promotion of human rights is clearly
contradicted by the institutions that it actively fosters. Several
items of the structural adjustment programme constitute premedi-
tated violations of specific rights set out in the Declaration.

The SAPs could not be better designed for abusing the right
to food. The programme requires that support measures for local
food production in the Two Thirds World have to be phased out.

The removal of subsidies ensures a rise of food prices, effectively impoverishing people, since there is no corresponding insistence on a rise in wages. This is generally implicit in the blanket condemnation of all government spending, which, rather than being an effort to cushion the people against the worst rigours of "liberalisation", is always presented as an obstacle and deterrent to "free enterprise". The arguments used are precisely those which Britain employed, with the effects that are well known during the great potato famine in Ireland in the 1840s. The extreme reluctance to interfere with market forces and with the efforts of private charity led to far more famine deaths than would otherwise have occurred. It cannot be said that the practices of the Western financial institutions are imposed in good faith. The ghoulish spectre of famine still stalks the jargon of their country-specific structural adjustment programmes.

Aware that their programmes impoverish people, the WB and the IMF benevolently insist that the poor should be provided with a safety net, the Public Distribution System (PDS), for essential food. But the removal of subsidies requires the government to raise the prices of cereals sold through the PDS, with PDS prices sometimes rising above even open market prices. The PDS has effectively collapsed.

High prices have compelled millions to reduce their consumption below sustenance level, or to spend more of their income on food with less available for medicines, education and other necessities. The impoverished say: "We used to have three full meals a day, now we can afford only one." Millions who were just at subsistence level now drop to malnutrition rank, those already suffering from malnutrition now starve, those earlier starving now die. The World Bank and IMF then smugly berate the Indian government for not caring for the poor they have themselves mass produced. In this way, while the WB and IMF claim credit for anything they can dress up as a success, they do not hesitate to blame those who implement the policies they have crafted for all failures. The circle is effectively closed.

A few tens of thousands of people in the world may have their human rights abused by physical torture and death, but there are hundreds of millions of people in India and elsewhere going to bed every night tortured by pangs of hunger, with the high probability of the violence of early death.

Outwardly, these deaths do not appear to be a direct consequence of the SAPs. They are rarely classified as starvation deaths,
but as mortality caused by one of the opportunistic diseases
associated with pathogens moving in to exploit the weakened
immune system.

In official reports and statistical returns, therefore, a right-to-
life problem becomes disguised as an unfortunate health condition, merely requiring more Western drugs or perhaps a little
improvement in sanitation. The avoidable violations of human
well-being thus become the source of vast new "business opportunities" for pharmaceutical and sewage treatment TNCs, giving rise
to rejoicing because of the rise in profits and GNP.

The WTO rules give the West the levers to prise open huge
new markets for the American food industry, and US officials say
they fully intend to use them. The Clinton administration has
decided to fight aggressively any trade barriers that limit US food
sales in foreign markets.[8]

Low cost wheat, one of the main items generously "donated"
as emergency aid, put farmers of importing countries out of
business and get the people addicted to a new cereal which, after
the emergency is over, can be sold to them at high prices. Quotas
or tariffs on imported food cannot be used to enhance food
security. This raises the possibility that imported food may become
cheaper than locally grown grains, forcing farmers to switch to
cash crops in order to survive. The import of food grains then
becomes necessary.

The US Wheat Associates (an association of eighteen American wheat-growing states) has been engaged since 1985 in persuading traditional rice-eaters in the Indian states of Tamil Nadu,
Karnataka, Kerala and Andhra Pradesh, to supplement their diet
with wheat. To this end, a series of projects has been funded by the
USWA in home science colleges and institutions.[9] The capacity to
alter the eating patterns of whole countries shows the extent of the
tyrannical invasiveness of an alien culture upon the rights of
peoples.

Where countries have the audacity to resist such policies,
trade sanctions are threatened. In 1988 Nigeria, Sub-Sahara's
largest wheat importer, imposed a ban on the import of wheat
because such wheat had depressed food prices and reduced
domestic production of food staples like cassava, yams and mil-

lets. The Cargill Corporation, Nigeria's main wheat supplier, lobbied with the US Government which promptly threatened Nigeria with a trade sanction on its textiles exports.[10]

Further abuses related to the industrialisation of food production, required by the liberalisation process. Food is no longer to be produced for supporting life; it must first serve as a raw material for the food industry. The processing of food adds value for the processors, not for the consumers.

The right to fresh and healthy food has to be exchanged for the "convenience" of unblemished, processed, packaged and therefore more expensive food, treated with quantities of additives and toxins, and deprived of its essential nutrients and therefore even legally guaranteed to diminish health.

Cereals, such as finger millet (*Eleusine coracana*), which earlier were made directly into porridge are not available for sale in some regions due to large purchases made by breakfast cereal manufacturers. People are thereby compelled to buy such breakfast foods marketed by TNCs, even though they have negligible food value in comparison with the millet porridge made at home.

The modern Marie Antoinettes tell those impoverished by liberalisation: "If you can't eat bread, eat Kentucky Fried Chicken and McDonald's burgers." The opening of the economy to such food TNCs has increased the demand for meat, with a corresponding decrease in cereal availability.

Agriculture, far from being a sphere of activity which supplies humanity with food and other essential products, has been made into an industry where profits are the chief criterion for its existence.

The WTO-enforced "opening up" of a country to imports is required by the West so that it can sell its products in Two Thirds World markets, this being essential for continued growth of Western economies. Unnecessary imports, from Benetton shirts to Mercedes cars, have all to be paid for in foreign exchange. In addition, billions of dollars are required every year for servicing the enormous debt incurred through financial institutions that were originally set up to solve foreign exchange crises. To earn foreign exchange all possible manner of exports, including food and other agricultural commodities are encouraged. The West welcomes these imports since they provide its citizens with a choice of exotic vegetables and fruits at relatively low cost.

Even though about 30 per cent of India's population does not have adequate food to eat, more than 90 per cent of agricultural exports from India consist of about 300 food items. For the impoverished, rice is a diet staple, pulses and fish their source of essential protein, fruit and vegetables provide other nutrients required for good health. In India, the average per capita availability of the latter foods is already below minimal nutritional requirements. The export of all these in increasing quantities can only be at the cost of increasing the malnutrition of the undernourished.

Food grains are also being exported because there appears to be a surplus, given that millions cannot afford to purchase their needs. Such export increases the possibility of massive famines occurring. Prior to the arrival of the British, in good years surplus grain was stored in individual farmers' homes in pest-proof containers, with paddy often remaining in good condition for more than twenty years. When a lean year occurred, such stocks filled the deficit, keeping food prices low. But the first railways constructed in India by the British connected the ports to the food production areas. In good years all surplus grain was exported to the UK, leaving nothing for lean years when prices rose. Widespread famines invariably followed.

Today the scenario is being repeated, with no guarantee that India will be able to import requirements quickly enough in lean years at reasonable prices. In fact, for instance, the moment it is announced in Delhi that there is going to be a low harvest due to drought, global prices of cereals shoot up.[11] The handful of TNCs which dominate such commodities globally, now control the fate of entire nations.

From such insecurity stems the downward spiral into impotence, increased dependency upon the West and its institutions.

The Right to Health

Article 25 promotes in practice the right to access the Western allopathic system and to use—if sufficiently well-off—the drugs its manufacturers produce. The allopathic system, for instance, claims that treatment with herbal drugs is not based on any studies but solely on superstition. Yet many of the pharmaceutical manufacturers have themselves patented such herbal drugs and are selling them now as allopathic drugs.

This institutionalisation of health care has focussed on the cure of disease and deprived people of their right to look after and treat themselves through local, self-reliant, free or low-cost, indigenous systems of health maintenance. In so doing, it is also destroying the creativity which led to the discovery of thousands of herbal medicines and which researched them for millennia.

Allopathy's narrow focus on drug therapy has resulted in the separation of food from health, leading to the exclusion of the use of a wholesome and appropriate diet from its therapeutic regimes. Such separation gives rise to ridiculous situations such as TB patients being treated with expensive drugs for over a year with no corresponding attention being paid to their nutrition during and after treatment. Relapses usually occur in such cases, with additional profit to physicians and drug manufacturers. A nutritious diet is essential for the maintenance of an active immune system. Any impairment of the latter decreases a person's ability to resist viruses, bacteria, parasites and immune-deficiency diseases such as cancer and AIDS.

The allopathic system claims that it has made notable advances in the detection and treatment of diseases, in comparison with other systems of medicine, the results being highly visible in the longer life-span of people in the West. However, much of the increase in average life-spans has occurred due to improvements in sanitation and water supplies, that is, through public health initiatives. In non-Western areas, the health situation often took a turn for the worse after colonial occupations impoverished people, reducing their ability to grow or purchase sufficient food.

Moreover, not "everyone" can have access to the allopathic system. There are those whom the system physically does not reach, being too remote from urban physicians. There are those who have been dropped out of the economy by the liberalisation process: they had earlier been made dependent on the system but are now deprived of its questionable mercies by rising costs of drugs and the removal of public health subsidies. The global expenditure on pharmaceuticals is estimated to be $220 billion per year, yet two billion people in the world have no regular access to drugs.[12]

The maintenance of health has, in fact, become incidental to the manufacture, prescription and sale of drugs in the allopathic system. Profits take priority over health, so we have a preponderance of useless drugs, irrational combinations, and "tonics". A Task Force on Prescription Drugs, established by the US Department of Health, Education and Welfare in 1967, found there were "too many examples of companies which have marketed ineffective products, dangerous or even lethal products, atrociously over-promoted products or products that received government approval only on the basis of fraudulent evidence, and which were not punished in the market place."[13]

Any attempt to make the system more rational by reducing the number of useless drugs on the market is vigorously opposed by TNCs. Bangladesh, in 1982, in an attempt to improve availability of allopathic medicine to all its people, tried to introduce a National Drug Policy (NDP) which promoted about 250 essential drugs recommended by the WHO instead of the thousands being imported by TNCs. The very same morning the news of the policy appeared in the papers, Jane Abel Coon, the US ambassador to Bangladesh, called on General Ershad, the Chief Martial Law Administrator, without prior appointment to convince him that as the policy was unacceptable to the USA it should not be implemented.[14] Ershad was invited to the US, where he met Vice-President George Bush, who had been a director of Eli Lilly—one of the largest US pharmaceutical firms—and who had substantial shares in other drug companies as well.[15] Bush's "advice" given to Ershad can well be imagined.

At the same time, the US TNCs in Bangladesh put pressure on most of the major Bangladesh newspapers to publish reports against the NDP. These reports were prepared by the Bangladesh Association of Pharmaceutical Industries (BASS), an organisation controlled by TNCs. The TNCs also bought up academics to resist the NDP.[16] British, Dutch and West German ambassadors called on General Ershad to express their dismay at the proposed drug policy. The Germans were particularly annoyed, threatening the policy would deter German investment in the country. The German ambassador claimed that Hoechst, the German TNC, had intended to expand in Bangladesh but was now reluctant to do so.[17]

On 6 March 1992, the Bangladesh government announced its decision to review of the National Drug Policy of 1982 (NDP 82) and formulate a revised drug policy by 30 April 1992. At this stage, the WB entered to put pressure on the Bangladesh government by "recommending" the directions the revised policy should take if the Bank were to sanction future loans. A letter from the WB threatened: "We would appreciate if these views are brought to the attention of the drug policy review committee urgently, specially since one aspect (import controls) of the above is germane to ISAC-II (Industrial Sector Adjustment Credit - II) negotiations."[18]

The policy was duly diluted in early 1992. Immediately thereafter, a nonessential combination cough rub, Vaporub, was approved, along with twelve other single-ingredient products of no proven superiority over existing ones. Three of the drugs were not even recorded in the British, the US and other pharmacopoeias. Pfizer won an appeal to get two drugs that had been banned under the NDP back on the market: Unasyn (ampicillin plus salbactum) and Daricon (oxyphencyclamine).[19]

Similar pressure has been exerted by TNCs, through their governments, in other Two Thirds World countries. When members of the faculty of Dar es Salaam University circulated a paper criticising the German company, Asta Werke, for marketing in Africa a drug which was banned in the UK and USA for safety reasons, the West German embassy sent a warning letter to the University, reminding it of its dependence on German aid for the construction of a new engineering school.[17] When the Philippines National Drug Policy was announced by President Aquino in April 1987, the US ambassador in Manila warned the Philippine health minister that the drug policy would discourage foreign investment.[20]

The WHO, under Dr Mahler, routinely exposed the drug industry's excessive promotional practices and the double standards it employed in marketing drugs.[21] But the US has consistently opposed the WHO's policies on drugs in the interests of its own TNCs. The WHO was soon forced to temper its public statements by indirect pressure from the US. When UN organisations promoted policies that went against US interests, the US simply withdrew its participation. It withdrew from the International Labour Organization (ILO) in 1978 and from the United Nations Educational, Scientific and Cultural Organization (UNESCO) in 1987, in both cases claiming that the organisations were becoming "highly politicised."[22]

The WHO has now been infiltrated by TNCs. Dr Hiroshi Nakajima, the present director, previously worked for Hoffman La Roche. The WHO Expert Committee on Essential Drugs includes industry representatives from the International Federation of Pharmaceutical Manufacturers, the World Federation of Proprietary Medicine Manufacturers, the Commonwealth Pharmaceutical Association and the International Pharmaceutical Federation. Representatives from Health Action International, the International Organisation of Consumers' Unions and the Public Citizen Health Research Group have always been excluded from such committees.[23]

Prices of medicines in India, at least those of essential drugs, were kept under reasonable control by the Indian government in the pre-GATT era. Earlier Indian laws allowed firms to manufacture patented drugs if the company holding the patent did not do so within a specified period. This forced several pharmaceutical TNCs to manufacture their drugs within the country. The WTO provisions for patent protection, however, treat the import of pharmaceuticals as equivalent to manufacture in the country. Several TNCs have now stopped manufacturing within the country and are importing the drugs, there being no price control on imports. The WTO's provisions openly serve to increase the industry's profits at the cost of people's right to health. The WTO has in effect eliminated the need for individual TNCs to fight individual policies of Two Thirds World countries. Its imperatives include all that TNCs have demanded for the their own profit at the cost of the right to health of their "beneficiaries".

In the US, those who make profits from providing health care include mercenary physicians and surgeons, the large for-profit hospitals, the health insurance companies and the employers who pay the latter's premiums on behalf of their employees. This cosy relationship has raised the cost of annual individual health care to about $27,000, far more than a family earning the median income ($30,000) can afford. US citizens have either to do without care or get heavily into debt in order to survive. It is estimated that roughly 100,000 people in the US die each year from lack of care - three times as many as die from AIDS.[24] Such is the commitment of the US to human rights in its own front yard.

For the impoverished, the allopathic system for all practical purposes does not exist, since it favours the rich, selecting only the wealthy for survival. The system is increasingly dependent on expensive high technology for diagnosis as well as treatment. Even the diagnosis varies with the level of affluence. French psychiatrist,

Pierre Janet, says "If a patient is poor, he is committed to a public institution and called psychotic. If he can afford a sanatorium, the diagnosis is neurasthenia. If he is rich, and at home under constant medical supervision, he is simply 'an indisposed eccentric.'"[25]

Another form of selection of the wealthy is the development of the organ transplant industry. It had become a common practice, until officially banned in India, for surgeons to literally steal a kidney of a poor and unsuspecting patient for grafting onto the rich. This, as N H Antia of the Foundation for Community Health says, "not only demonstrates the extent to which the ethics of the medical profession has deteriorated but also depicts the levels to which the morals of those who feel that they can buy anything with money has dipped."[26] It was recently revealed that patients were coming to Mumbai from Spain, Germany, France, Saudi Arabia, Yemen, Qatar, Turkey, and other countries to have their diseased kidneys replaced by stolen Indian ones.[27]

The medical system also selects by race. According to an analysis by the International Mortality Chartbook of data for 1991, the death rate of Blacks in the US is one of the highest in the industrialised world—around 40 per cent higher than those for whites.[28]

The ethnic bias is applied worldwide by Western legislation that permits the sale of banned drugs in the Two Thirds World. WEMOS, a Dutch medical organisation, reported that European pharmaceutical firms are dumping at least seventy-five drugs in Two Thirds World countries, which have been pulled out or banned in one or more EC countries.[29]

One of the painkillers most widely sold in India is analgin, with approximately 200 formulations based on it currently available. This drug may increase the tendency to bleed and produces a severe loss of white blood cells which damages the user's immune system. A major manufacturer of analgin is Hoechst, whose worldwide sales of this drug alone was $75 million in 1984-1985. However, the pressure of activists in Germany compelled the company "voluntarily" to withdraw the drug—but only in that country.

Most of the developed countries have either banned or severely restricted the sale of analgin. However, Hoechst has openly stated that it will not stop selling the drug anywhere else unless forced to do so.[30] One wonders how much the spread of

AIDS and other diseases is a result of damage to the immune system due to drugs such as these.

Other examples of such racism abound. Cyproheptadine is marketed in the UK by Merck Sharp and Dohme for allergic rhinitis and various allergies. The same product is marketed in India, Pakistan and other hunger-prone countries as an appetite stimulant. Pentoxifylline is marketed in the UK and the USA by Hoechst for peripheral vascular diseases only. Hoechst markets the same drug in the Two Thirds World for cerebral vascular problems and for the treatment of confused states of mind, loss of social contacts, sleeping disorders, vertigo and dizziness, loss of memory and loss of concentration.[31]

Many allopathic drugs make themselves obsolete, an apparently inherent defect in the system. The promotion of approved drugs for unrestricted use by pharmaceutical companies and physicians has led to drug-resistant disease microorganisms. There has been a consequent resurgence of TB, malaria and other illnesses, which the allopathic system had earlier boasted it had eliminated. More than 90 per cent of staphylococci strains are now resistant to penicillin and similar antibiotics. Resistance to vancomycin, the potent weapon once available against deadly hospital-acquired infections, was twenty times greater in 1993 than in 1989. Tuberculosis microorganisms are now resistant to many drugs.[32]

The drug industry, based as it is on profits for itself, not health for its clients, cannot provide for such a situation. Few new drugs are being developed since the target microbes are developing resistance so rapidly that companies find it unprofitable to invest in bringing an antibiotic to market, as it may be useful for only a few years. Further, dependence on such a system could result in a public health disaster.[32]

Such resistance would not have arisen if professionals had concentrated on the maintenance of health rather than the cure of disease. However, neither doctors nor drug companies can make money from promoting health maintenance while both can do so from attempting cures—in many ways. In addition to the straight sale of cures, there are the cures required for the side effects of cures. Then, there are the cures for the side effects that industrial society is so liberal with: illness due to poisoned food, water and air, illness due to physical and mental stress, and so on. There is now incontrovertible evidence from the US and elsewhere linking the rising incidence of mental illnesses with the tensions associated with the marginality of physical existence.

Since the political process (and with it the kind of political options voters face) in all late-capitalist societies offers victims of economic deprivation virtually no avenues for redress, an explosive pathology can easily develop. This leads to acts of "random violence", which are blamed upon deranged individuals, and from the creation of which society conspicuously seeks to exculpate itself.

Acts such as the killing of schoolchildren in Dunblane lead to anguished social debate in the West about "improved security in schools", the policing of crazy individuals and the control of guns, but never about the social pathogens which wound and mutilate increasing numbers of people in the enclaves of privilege which the West is perceived to be.

But there is another related factor at work as well. The ultra-atomised society of North America and Europe—with its dangerous fetish for individualism nurtured by movies and television—ensures that more and more people are cut away and allowed to drift towards the fringes of society. There they fester, harbouring grudges—some real, some imagined—and planning their retribution.[33]

A major claim which the allopathic system makes to assert its superiority over other systems of medicine is that its drugs are thoroughly tested by clinical trials before being approved for sale. However, the American Medical Association estimates that of the 2.1 billion prescriptions written by doctors in 1994, 40 to 60 per cent were prescribed for off-label use, that is, to treat conditions for which they are not approved and, in some cases, not even tested. More than 70 per cent of the drugs used to treat cancer are prescribed off-label, as are 60 per cent of drugs for children.[34]

In the 1980s, off-label use of several potent heart drugs killed thousands of patients, while similar use of antipsychotic drugs for mentally retarded patients produced disabling side effects. In the US about 200,000 children are currently being prescribed an adult high blood pressure drug, clonidine, to treat their attention deficit disorders. The risk of giving clonidine to children is unknown, since there exists little data to back up its use, and there is concern about side effects and other reactions that may cause death.[34]

Yet a bill has been introduced in the US Congress to allow drug companies to market drugs for such off-label use. The legislation is being promoted by the Pharmaceutical Research and Manufacturers of America.[34]

Such use of drugs for non-registered purposes illustrates the extent to which allopathic practice is based on physician's individual experiments rather than on clinical study. An American Medical Association expert says medical practice, by necessity, always will be based on trial-and-error.[34] But then, what differentiates the allopathic system from other medicinal systems which do not use clinical trials? Its total dependence on profit-making pharmaceutical companies, perhaps.

Another claim made by allopathy is that it is the only system which employs surgical methods on a wide scale. However, there is no allopathic speciality based so little on science. "Anything that hasn't been shown with hard data to be an effective treatment is experimental", says Richard Greene of the US Federal Agency for Health Care Policy and Research. "That would go for virtually 85 to 95 per cent of all surgical procedures." Surgeons have little tradition of research. Claiming that they are using state of the art techniques, surgeons employ untested procedures and implant experimental devices, often without the knowledge or consent of the victim. For example, a new, high-tech brain surgery—performed on several thousand patients a year—was found to be ineffective at best and actually harmed some patients by causing strokes.[35]

With the increasing cost of discovering new allopathic drugs, Western pharmaceutical industries are turning to investigating traditional herbal medicines, proving—if such proof is necessary—that these medicines, often tested by centuries of use, are effective. This path results in lower research and development costs since no compensation need be paid for the considerable earlier research carried out by herbal developers, intellectual property rights being expressly denied them. In addition, the large scale, unsustainable harvesting of wild herbs deprives those who use them directly for health, while causing a major loss of biodiversity.

The "advances" of biotechnology have introduced new sources of violence to the very people it claims to help. The use of genetic screening can produce, as an article in The Lancet starkly puts it, "a subcaste of genetic lepers who are refused jobs, health insurance, and life cover, and who find it difficult to find a marriage partner."[36] With testing for susceptibility to more diseases becoming easy, insurance companies could attempt to raise rates for persons suffering from such commonplace conditions as asthma, eczema, cataract, hypertension, obesity and arthritis.

An earlier example illustrates the possibilities. In the 1960s in the US a national screening programme for sickle-cell disease—a disease mainly hereditarily restricted to Blacks—was initiated. But mere identification of persons carrying the gene responsible for the disease does not help its carriers. Sickle-cell disease is not preventable and it does not need treatment except during sickling crises which occur when oxygen levels in the blood drop. The screening programme was not accompanied by adequate education, with the media publishing much misinformation. Blacks faced further discrimination in the job market and had to pay higher health and life insurance premiums. The occasional false-positive result led to accusations of infidelity or illegitimacy. Some US States decided that sickle-cell was a communicable disease.[37]

The workings of the health care industry lobby are representative of US-style democracy in action. One of the ways in which the lobby exercises power is by funding the election campaigns of members of Congress. From 1981 to the first half of 1991, for instance, the health insurance industry's political action committees (PACs) contributed $60 million to members of Congress, with much of the money going to key members of health-related committees. These same people also received $28 million from the medical-professional PACs, $9 million from the pharmaceutical PACs, and $6 million from the hospital PACs.[38] Pro-industry legislation is further ensured by the "revolving door" mechanism—the movement of ex-politicians and the staff of the major health-related congressional committees to jobs in the medical-industrial complex and vice versa.[39] This shows again that the US has the best Congress money can buy and that it is a plutocratic, not a democratic system. In the words of Ronald W Lang: "The drug industry lobby buys Congressmen's votes the way you and I buy aspirins."[40]

As a result of such collaboration, the profits of the top twenty drug companies increased 15 per cent per year over the past ten years, compared with an average annual increase of 3.2 per cent for the top *Fortune* 500 companies.[41] The profits of course come from patients who have to exercise their rights to health within the Western allopathic medical system.

It is notable that Western commentators increasingly refer to "the health of the economy", "a healthy trade balance", "the ailing textile industry", markets that are "sluggish", "volatile", "buoyant". It is clear from all the rhetoric that the health of the economy now clearly takes priority over the health of the people; and this is duly reflected in discussions about health care.

Drug Abuse

The use of addictive stimulant and narcotic drugs, illegal or prescribed, is one of the largest single causes contributing to ill-health and early death today.

Some of the drugs which are now considered among the most harmful narcotics were earlier widely prescribed by the allopathic system with the profits from their sales forming the financial basis of some of today's large companies.

Heroin was first developed by the A G Bayer Company of Germany in 1898 as a painkiller. Bayer is today one of the largest pharmaceutical firms in the world. Nelson Rockefeller's great-grandfather was a dealer in bottled medicines which often contained opium as an active ingredient.[42] The Parke-Davis Company provided coca and cocaine in fifteen forms, including coca-cordial, cocaine cigarettes, hypodermic capsules, ointments and sprays. The Coca-Cola company introduced Coca-Cola in 1886 with cocaine as an ingredient.[43]

Today the poverty of the people living in the US inner cities is sourced to the liberal use of illegal drugs rather than to the endemic racial, social and economic problems which result in intolerable living conditions. The US cannot solve these problems without extensive changes in its system, changes which must result in a reduction in affluence of those in power.

Instead of attempting to cure the problem of drug demand at home, the US seeks to wield its power to demand that other countries which serve as drug sources control the supply.[44] Needless to say, programmes to rehabilitate and "cure" drug abusers furnish ample business opportunities and employment possibilities for others.

The US has, however, been responsible for setting up and nurturing many of the drug barons who control narcotic drug supplies. Central America became the transit point for cocaine during the covert war the US waged against the Sandinistas in Nicaragua. Colonel Oliver North and Admiral John Poindexter, of the Iran-Contragate scandal, financed the war by trading in drugs to get round a Congressional ban on aid for the Contras. Manuel Noriega, then President of Panama, was employed by the CIA to open accounts with the Bank of Credit & Commerce International (BCCI) to launder money for the Contras. When found to be an uncontrollable embarrassment, Noriega was finally abducted and convicted in the US for drug trafficking. The Colombian drug cartels used the same BCCI offices in Panama to launder drug money. The CIA itself maintained BCCI accounts.[44]

The "Golden Triangle"—source of much heroin—on the borders of Myanmar, Laos and Thailand is run by men whose careers were launched by the US CIA during the Vietnam War. In Afghanistan the US was well aware that some of the anti-USSR Mujaheddin groups it supported were running their own drug smuggling operations.[44] On the one hand, the US government claims that drug suppliers are to blame for drug addiction in the US; on the other, the CIA has been regularly using these same suppliers in the covert expansion of American influence abroad. The latter objective takes priority over the health and happiness of its own, mainly Black and Hispanic, citizens.

Cocaine, heroin, marijuana and other drugs are declared illegal and are not marketable by legitimate US business which claims that it is thereby losing billions of dollars in profits. So, free market economists have initiated moves to have narcotic drugs treated on par with other legal drugs like alcohol and tobacco.

However, these legal drugs actually harm and kill many more millions than the "illegal" ones. Today, nearly 14 million American adults—more than 7 per cent of the population—have a problem with alcohol. The problem is worse among men than women, and more common among people between eighteen and twenty-nine years old than among the older population.[45] Tobacco kills an estimated three million people in the world today, of which 800,000 deaths occur in India.[46] The market claims an inalienable right to promote such drugs, often as status symbols, even though they produce serious health problems, possibly leading to death.

Health and the Environment

The right to health is negated by numerous other practices inherent in the Western industrial system. The right to health should include the right not to be exposed to industrial, vehicular or agricultural pollution, extra ultraviolet radiation through ozone holes, nuclear radiation from leaky reactors, major changes in the climate, or to any other known or suspected environmental health hazard. But the production of harmful pollution is so ubiquitous that classifying this as a human rights situation, and acting to reduce pollution drastically, would result in the collapse of the Western industrial system.

The Western system considers the right to health subordinate to its right to profits through the sale of toxic chemicals. Synthetic pesticides are among the most toxic substances deliberately sold for introduction into the environment. The manufacturers claim that if their pesticides are not used, food production would drop considerably and people would die of starvation.

This is a wholly false claim since there are many other ways by which sufficient food could be made available to consumers, though all of these would unfortunately also reduce industrial profits.

Some fifty-three carcinogenic pesticides are registered for use in the US on major food crops. The US Environmental Protection Agency (EPA) allows residues of a single carcinogenic pesticide on a single food item, at levels posing a "negligible cancer risk" of 1 in 100,000 excess cancers. Thus, consuming a normal meal contaminated by residues of some thirty carcinogenic pesticides would result in about 30,000 excess cancers each year, on the conservative assumption that risks are simply additive rather than synergistic.[47] Scientists talk about an "acceptable risk" of one in a hundred thousand or one in a million deaths, but such a risk cannot be acceptable to those who are thereby denied the right to life.

Current US law allows American manufacturers to export products which are known to pose high health and environmental risks. A survey of 1991 exports found that nearly 30,000 tonnes per year of banned, never-registered and restricted-use pesticides were exported, among which were almost ninety-six tonnes of DDT, which had been banned for use in the US more than twenty years ago.[48] The US protects some of the rights of its own citizens but sees no harm in denying these same rights to the people of other countries.

The Occidental Petroleum Corporation in the US manufactures DBCP, a chemical known to cause sterility and cancer. The company was not concerned about the user's rights to health and life but about the possibility that it could have to pay compensation to its victims. A memo, concerning the assessment of the potential liability to the company, requested company personnel to estimate the maximum number of people exposed to DBCP during manufacture, transportation, distribution and use. Knowing the "normal" rate of induced temporary and permanent sterility and of cancers, the potential liability was calculated, assuming that only 50 per cent of those affected would file claims. "Should this product still show an adequate profit, meeting corporate investment criteria", the memo concluded, "the project should be considered further."[49]

Other types of toxic pollutants are treated similarly. A Gulf Resources and Chemical Corporation vice president estimated how much the firm would have to pay if it continued to expose children in the town of Kellogg to lead emissions. The note's calculations were based on an earlier lead poisoning incident in Texas, where the liability was set at $5,000 to $10,000 per child. The calculation estimated that the cost to the company of poisoning 500 children in Kellogg would be $6-7 million.[49] People, children included, are merely one more raw material whose cost is to be estimated like any other to determine profits.

Industries in general determine the pollution they can emit by the illness potential of healthy humans: how much smog can fresh lungs stand before lung diseases appear, how much of carcinogenic chemicals can people consume before cancer appears, how much of mutagenic substances can parents absorb before a statistically significant number of babies are born defective, and so on. Genetic testing may even allow higher levels of pollution in industry, with employers only hiring workers whose genes show they would be able to withstand those levels.[50]

Another violation of the right to health comes from transferring Western toxic wastes to Two Thirds World countries, pollution related illness and health rights being considered exchangeable commodities.

Western companies dumped over 24 million tonnes of hazardous wastes in West Africa alone during 1988. In 1989, a Norwegian company unloaded hazardous waste from Philadelphia on an island near Conakry but was forced to haul it away. An Italian waste disposal firm shipped 8,000 drums of highly toxic waste, including about 150 tonnes of PCBs to Nigeria.[51] One firm sent huge volumes of outdated pesticides, industrial chemicals and solvents to India, South Korea and Nigeria. These particular wastes came from US government agencies such as the Department of Agriculture, many city governments and the Environmental Protection Agency itself.[49] The latter must have known their destination, but let the firm carry on its business of abusing the right to health of others. No records are liable to be kept of the ill-health and deaths resulting from these deadly mercantile transactions.

CHAPTER 7

The Rights to Education and Work

E *veryone has the right to education. Education shall be free, at least in the elementary and fundamental stages. Elementary education shall be compulsory. Technical and professional education shall be made generally available and higher education shall be equally accessible to all on the basis of merit."* (UDHR, Article 26.1)

"Education shall be directed to the full development of the human personality and to the strengthening of respect for human rights and fundamental freedoms. It shall promote understanding, tolerance and friendship among all nations, racial or religious groups, and shall further the activities of the United Nations for the maintenance of peace." (UDHR, Article 26.2)

"Parents have a prior right to choose the kind of education that shall be given to their children." (UDHR, Article 26.3)

The Right to Education

The right to education in the UN Declaration ensures that the "educated" are supportive of the Western system even while destroying more life-sustaining knowledge.

The formal education system in India has been controlled since the time of Macaulay's infamous Minute with his orders to produce "a class of persons, Indian in blood and colour, but English in taste, opinions, in morals..."[1] Julius Nyerere confirmed that education was used for the same purpose in other colonies: "The education provided by the colonial government...was not designed to prepare young people for the service of their own country; instead, it was motivated by a desire to inculcate the values of the colonial society and to train individuals for the service of the colonial State."[2]

Today, the Western-oriented formal system in India still serves as a means of conveying the West's ideology, while devaluing and disgracing local cultures. School curricula, not too subtly, promote an authoritarian, hyperconsumptive society, conditioning children into docilely accepting, fitting into, and then propagating the Western system.[3]

Education has become an exercise in manipulation rather than a means to develop the human personality and acquire a livelihood. Schooling is given a value in itself as a human right, irrespective of its utility to the schooled, indeed, even if it tends to reduce her/his chances of survival. The formal educational system does not teach the adverse side of the Western development system, its injustice and unsustainability, the fact that it cannot provide jobs for all. Indeed, students are so narrowly educated they are able to survive only within the Westernised system.

Even if the content of the curriculum were satisfactory and if "everyone" had a right to enter school, the institution of the school ensures that the children of the elite pass through its portals with much greater ease than the children of the impoverished, since part of the injustice in the system results from the hierarchical nature of employment classes, with menial, unskilled jobs at the bottom and managerial and administrative positions at the top. To supply candidates for the former, filters are installed in the education system which keep out or deliberately drop out children at varying levels.[4]

Perhaps the most revealing book on the falsity of the Declaration's "rights" has been written by three Italian school students who have themselves experienced this whole degrading process.[5] They show, with a wealth of statistics, that the formal school system is heavily biased against the poor with the result that most of those who obtain its certificates are children of the power-holding elite.

The failed and the dropped out are the innocent victims of the triage morality underlying modern "development": those who cannot climb into the lifeboats of the system can drown. Tragic psychological damage is the reward reserved for those not considered good enough to become full members of the Western system.

Such systems in no way meet the requirements of Article 26 (2) of the UDHR which insists: "Education shall be directed to the full development of the human personality..."

The apparently thoughtful provision of "technical and professional education" is merely a means of ensuring a supply of skilled and semiskilled personnel to keep industry running, even while confirming the lower position of those who are forced into this stream. Further, deskilling—accomplished by rapid technological "advances"—renders much knowledge acquired with great effort unusable.

"Professional" and "higher" education is limited by wealth and family advantages to children of the rich. As John Kenneth Galbraith admitted: "Higher education is, of course, extensively accommodated to the needs of the industrial corporate system."[6]

Several of the Indian institutes of "higher" education are partially funded by Western foundations and governments, with the knowledge imparted more suitable to the needs of the Western economies than to the needs of India. The successfully Westernised students, qualified and skilled in "high technology", are welcomed as immigrants in the West. This brain drain constitutes an enormous subsidy paid by the Two Thirds World to increase the affluence of the West.

The professionals, the scientists, physicians and other "experts", enclose spaces of knowledge, in the process denying the majority of people their rights to their own traditional wisdom. Such enclosures also ensure that information that would raise questions about the validity of the "experts'" knowledge or practices is kept hidden.

The structure of the school has to be authoritarian in conformity with the hierarchical structure of society at large, with the consequence that such heresies like true democracy and cooperation cannot be taught within the system. As Chomsky explains: "The rabble must be instructed in the values of subordination and a narrow quest for personal gain within the parameters set by the institutions of the masters; meaningful democracy, with popular association and action, is a threat to be overcome."[7]

The co-option of academics into supporting the dominant system has been made easier by depriving them of public funds, and compelling them to become subservient to industry. But even prior to this, the process of purchasing academics has thrived. As long ago as 1972, Judge Lewis Powell wrote a memo to the US Chamber of Commerce urging business "to buy the top academic reputations in the country to add credibility to corporate studies and give business a stronger voice on the campuses." Academics, it appears, are easily bought, ensuring that the public-policy area "is awash with in-depth academic studies" that have the proper conclusions.[8] Indeed, there has never been any dearth of clever and able people in the world willing to declare under any regime that black is white and evil is good. The temptation to intellectual dishonesty is always greater when livelihood, professional survival and prestige are dependent on it.

The spread of Western culture has been aided by the UN Educational, Scientific and Cultural Organisation (UNESCO). Among its contributions are the annual "Study Abroad", a comprehensive index to foreign study opportunities, seminars for teachers on methods to increase international understanding, and so on.[9] One does not find the reverse process at work: Western students being encouraged to study, for example, traditional sustainable knowledge and its modes of transmission.

Modern media allow even more direct promotion of the West's values. Channel One, a US school television programme, transmits advertisements for candy bars, fast food, and sneakers directly into the classroom of more than 12,000 schools. In exchange for a satellite dish and video equipment, the school must agree that Channel One will be shown on at least 90 per cent of school days to 90 per cent of the children. Teachers are not allowed to interrupt the show or turn it off.[10]

The UN UDHR holds national governments responsible for providing education to all, even as the SAPs require that all subsidies be removed and that education be privatised. The high costs of such education will serve as one more efficient filter to keep out the "lower" classes, but the main aim is tighter thought control with high profits.

The chief purpose of education should be to make people think critically so that they can act to preserve just and sustainable ways of living and change those that are not. But this is what the system dreads and every attempt is made to make independent thinking difficult. The little deviance that is permitted has to be within the parameters of the Western system itself. People in fact are unable to imagine a type of society so different from the Western system as to be "outside" it. This is a fundamental denial of the right to education.

It is this point that the NGOs at the 1994 Social Summit missed when they insisted that: "Education must be granted as the main instrument to empower youth to take their rightful place in society, enabling them to take control of their lives."[11] While education is necessary, what is taught and how are of equal importance.

Article 26 (2) is self-reinforcing in that it promotes its own Western set of human rights. Other societies may have different "rights" according to their cultural values and priorities, but no latitude is permitted here. The same Article also promotes "tolerance and friendship among all nations", thereby ensuring that the exploited amicably tolerate their exploiters.

The "prior right to choose the kind of education" (Article 2 (3)) is meaningless when formal education is made compulsory and traditional education is not recognised as sufficient for survival and perhaps better for justice.

With illiteracy equated with ignorance, the formally "educated" are trained to consider themselves superior to the "illiterate", though the latter—whether "illiterate" Adivasis or others—may have a much greater store of knowledge regarding how to survive sustainably than the conventionally literate. The knowledge of the "illiterate" is transmitted from parents and elder siblings to the young, forming a holistic education system for living. The insistence on compulsory formal education ensures the destruction of traditional self-reliant and sustainable knowledge and of its integral methods of transmission.

Western countries which pride themselves on their high levels of literacy have actually produced a majority of citizens who choose to read only newspapers (a skill which requires a reading age of about eight years). Those who can acquire information about the latest sex scandal or the most horrific crime or royal divorce are deemed to be "literate"; an achievement which shows up favourably in the United Nations Development Index. Whereas the wisdom, the vast stores of orally transmitted knowledge of a person in the Two Thirds World shows up simply as "illiteracy" and is therefore deemed to be "underdeveloped". Just which one is the more competent functional human being is not in doubt.

Those brought up in non-mainstream education systems are effectively out of control. Hence the desperate need for the Western mainstream to insist on the "right" to compulsory formal education.

There is, moreover, an increasingly obvious lack of congruence between "education" and "employment". The existence of scores of millions of unemployed graduates in the world, as well as of countless people performing labour far below their capacities, shows just what a mismatch exists between the resounding declarations of educational intention and the demeaning forms of labour required of people. Yet "education" still continues to be offered as an incentive and a source of hope to those for whom it will guarantee neither work nor security nor self-fulfillment.

In any case, official channels of education have been effectively bypassed by more urgent modes of instruction to the young, notably, advertising, publicity and communication machines of the transnationals. Such channels directly address the young, independently of the influence of parents, teachers and elders.

The Right to Employment

"Everyone has the right to work, to free choice of employment, to just and favourable conditions of work and to protection against unemployment." (UDHR, Article 23 [1])

"Everyone, without any discrimination, has the right to equal pay for equal work." (UDHR, Article 23 [2])

"Everyone has the right to just and favourable remuneration ensuring for himself and his family an existence worthy of human dignity, and supplemented, if necessary, by other means of social protection." (UDHR, Article 23 [3])

"Everyone has the right to form and to join trade unions for the protection of his interests." (UDHR, Article 23 [4])

The right to employment is apparently of nominal value since other Western policies directly contradict it.

Here too, the use of the term "everyone" is obviously misleading. In India, most parents push their children through the initiation ceremonies of tortured years in school, seeing formal education as essential for entry into a highly competitive job market. But the fine print states that the system's "right to work" does not guarantee a job, let alone a satisfying "free choice". With people being continually replaced by machines, full employment is impossible within the Western model. The "right to work" then becomes merely "the right to compete for the limited jobs available".

The huge industrial restructuring programmes imposed by the WB, IMF and GATT, have resulted in millions being disemployed as employers are encouraged to "downsize" in order to reduce expenditure on labour so that management can be paid fatter salaries. With anxious competition for the reduced number of jobs available, workers are abandoning trade unions and taking whatever meagre salary is doled out. Globalisation is leading to increasing insecurity, anxiety and fear in the people; a process which militates against the fine ideals enshrined in articles 23 (3) and (4), but which, in the curious selective blindness of the global elite, is not perceived as an infringement of anyone's rights, but is seen as part of the natural order of things.

The bias in the system is glaringly evident here. The particular interests of the employers, not covered by any human rights, are allowed to override the basic rights of millions of workers. In fact, those who "successfully" downsize are praised for their managerial competence, which is in reality the power to efficiently abuse the rights of their workers.

In the US particularly, determined efforts have been made to undermine unions, to deny workers the rights that had been won by unions earlier. The right to unionise is very effectively negated by big business through threats of further unemployment or of moving factories out of the region completely. The maintenance of an ocean of unemployed is essential for Westernised industry's survival since it forces workers to accept low—often below subsistence—wages, thus making the industry "globally competitive" by transferring employment to other countries. The deliberate creation of a labour surplus denies the very possibility of implementing Article 23 (1).

It is not to be wondered at, therefore, that globally today there are 920 million people, unemployed and underemployed, denied these basic rights. 30 per cent of the world's workforce has no work, a record surpassed only during the great depression of the 1930s.[12]

A survey carried out in 1995 in an industrial estate consisting of approximately 5,000 small units near Mumbai showed that monthly salaries were down to the Rs 500 level, far below the government's notified minimum wage.[13] This amount is insufficient to support a single person, let alone a family, so children have to take up jobs, too. India is then accused of abusing the rights of children.

In nearly all countries the proportion of unemployed is increasing, though changing definitions of employment and statistical manipulation may make it appear otherwise. For example, part-time and casual workers are now not included in the figures of the unemployed.[14]

The production of unemployment—liberation from work— is not considered an abrogation of human rights since future, fully satisfying, employment is easily promised. But there is no sign of this happening anywhere, even without resource and environmental constraints preventing much further industrial expansion. The whole history of industrial society has been a crusade to diminish, dispense with and disgrace labour; to find ways of replacing rebellious human beings with machinofacture, mechanisation, automation and now *jidoka*—the use of machines endowed with human-like intelligence. Such a system cannot provide employment for all.

Liberalisation no doubt produces some employment, but the jobs it creates are in the West. The WTO rules insist that raw cotton and cotton yarn be allowed to be freely exported, thus providing cheap raw materials for the textile industries of nations which do not grow their own cotton. This produces, in countries like India, a local shortage which raises costs of textiles. The simultaneous insistence on the removal of all government subsidies ensures that the local handloom workers cannot afford to purchase yarn. With the wiping out of their skills, the West obtains a permanent competitive advantage in the global market. Today the Western textile industry can only exist and expand by further disemployment of Indian and other Two Thirds World textile workers. This is an unedited replay of the exploitative processes that occurred during the early days of the Industrial Revolution.[15]

Again, because of liberalisation, TNCs can bring in any number of foreign workers and pay them as much as they wish. One German pharmaceutical firm recently dismissed nearly all its

Indian research staff and replaced them with Germans, much more highly paid and provided with plenty of expensive perks. A further advantage of having German researchers is that when a particular investigation looks promising the research is shifted to Germany and the results patented there. Thus all the expenses are borne by India, while Germany gets the benefits.

The contradictions in the Western system are becoming more apparent as WTO rules begin operating. TNCs have insisted that, before they condescend to set up industries in India, labour laws need to be diluted to the level of impotency. The right to form trade unions needs to be withdrawn, employers should be given full rights to hire and fire workers when they please, there should be no set minimum wages and so on. All of these militate against the rights mentioned in Article 23 (2). In fact, this is what comparative advantage is all about.

Manufacturers in the West, afraid of competition from industries—often their own TNCs—using cheap labour in the Two Thirds World, are now insisting that a "social clause" be inserted in the WTO agreement which will compel employers in the Two Thirds World to pay much higher wages, thereby losing their comparative advantage. The Indian government is evidently not ashamed of insisting that Indian employers be permitted to pay workers poorly, just in order that a tiny section of the population with whom the country is identified, benefits.[16]

The insistence by the West on the inclusion of social clauses governing employment abroad is strangely at odds with the process of reducing protection for workers at home. In the US, for example, the wages of the poorest one-third of employed people have not kept pace with the rate of inflation in the past two decades. Jobs have been created, but at income levels that barely suffice to sustain life in an intensive market economy.[14]

Liberalisation of trade not only allows the West to sell its goods in the Two Thirds World but also permits the Two Thirds World to sell its products in the West without the old systems of quotas and other restrictions. It seems as if the unemployment that this would create in the West was foreseen and that sufficient non-tariff barriers were kept in reserve to control that eventuality.

Slavery—relatively low cost labour—liberally used in the past, contributed greatly to the initial accumulation of wealth by the West. Article 4 specifically states that "No one shall be held in slavery or servitude; slavery and the slave trade shall be prohibited in all their forms." But it says nothing about compensating the descendants of slaves. The National Coalition of Blacks for Reparations in America has continued to demand $3 trillion as reparations.[17]

There are several arguments used by the whites in the US to deny this rightful claim. Some maintain that the debt the people of America might have owed to the slaves, was paid in full with the lives of the 620,000 men who died in the Civil War and that seeking to punish people for acts done long in the past goes against the moral principle that sons and daughters are not responsible for the acts of their forebears.[17] However, if people benefit from the illegal acts of their forefathers, they are morally bound to make reparations.

In India there are millions of bonded labourers, effectively slaves to moneylenders, big farmers and owners of small industries. Such a situation can only get worse as SAPs produce more poverty.

Virtual slavery also exists in regions where there is vast unemployment. Those lucky few who have jobs are bonded to their employers, no matter how hard and harsh the working conditions may be. Whether the slave is shackled by steel or by necessity, slavery is equally effective and violent. Economic slavery—not covered by the UN UDHR—is so much simpler to manage, as well as less visible and contentious, than physical bondage. And it doesn't place upon the "slave owners" the burden of their workers' "maintenance". Moreover, the new slaves cannot afford to be free, since they have no welfare provisions to fall back upon. The factory becomes a prison without bars or walls which the unemployed desperately want to enter, because even this seems to be a more desirable option than cageless incarceration in destitution.

There is much moral indignation in the West against bonded labourers in the Two Thirds World—and rightly so. But there is little condemnation of, for instance, the trafficking in women from Burma and Thailand to serve as sex workers in Europe and Japan. Many such women remain captives in closed houses. They contract vast debts to their owners which they may never be able to pay back. Many receive no wages. They are punished, beaten, tortured and killed at the whim of their owners. Many have disappeared without trace outside the country of their birth.

Article 13 (1) defines a right to freedom of movement and residence within the borders of each State only. Article 13 (2) states that "Everyone has the right to leave any country, including his own, and to return to his country." But without a corresponding right to enter any other country, this right is of little value. It was precisely this right to enter any country which was used as justification for the invasions and occupations of the Americas and other regions by the Europeans and it is this right which is today being denied to intending immigrant workers.

The creation of the "fortresses" of Europe, North America and Japan, against those whose right to enter is delegitimised by calling them "economic migrants", represents a further example of the mass violation of rights. For many such potential migrants are doing no more than testing the vaunted free markets of the West. Furthermore, many of them come from areas of the world whose original economy and culture has been violently disrupted by colonial incursions, and continue to be ravaged by all the impoverishing dictates of structural adjustment and so-called reform. The Western governments then deny entry to those very people whose lives and livelihoods they have ruined.

The "favourable conditions" mentioned in Article 23 (1) must include workplace safety. But nearly all industries, including TNCs, ignore this. That they can do so with impunity is one of the reasons why the latter shift production to the Two Thirds World in the first place.

The health of workers is an essential raw material for polluting industries. Just like the pollution potential of a pure environment, workers too have an illness potential. If they possess no needed skills, there are always temporary jobs available in highly polluting industries where they can be exposed to carcinogens, mutagens, ionising radiation, and other hazards, until they fall ill. Their illness potential being fully utilised, they are then discarded as human waste. This is particularly evident in the case of asbestos factories, stone quarries, cotton spinning mills and nuclear installations. In the last, their illness potential is actually measured and when they have been exposed to arbitrarily fixed radiation doses, they are summarily dismissed.

Ingenious schemes have been devised to discourage workers from reporting workplace accidents. In one German TNC factory near Mumbai, workers have been divided into several groups, with a monthly bonus promised to the group that reports the least number of accidents. If an accident does occur, the victim concerned is pressurised to remain silent by his own companions.

The right to work, to occupy oneself purposefully, is fundamental to the survival of all human beings. People living in traditional societies are generally involved in fulfilling their basic needs with varying degrees of self-reliance, a generally satisfying objective. Western technology, however, has changed the function of work. By offering a wage for jobs which rarely relate to personal needs, dependence on the market economy is ensured. Thus, sometimes willingly, sometimes kicking and screaming, ever more people are drawn into the market economy. Cut off from the satisfaction of basic needs, all are presented with every encouragement to develop unlimited wants. In this way, they cease to become self-determining, but become part of the invisible drive of "demand" which feeds the engines of perpetual economic growth and expansion. They have been caught up in a vast machinery which they must serve, even while they are persuaded it is serving them.

Several of the rights of workers listed in the UN UDHR are required only within the mainstream employment system. Traditional artisanal systems avoid the problems which require public declarations of such rights.

CHAPTER 8

Cultural and Communication Rights

E *veryone has the right freely to participate in the cultural life of the community, to enjoy the arts and to share in scientific advancement and its benefits."* (Article 27 [1])

"Everyone has the right to freedom of opinion and expression; this right includes freedom to hold opinions without interference and to seek, receive and impart information and ideas through any media and regardless of frontier." (Article 19)

Cultural Rights

Colonial conquests as well as modern global communications systems have contributed to the spread of Western culture with its accent on high consumption. The history of Western colonialism is a story of cultural contamination, with whole peoples dying of grief for their ravaged civilisations. Cultural genocide is of a piece with colonial adventures which usurped the land and riches of indigenous peoples in North and South America, Australia and all the other land masses Western colonialists claimed were "unoccupied."

About 10,000 years ago, there were somewhere between 10,000 and 15,000 languages, of which about 6,000 survive today. But linguistic experts predict that at least three-quarters of these will vanish during the next century.[1]

Probably the greatest loss of cultures occurred in the Americas, where some of the most benign populations existed. There is little trace of the 400 different aboriginal tribes and their fifty-five language families.[2] Innumerable aboriginal cultures everywhere have vanished and those that are still left are fast disappearing. In spite of the world outcry against the destruction of the Amazon rainforest, ranchers and prospectors are still encouraged to lay waste the culture and civilisation of tribal peoples living within it.

The world echoes with the cries of indigenous peoples whose existence is now almost at vanishing point, from the Yanomami in Brazil, to the Penan of Sarawak and the Lumad of the Philippines. The best that is being offered to those who can survive is a hut in some city slum and the consolations of cheap liquor. This option is sometimes described, even by the present-day governments of these countries—and in language used by their own former colonial masters—as "bringing backward peoples into the mainstream", or "granting them the benefits of civilisation."

The "great" cultures, by Western norms, are those that have provided plenty of artefacts for colonial plunderers. These artefacts now lie in the museums of the West. Also included in this category are those societies which built not-so-easily-portable monuments, mostly through the use of slave labour. Recent excavations in Egypt have uncovered a mass grave where hundreds of slaves who worked on the great pyramid of Cheops lie buried. Most of the workers' skeletons show worn out joints, damaged spines and abnormal bony outgrowths: symptoms caused by chronic heavy labour. The slaves worked themselves to early death between the age of thirty to thirty-five, compared with the average life span of between fifty and sixty years of the affluent at that time.[3]

As Germaine Greer states: "People who left nothing for us to plunder, who left no permanent scars on the ecology, are rewarded by being totally forgotten."[4] Their real culture, their languages, their values, their social systems, have been extinguished long ago, swept away by "mainstream" pressures. Confining people within the cultural "reservations" of the mainstream system is the most common current method used for destroying cultures.

The West likes to advertise its "pluralism" and "diversity" by incorporating exotic African styles of music, tribal paintings, writers of novels about India, Egypt or Kenya, within its own cultural hypermarket. Here the work of art, detached from its roots or context, becomes yet another commodity fit for Western consumption.

The spread of Western monoculture today extinguishes cultural diversity so that manufactured culture and its products can be the more easily mass marketed. The right to "impart informa-

tion and ideas through any media and regardless of frontier",
licenses the modern communications media not only to cross
national boundaries but also to invade the minds and imaginations
of people, enabling the new colonialism to gain a swift and
apparently irreversible hold over people. The promotion of the
"global village" overrides the right to cultural diversity.

Under the new economic colonialist regime cultural rights
continue to be overruled, in particular the rights to the maintenance of traditional husbandry and medicinal and sustainable
industrial systems. These are reviled as superstitions or as archa-
isms unfit to survive in the modern world. The elimination of
cultural systems which promote a frugal use of resources and a
sustainable life-style is essential to the promotion of the market
economy, so that those who adhere to the older principles can be
converted into faithful hyperconsumers. By this destructive invasion, the most harmonious, beautiful and intricate cultural practice
must inevitably go down before the right to sell hamburgers and
colas.

Cultural rights are further negated by the existence of tribes
of experts who determine what is "progressive" art and science. It
is noteworthy that the "right to the moral and material interest
resulting from scientific, literary or artistic production of which he
is the author" does not exist in most indigenous systems where all
such goods are considered community property.[5] The existing
equitable systems have, therefore, to be smothered by the demand
for intellectual property rights lobbied for by those who wish to
commercialise the products of traditional technologies for their
own personal profit.

Communication Rights

The knowledge of whole cultures has been transmitted from
generation to generation for millennia by means of speech, signs
and expressions. Much is still done so. These are methods of
communication which are universally available. However, the
gradual development of technology for mass communication has
enabled the powerful to take control over the multitudes.

The art of writing limited the right of transmission of knowledge to those who knew how to write, who could spend time on
writing and who could afford the expensive clay tablets, parch-

ment and other materials required. Reception of such written knowledge was restricted to those who were literate and had access to the manuscripts, mainly the professionals and academics. Because of these limitations, writing had little adverse effect on those who used oral communication to transmit traditional knowledge and who developed the memory to retain and use that knowledge.

All subsequent development of communication was by "advances" in technology, with each upgradation more complex and expensive to use. The communication avenues also grew narrower because of their inherent technological constraints. While these advances enabled an increasing number of people to receive information, each of them produced an even deeper deprivation of the right to transmit one's own knowledge and ideas. The right to impart information through the commercial media is not available to the vast majority of people, the ordinary newspapers as well as the communication superhighways being mainly one-way avenues, reserved for the affluent. This is how we now come to hear of such exotic castes of functionaries in the West as "opinion-formers", whose high democratic purpose is, presumably, to shape the opinions of the people so that these conform with the ideas of those who rule them.

Such technological advances favour the transmission of selected sets of knowledge, reducing cultural diversity.

The first of the technological developments was the invention of printing by the Chinese which allowed their knowledge to be spread widely and to be easily carried forward from generation to generation. Movable type was invented in China in the eleventh century. This technology was developed and widely used in Europe from the fifteenth century onwards.⁶ Books could be printed in large numbers and read by still more people, provided they were literate. The publication of books was, and still is, mainly limited to the dominating affluent.

Further "progress", the cinema, radio and TV broadcasting and now electronic networks and satellite communications, additionally restricted transmission rights but widely extended some reception rights. The visual media transcend literacy and language barriers, since even those who are unable to read or to understand the language of transmission get the message of many of the advertisements which are in effect a reversion to sign language.

The term "mass communication" is itself an admission of human rights violations, since its basic assumption is that individuals lose their identity in the "mass" and hence need not be given information suitable to their particular needs. Some variation in programmes is available, but nothing to cater to the vast multitude of cultures that exist or at least existed till mass communications spread.

The right to freedom of speech can be promoted by the West with impunity now that people have been "educated" not to threaten the system. Further, this freedom is strictly limited to its literal meaning, oral communication.

Mass communications are ideal for indoctrinating individuals with the values, beliefs and codes of behaviour that integrate them into the structures of society controlled by the wealthy and powerful. The main aim of modern communications media is not to enlighten people with the truth, but to promote the myths which create wants, to propagate the Western high consumption way of life as essential for happiness, indeed for existence itself. To this end, the information provided is controlled by ownership of the media, by reliance on data from industrial and scientific "experts" only and by the use of expensive advertising.

Communications media transmitters today require very large amounts of capital, and so their ownership is now being concentrated in the hands of just a few powerful individuals and corporations. These media routinely violate Article 19: the right "to seek, receive and impart information and ideas through any media and regardless of frontier."

Even the print media are closely controlled. *Reader's Digest*, a family business, is printed in eighteen languages and is available in over 160 countries.[7] Though appearing to be a family magazine, it is a major vehicle for subtly promoting Western ideology. Other major players in the propaganda league are *Time*, *Newsweek*, and *The Economist*.[8]

The Internet—which is often touted as giving any individual the freedom to communicate with all the rest of the global population—can be accessed only by those who can purchase a computer and modem and who can pay for expensive telephone calls. These are the people who have already benefited from the system and are hardly liable to question its basic utility. Just as the normal highways clog up if too many people attempt to travel at the same time, the Internet already shows signs of jamming as more people attempt to search for the information they require. In fact, such technologies are built on the assumption that most of the six billion earthly inhabitants will *not* use them.

It is invariably claimed that the electronic networks have unlimited information available, but the information from, for instance, the much-publicised databases, is limited to promoting the Western system. Databases on the traditional use of herbs for medicine are oriented towards their commercialisation, rather than the promotion of traditional healing methods.

Expert Filtering

The news media, though assumed to be independent and committed to discovering and reporting the truth, is part of the system. There is, therefore, continuous and efficient self-censorship, which makes more obvious methods of control superfluous. Since "freedom of speech" does not mean that the truth and the whole truth need be spoken, the media feels free to convey half-truths or even falsehoods.

The filtering out of uncomfortable facts, the sanitisation of news which does not contaminate the publicly accepted ideology, is essential to avoid true debate on what goes on in a "democracy". This task is admirably accomplished by economists, scientists and other "experts". Though token challenging opinions are allowed to be expressed, quantitatively, pro-mainstream opinion far exceeds the anti-mainstream voices.

Self-censorship and the selective filtering of news is so effective that it can make invisible even obvious truths. For example, the US media promoted the US government's claim that it was helping Guatemala in 1954 on the path to democracy, although the CIA-sponsored invasion supported elite rule and helped to organise the State's terror campaigns. The media proclaimed that "democracy" was being promoted in Brazil, Chile, the Philippines and Nicaragua by the US when it was actually being actively subverted. When the US supports terrorist dictatorships the media mildly claims that it is "constructively engaged" with them.[9] Such photographic development of positive images from negative reality occurs continuously.

Industry efficiently controls the flow of information through its advertisements. The high cost of advertising ensures that only those who have funds can get their message across—the message naturally, always being the tenets of the religion of Mammon. The press and TV in particular apparently feel they have a duty to their advertisers which transcends their readers' or viewers' right to correct information. While the misleading advertisements of those who pay up are unabashedly published or aired, it is extremely difficult for the non-paying person to get in a word.

The "higher" the technology, the larger the audience required to be entrapped by it, otherwise manufacturers do not find it profitable enough to advertise on the medium. Such sums as are required for the purpose are only affordable by producers of mass consumption items, with their accompanying mass use of nonrenewable resources and mass pollution of the environment. The extensive injustice produced as a necessary adjunct of excessive consumption has to be kept hidden by the media.

In TV, it is the sponsor who controls the content of the programmes transmitted. Large corporate advertisers do not sponsor programmes that engage in serious criticisms of the dominant system. Viewers need to be lulled into feeling that "all's right with the world" so that they will continue purchasing the environmentally damaging products advertised. In an inhuman inversion of roles, viewers have become in effect mere products to be sold on the free market by the advertising agencies to the businesses which advertise.

The available advertising space in printed matter, and time on radio and TV, are limited, and TNCs have to compete for it by offering to pay ever-increasing rates, thus ensuring not only that individuals are completely left out but the small and medium manufacturers, too. Even among the largest, the tendency now is to fund whole television programmes, rather than to buy slots of a few seconds, making it much easier to seduce the viewer by subliminal or clear messages.

Unilever Magazine complains that "media ownership is moving towards being concentrated in the hands of one or two powerful individuals." It continues: "Companies which may want to buy airtime, or to get better airtime deals, are becoming increasingly involved in funding television programmes. Many advertisers, agencies and television companies alike are quickly reaching the conclusion that in seducing the viewer it will be the quality of programmes that wins the day....If the programme proves popular enough, then possibilities for world sales would open up."[10] This was proved in the popularity of the soap, *Riviera*, produced jointly by Unilever and EC TV on a $40 million production budget.[11]

Large companies try to control the media by withdrawing, or threatening to withdraw, their advertisements when attempts are made by NGOs to tell the truth. Procter & Gamble (P&G) sells Folger's Coffee, a bestselling brand in North America. In 1990 a US NGO, Neighbor to Neighbor, placed two thirty-second advertisements on WHDH-TV, an affiliate of CBS, urging consumers to boycott this brand of coffee, since P&G buys some of it from El Salvador. The advertisement said that wealthy coffee planters funded the right-wing death squads who were responsible for the disappearance and murder of tens of thousands of people in El Salvador during the 1980s.[12]

The day after the advertisement was shown, P&G announced it was indefinitely suspending all advertising on WHDH-TV for its entire range of products, depriving the TV station of revenue of around a million dollars a year. P&G also threatened to withdraw all advertising from any TV station that broadcast the anti-Folger's advertisement. Television stations forced to choose between carrying commercials from P&G or from Neighbour to Neighbour, found it economically necessary to choose the former. P&G is America's biggest advertiser, spending more than $600 million a year on television advertisements for Pampers nappies, Tide detergent, Charmin lavatory paper, Crest toothpaste and scores of other products.[12]

P&G's corporate censorship, however, boomeranged since the resulting publicity only made the Neighbour to Neighbour campaign more widely known. Moreover, P&G is being portrayed as a corporate bully that denies its critics the right of free speech—even when they are willing to pay for it.[13] But, more often, the TNC wins.

The emphasis in Article 19 on the right to freedom of speech is being misused to promote harmful advertising. Smoking has been proved to cause cancer, resulting in the early and painful death of millions of smokers, active and passive, every year. The

Indian government had proposed not to ban cigarettes, but only to ban advertisements promoting them. The potential loss of the Indian market so alarmed the international tobacco lobbies that they joined hands with the World Federation of Advertisers in Brussels to fight the proposed ban. In a letter addressed to the Indian Prime Minister, the director general of the Federation claimed that a "ban on advertising would be an infringement of Article 19 of the Universal Declaration of Human Rights which has been supported by India."[14] This distortion of the Declaration gives the right to free speech precedence over the right to health and life.

Typical of common misleading advertisements are those for processed foods and "health" drinks. People are persuaded by partial information that, for instance, the particular concoction of the manufacturer can increase a child's intelligence. The nourishment they could have obtained cheaply from direct use of cereals and pulses they seek vainly in a small quantity of expensive powders. Again, the inhuman right to sell for profit takes priority over the right to health.

Pesticides which are decidedly harmful to human beings and other living creatures are now being sold in advertisements as "working in harmony" with nature and being "environmentally-friendly".

The spectacle of the "good life" presented in advertisements is so entrancing, the need to keep up with the neighbours so essential for peer acceptance, that the impoverished are tempted to take by force what they can never hope to enjoy as of "right". Hence robberies and even murders for the sake of items like branded shoes.

A recent half-page advertisement in the *Times of India* shows how crime itself is promoted. Philips, the international electronics giant, advertised its CD System AZ6840, with the following (decoded) message to the young:[15]

• You have the right to play around all day; if your parents object and there is "too much order in life" "we suggest you leave home." (This is an inducement to idleness, disobedience and then to mental and physical alienation from the family.)

• No ordinary equipment will do for you. (This is an attempt to inflate the self-esteem of the purchaser by implying that she or he is superior in aesthetic, musical and technological appreciation to those possessing "ordinary CD players.")

• If you don't demand this product it shows you must be afraid to face the music of parental objections. (A concealed challenge which many teenagers would find difficult to resist.)

In addition to the adverse physical effects of sound equipment used at a level "to test your ear drums", there have been serious social consequences resulting from attitudes induced by such messages, absorbed over a period of time by young people in the West. These include an alarming increase in crimes committed by 12-25 year olds, growing levels of alcohol and drug addiction, the appearance of young people begging and "sleeping rough" in towns and cities, exacerbation of conflict within the family if parents are unable or unwilling to meet repeated demands for "designer" products which often cost more than their own weekly or even monthly wage, the suicide of children derided by their peers because they did not possess such status symbols, the appearance of the battered parent and grandparent and the escalation of anti-social public behaviour ranging from the aggressive use of insulting or obscene language to wanton attacks on the police, ambulance personnel, fire brigade officers and hospital staff. In India, these consequences will be further aggravated by the wider differences in income levels.

When a complaint along the above lines was sent to the Advertising Standards Council of India, it replied that its Consumer Complaints Council had "concluded that the advertisement was not considered offensive or objectionable in respect of the Code".[16]

Thought Control

Perhaps the most insidious means used by the West to manipulate people is the use of thought control. This is most easily done by changing the meaning of words used. The colonising of the rhetoric of their critics by the West, leads to incoherence and an intellectual confusion which serve as a useful smoke-screen behind which cynicism, business-as-usual and institutionalised injustice may continue their majestic progress through the world. The interpretation of the rhetoric used by the globe's international institutions would require a comprehensive lexicon to unravel. The meaning of language has been subverted to mask the almost unchallenged triumphalism of wealth and power. Hence, words like empowerment, sustainability, participation, conservation, equity, social justice, have become mere ornaments, an exotic form of adornment on the face of privilege.

The dissemination of distorted information results in thought control, more effective because it is so subtly carried out. The right to information as implemented is a restricted right, with information not often given even when demanded. People are rarely informed of all the possible environmental, health or impoverishing and culturally damaging effects flowing from any policy, product or activity.

That symbol of rampant consumerism, the supermarket, exhibits the abysmal level to which the ability for independent thought has been driven in the West by the techniques of advertising. A columnist wrote the following about purchasers in supermarkets: "Like sheep they follow marked paths and graze at shelves along the way. They buy on credit what they don't need, not because the price is good but because the discount is attractive."[17]

The fear of losing this much-promoted freedom of choice is what drives people to vote for political parties that promise even more of such doubtful freedoms. "Freedom of choice" has become a major slogan of the Western way of life, and indeed is now something of a substitute for freedom itself. The right to spend money as one chooses is one of the paltry consolations for our lost liberties, the most precious of which is the liberty to choose other ways of answering our basic needs.

Correct and full information, for instance, about food products (their real nutritional value in relation to their cost, the nature of the additives used, genetic modifications, if any), about pesticides (their health and environmental effects), about medicines (side-effects, alternatives) and so on, has to be wrung out of the system, instead of being given as a matter of right. But if people were fully informed, the sales of most such products would certainly drop drastically.

So much relevant information about the system has to be concealed if it is to survive, that the communication of ignorance seems to have become the principal aim of the media. The new communications right is the right "not to know", since much knowledge could disturb the consumer's complacency. It would not do for consumers to know the consequences of their life-style, the poverty it creates elsewhere, the cost to the fabric of the planet itself. In this way, the blood, violence and sweat that invariably attend the presence of the products and services are no concern of those happy people whose right to dispose of their self-earned money as they choose is sacrosanct.

Mass communication has enabled the West to project itself— on the whole—as immaculately pure even while portraying its "enemies" as major offenders. The war against Iraq showed how information served military power, with the war itself initiated and controlled by the manipulation of the communication media.

Theoretically, the skies are "open": the data from the civil satellites, even that covering militarily sensitive areas such as nuclear test sites, can be acquired by anyone. The orbiting cameras hypothetically allow anyone to check the validity of government claims. Anyone, that is, who can afford to pay the commercial rate of more than £1,000 per image.

In those crucial days before the war, the US sought to convince other nations that Iraq was a danger to the whole world, even though the US knew that it was not.[18] More important, the US had to terrify Saudi Arabia and other Islamic Gulf countries into allowing—in fact inviting—an army of infidels to occupy their lands. This was accomplished simply by misrepresenting the information that the US controlled.

The Pentagon alleged that satellite images showed that on 13 September 1990, there were more than 250,000 Iraqi troops inside Kuwait, together with 2,000 tanks and thousands of support vehicles. This was cited as evidence that Saddam's ambitions went beyond the occupation of Kuwait and that containing Iraq required the US to send a large contingent of forces into Saudi Arabia.[18] But the military had taken care to hide the evidence that the troops were digging in at the Kuwait-Saudi border, a defensive rather than offensive posture, though at that time the Iraqis could very easily have marched into and occupied much of Saudi Arabia itself.

During the war, images of US bombs destroying "only" military targets in Iraq were circulated by the Pentagon, but none of the suffering innocent Iraqi civilians who were heavily bombarded by the multinational force.[19] This allowed Bush to claim that the allied forces attacked only military targets, keeping civilian casualties to a minimum. Contrary to Bush's claims that the US had gone to "extraordinary" and "unprecedented" lengths to avoid hurting civilians, the bombing campaign against Iraq was intended to destabilise the Iraqi government by creating wide-spread disruptions to civilian infrastructure. This was a violation of international legal restraints on warfare and clearly exceeded the UN mandate authorising the use of military force should Iraq not withdraw from Kuwait by the January 15 deadline.[20]

The "independent" TV media gave a noticeably one-sided view of the conflict flavoured with racial bias. Typical phrases for disparaging the Iraqis, in order to fashion them into hated enemies, were liberally employed. One newspaper reported that the "international thug" Saddam Hussein's "beastly soldiers" were carrying out "fiendish sex attacks" on women hostages after invading Kuwait.[19]

There is telling evidence of the success of the West's communications systems in controlling the rest of the world's peoples. The latter have accepted the West's propaganda that all the institutions it promotes, the UN, WB, IMF, WTO and others, are meant only to help the Two Thirds World "develop". The latter have accepted that the West's concepts of development, economics and its culture are the only valid ones. They have accepted that the West, the US in particular, has a right to "police" the world and keep other nations "in their places". In sum, they have accepted the "right" of the US to dominate and exploit their own countries.

This is, in a way, the ultimate triumph of colonialism.

The peoples of the world have been diminished, inferiorised, made uncertain of their identity, disempowered. This has nothing to do with self-determination, emancipation or freedom, but is the most total and abject form of imperialistic subjugation the world has ever seen. The fact that "economic forces" are a more effective soldiery than the flesh and blood occupancy of the lands of others, should not distract us from the melancholy reality.

Distracting Entertainment

Thorough thought control requires the occupation of all mental spaces and moments by suitable propaganda or distractions. Incipient protesters are sedated through sports, "cultural activities", dramatised political confrontations and violence—the modern circuses with integrated commercials.

As mentioned earlier, in fifteenth century Europe, public torture and executions of criminals were enjoyed by the spectators like an entertainment at a fair. Today violence as spectacle is provided under discreet domestic cover by multiplying channels of news on millions of TV screens, daily, and in close up: victims of disasters—natural and human-made, skeletonised children dying of hunger, torn bodies resulting from terrorist actions, and just everyday crimes of "normal" violence. An increase in do-it-yourself crime by children and adults follows—whether rapes and murders—in imitation of screen crimes.

Modern communications have displaced the traditional cultural leisure activities which promoted creativity rather than destroying it. Radio and cinema grew rapidly after 1918, and these technologies, in effect, transferred the incomes of thousands of village entertainers and story tellers to the pockets of a few "stars", their managers and directors, who could then be highly paid.

The Invasion of Privacy

The extensive and intrusive communications systems also nullify the right to privacy. Article 12 states: "No one shall be subjected to arbitrary interference with his privacy, family, home or correspondence, nor to attacks upon his honour and reputation. Everyone has the right to the protection of the law against such interference or attacks."

Technological "advances" are making these rights impossible to enforce. Computers and communication systems tend to make the State more powerful and tyrannical, since personal databases, built up for credit and census requirements, can be taken over by the police for "benign" preventive surveillance. They can also be misused by business for promoting its interests and by criminals for their own ends.

The sale of surveillance equipment—specially manufactured to invade the privacy of others without their knowledge—is uncontrolled and booming. Such equipment is widely used to monitor the activities of workers and political dissidents and not only criminals.

The *Wall Street Journal* reported that, at the request of Procter & Gamble, the Cincinnati Bell telephone company searched the records of more than 800,000 telephone calls made to a journalist who had written an unfavourable story on the company. This enormous undertaking was carried out solely in order to find which company employee had leaked the information.[21] When vigorous protests were made by the press, P&G claimed that this was merely a public relations failure, and that in any case P&G was legally and ethically right.[22]

With global electronic communications controlled mainly by the West, the US can tap and scrutinise conversations and data transfers for information that could be useful to the US government and its TNCs. This electronic eavesdropping is routinely carried out by the National Security Agency of the US.[23] The Clinton administration has insisted that the encryption keys for coding private information on the Internet be given to the NSA for such surveillance. This is a gross violation of Article 12.

Such is the importance of a monopoly on communication technology that the West makes determined efforts to block other nations from acquiring the technology itself. When the UNESCO tried to provide Two Thirds World countries with access to international communications, the US led a fierce attack on the institution that effectively eliminated it as an independent force in world affairs.[24]

CHAPTER 9

The Rights of Children

M otherhood and childhood are entitled to special care and assistance. All children, whether born in or out of wedlock, shall enjoy the same social protection." (UDHR, Article 25 [2])

This is all that the UN UDHR has to say for children, though later UN resolutions have elaborated on their rights. One such resolution regarding children was adopted unanimously by the UN in March 1995. A resolution similar to it was adopted by the UN Human Rights Commission three years earlier, with an action programme whose implementation is still to get under way.[1] The UN Convention on the Rights of the Child was adopted by the General Assembly in 1989.

The Convention claims to be guided by the principle that the essential needs of children should be given highest priority in the allocation of resources at all times. It emphasises, among other items:

• The right to survival which includes the right to life, the highest attainable standard of health, nutrition, and adequate standards of living.

• The right to protection which includes freedom from all forms of exploitation, abuse, inhuman or degrading treatment, and neglect including the right to special protection in situations of emergency and armed conflicts.

• The right to development which includes the right to education, support for early childhood development and care, social security, and the right to leisure, recreation and cultural activities.

• The right to participation which includes respect for the views of the child, freedom of expression, access to appropriate information, and freedom of thought, conscience and religion.[2]

Such care and concern manifest in the 1989 Convention is surely hypocritical when one finds that children today, from the moment of conception, have also been given an inalienable "right" to be exposed to environmental, food and other toxins. They enjoy the right to be born deformed, physically or mentally. They have a right to be educated in a system which cannot guarantee a job. They have the right to a future which is constrained by possibly insoluble problems which the past and present generations have so kindly bequeathed to them; a future in which there may be no fossil fuels to power the industrial and transport systems on which Western society has made them totally dependent; a future in which the destruction of the stratospheric ozone layer could afflict them with malignant tumours; a future in which the climate could be so altered that food production could be reduced to famine levels; a future in which they could be continuously exposed to toxic and nuclear wastes, causing an unlimited range of new diseases for which they have a right to expensive medical treatment. They have the right to be exposed to the merciless attentions of advertisers, of an intrusive commercialism which becomes a part of their upbringing, and hence, part of their identity.

Children do not ask to be born. They are vulnerable human beings who need love, respect and nurturing if they are to become responsible, considerate and mature adults. The acceptance of the false rights of children by the UN, followed by the cynical negation of even these by inhuman economic rights, is one of the saddest illustrations of the amoral operation of the Western system.

The right to "early childhood development" is abused even before children are born. Germaine Greer points out that the "foetus, *in utero*, if assailed by drugs like alcohol, nicotine and caffeine in its mother's bloodstream, or starved of essential vitamins and trace elements, or exposed to environmental poisons like lead and radiation, or blinded by rubella, damaged by potent medications or desexed by steroids, loses some of its potential for development."[3]

According to a report published in the *Journal of Family Practice*, every year in the US, mothers who smoke kill around

115,000 foetuses and 6,000 babies. In addition, 53,000 babies have low birth-weights and 22,000 require intensive care at birth. A further 3,700 children die by the age of one month each year from complications caused by tobacco smoke during the mother's pregnancy.[4] Such inhumanity is vigorously promoted by Western society's tobacco, alcohol and other "legitimate" industries.

Children today are the primary victims of hunger, malnutrition and disease. James Grant, late Executive Director of UNICEF, lamented the 40,000 preventable child deaths which are estimated to occur each day.[5] In their case, the right to life is not even conceded as a basic human right. This nullifies their other rights, since without the right to live and the right to grow to maturity with dignity, all the rest is empty rhetoric. Those children who escape death may still be physically and mentally damaged by malnutrition or environmental toxins and thus remain deprived of their right to realise their full potential.

The rights to adequate prenatal and postnatal care and to satisfactory nutrition are vitiated by the same "progress" that keeps Western adults unhealthy, the promotion and consumption of processed, fast foods. The process begins with the commercialisation of breast milk in the form of artificial infant foods. It has been estimated that the sale of processed milk powder, as an alternative to breast feeding, has caused the death of millions of children.[6]

TNCs play a major role in this process. Nestle's promotion of breast milk "substitutes" is notorious. In January 1995, a criminal complaint had to be filed against Nestle India Ltd for violation of laws regarding the promotion and marketing of infant milk substitutes. The company had arrogantly refused to observe product labelling requirements, advertisement guidelines and mandatory warnings as laid down in the "Infant Milk Substitutes, Feeding Bottles and Infant Foods (Regulation of Production, Supply and Distribution) Act 1992.[7]

While children in traditional societies live and play with adults constantly around, those in the West are often considered a nuisance to be secluded in separate rooms. There they spend hours watching television programmes or playing on their computers, and more recently, accessing the Internet, isolated from reality. Children can no longer distinguish reality from the fiction on the screens. Such deprivation results in anti-social behaviour, a dislike for adults—even their parents—for which the children are blamed.

The outcry against the abuse of children by the West is disingenuous; for the Western system routinely exposes children from the earliest years, by means of television, to the abusive attentions of advertisers, hucksters and salespeople. Strategies to reach infant consumers bypass the controls, constraints and wisdom of parents, and the imperiousness of the wants of children—which in all other societies have been tempered and filtered by the sagacity of parents—becomes a dominant influence upon the parents themselves, who feel it is their duty to satisfy the implanted wants and needs of children as defined by the market. In the US, small children are said to have control of billions of dollars worth of spending power within the family, since they now influence such decisions as what car the family will buy, where it will go on vacation, what it will eat. No wonder children are the secret target of so much manipulation. A form of covert operation is waged against childhood to ensure children will grow dependent upon a market system from which they will later have neither the resources nor the imagination to escape.

One of the most damaging consequences of the Western way of child-rearing is that it denies children any purposeful role in contributing to the work of society. Childhood is seen—sentimentally—as a kind of holiday from life, during which the only function of children is to become apprentice consumers, denied any creative outlet for their energies other than intensive immersion in a culture of wanting.

More harmful, mentally, is child abuse by parents through deliberate injury or plain neglect. In 1993, the last year on record, roughly one million abuse and neglect cases were confirmed in the US, says the National Committee to Prevent Child Abuse. About 1,300 of those ended with the child's death.[8] No study of the effects of the basic philosophy of individualism on child abuse has been undertaken.

Education and Working Children

Childhood, it is claimed, gives the child a few carefree and happy years before she or he is forced to move into the rough and tumble of real life. But the years that Indian children spend imprisoned in classrooms, terrorised by thoughts of authoritarian teachers, inflexible discipline and oncoming exams, cannot be considered years of carefree happiness. An increasing number of suicides among children who dread the intense competition with classmates with the ever-present possibility of failure occur in India and other countries. Immediately after the 1995 Secondary School Certificate examination results were announced in Mumbai, four girls who failed killed themselves, by hanging, shooting and burning. Add to this the rising bullying and violence in many schools and the myth of the carefree child lies shattered.

The right to have an education, defined narrowly as school-ing, is part of the design to indoctrinate children into unquestion-ing membership of—and complicity in—the high-consumption Westernised society. Such an education is designed, not, as it asserts, to release the potential of each child, or to provide the knowledge and skills for maintaining a just, sustainable life-style, but to school her/him to the requirements of the labour and consumer markets, whatever be the damage done to spirit, intel-ligence and creative capacity. Schooling today has nothing what-ever to do with the pious enunciations by the United Nations, governments, or anyone else about the rights of children.

When their carpet trade was being taken over by Asian manufactures, Western industrialists suddenly discovered that Asian children had rights. They claimed that children should not be made to work as it does not allow them to be educated.

It is true that an enormous number of children are often forced to work for a living. According to the ILO, 5 million children in India regularly work, several million in agriculture, around one million in brick works, stone quarrying and in construction industries and hundreds of thousands in carpet weaving and diamond cutting. The children in domestic service are too numerous to be counted.[9] There is no doubt that much exploitation does exist, and that working conditions need considerable improvement.

The West's concern, however, appears to be limited to child workers in the carpet, textiles, footwear and other industries which compete with their Western counterparts. The real intention behind the campaigns for the rights of child workers is to force up the cost of production of Indian products so as to price them out of the international market.

The West exhibits no such tenderness for the fate of children who work in private domestic service, in small restaurants or markets, who labour in recycling wastes, or in other small units, garages and workshops, because the products with which they are involved are not destined to enter the world market. Even less care is shown for the children who are not employed at all, who beg at the traffic lights, who waste away on the sidewalks, who become the hirelings and runners of criminals, or who sit in the dusty corners of railway stations, chasing the dragon or abusing themselves with solvents.

The hypocrisy becomes more evident when we observe that childhood in the West is regarded as being a time of gilded inutility. The absence of opportunity to participate in the labour of society is also abusive of children, as the high levels of juvenile violence, crime and emotional disorders attest. In the spectacular efforts by the West to detach the workings of the economy from its social consequences, the connections between them are rigorously suppressed and denied.

The concern for child workers is again a replay of earlier colonial practice. At the turn of the century, business chambers of England and Scotland had petitioned the Crown against the miserable condition of women and children working in India's textile and jute mills, mainly owned and managed by Englishmen. They demanded legislation to improve their working conditions, laws in their own land having forced them to employ more expensive adult labour.[10] The British had conveniently forgotten that the Industrial Revolution was successful mainly because of the widespread use of child labour in the early textile mills, with certain kinds of work reserved only for children.[11]

The selectivity of Western concern is further emphasised by the absence of any voices raised against the extensive use of child labour in sugarcane and banana plantations in South America, these being mostly owned and operated by Western TNCs. There are also child labourers in the West, delivering newspapers and milk, mowing lawns and using other means which enable them to pay their way through the education system or merely survive.

It is essential to distinguish between child labour as apprenticeship in the acquisition of a skill for living and child labour which is merely an earning process of endless drudgery continued into adulthood. The inability of the West to distinguish between these two quite distinct categories leads to the confusion and hypocrisy which surround the question of what might be a dignified and fitting role for children in society.

In traditional societies knowledge of how to live is mainly transmitted by parents, elders and older siblings individually tutoring children. With education and work integrated, children were—and still are—taught the practice of agriculture or helped to acquire a skill in a remunerative and often creative handicraft, enabling them to support themselves through life, to become useful members of a sustainable society. Hence it becomes a duty of the parents to "impose" such labour on their learning children. Even such apprenticeship in living is often considered an abuse of children's rights today since it may deny the child's access to a formal education.

Once again, therefore, the question may be posed: which are the more integrated and properly functioning human beings, the rising number of the dropped out, excluded, disordered children of the West, or the child of the tribal family who knows all the secrets of her environment, the sites of nutritious, medicinal and useful herbs, plants, trees, roots and fruits, who can look after younger siblings, as well as tend cattle and grow food, and still find time for play, story-telling and games in the forest?

The formal educational system, totally isolated from work, teaches particular skills that are in surplus in the real world, and promotes knowledge that has little life-survival value. This is real abuse of the child's right to learn to live. And even when, as is the case now, Western politicians and industrialists propose that school should become a kind of outpost of work, a kindergarten, as it were, for the work-site, can this be regarded as liberating or fulfilling of childhood potential?

At the height of the controversy regarding child labour in the carpet industry, a social worker in a tribal village in Gujarat came to know that the village headman had set up a carpet loom in his house and was employing several children. She accosted the headman, politely pointing out that he was exploiting the children. Patiently, the headman explained that the children were at least earning some income, that if not occupied they would be wasting their time loitering around in the village, drinking and watching television. The children, he added, were those who had been dropped out by or had passed through the formal education system but could not get a job in the Westernised mainstream, while their education made them unfit for agriculture or other traditional village work.

Most indigent parents are forced to send their children out to work in factories, either because the market for goods made using their traditional skills has been destroyed by industrialisation or because they are not being paid adequate wages, or because their wages are rapidly declining in value due to liberalisation.

The UN resolutions declare that children have certain inalienable rights. However, several practices, often also derived from other UN resolutions, ensure that the rights can never be implemented within the Western system. Human rights are used merely as a management tool for increasing Western sales and profits. Consequently the rights of millions of children who die every year of starvation and disease are not given due attention by the West, which points instead to the abuse of the rights of those who, in order to survive, are forced into arduous and monotonous work by Western economic policies. For millions of parents in the Two Thirds World, the fate of their children is not measured by the selective monitors of Western human rights, for their brief existence is cancelled not by flesh and blood executioners and torturers, but by the workings of an elaborately constructed human-made determinism called economic necessity.

Children as Consumers

The rights to have a happy childhood and to enjoy full opportunity for play and recreation, are determined mainly by their present and their future value as consumers. The manufacture and sale of toys is a billion dollar business.

Toys, in Western society, are expensive objects with which children, encouraged by advertising, are placated by parents. Children in traditional villages make their own toys, which are often creative miniatures of the implements they will use in later life. Rich children, however, need expensive manufactured playthings, with creativity transferred from the children to the manufacturers' designers.

The subversion by commerce of a basic childhood need for creativity leads to the production of such curious objects as Barbie dolls, which are idealised, lifelike and detailed in such ways as to leave the child's imagination no scope to work. These objects, also serving as models for young girls of Western notions of glamour and beauty, become a deterministic influence on the growth and development of the young.

As Jeremy Seabrook writes: "The principal role for children in the West has become apprenticeship in consuming, in learning to want things which the busy market place seeks to sell to them, whispering into their ears seductive messages of desire, bypassing the wishes of their parents. [See Philips advertisement, referred to in chapter 8.] This one-sided development and absence of deeper purpose takes its toll in Western society. For there, children cannot wait to grow up. They regard childhood not as a time of sweet privilege but as a conspiracy of adults to keep all the good things in life from them, and for themselves. This is why they so swiftly become miniature grown-ups, infants who are intensely fashion-conscious, children who must instantly have what their peers have, adolescent girls who become pregnant, as they desperately seek in the role of mother an answer to the purposelessness of their young years....But in a culture where children are without function, where they imitate adults, become prematurely sexually aware, where they are assiduously courted by a market system which sees in them a long secure future for its endless products and services, childhood itself has been violated, used up, consumed. No disorder, no distortion should astonish us in a society where the market place is allowed to become a major determinant in the social formation and upbringing of children."[12] Parental authority is limited to training their children to be good consumers of the system's products.

The US opposed the 1989 UN Convention on the Rights of the Child on the grounds that it would undermine parental rights.[13] Parents can vote, children cannot. Adults are simply greater consumers than children, and therefore their right to consume needs to be protected even if it results in the abuse of children's rights.

CHAPTER 10

The Rights of Women

The question of women's rights is a vast and complex subject. As in the other chapters, only the rights appropriated by the Western system for its own ends and those that are in conflict with other rights will be discussed here.

The Declaration of the Vienna Conference held in 1993 stated: "The human rights of women and of the girl-child are an inalienable, integral and indivisible part of universal human rights."[1] This was a repetition of the rights the UN UDHR listed decades earlier: the latter applied to "everyone", men, women and children.

At the Beijing Conference of 1995, the governments, having so dismally failed to carry out their own earlier solemn resolutions, promised again to ensure "the full implementation of the human rights of women and of the girl child as an inalienable, integral and indivisible part of all human rights and fundamental freedoms."[2] Such routine statements reveal that the main purpose of these pronouncements has little or nothing to do with the promotion of women's rights.

Women in all societies are victims of the same systemic exploitative mechanisms as men; but they are also subject to a vast range of gender-specific abuses. While many of these abuses are the responsibility of the Western system, men also add their share. It is important to avoid easy distinctions between traditional versus modern (or Western) experience, because few societies, except perhaps a few vestigial indigenous or tribal cultures, have exhibited an adequate concern for the rights of women, or have shared the burdens and joys of life equally between the sexes.

In arguing in favour of giving particular attention to women's rights, just a few of those practices which damage women specifically may be mentioned. Sexual slavery, rape, including marital rape, sexual harassment, dowry-deaths, amniocentesis designed to abort female foetuses, female infanticide, prostitution, gender discrimination, genital mutilation, polygamy, and mail-order brides, represent a short list of the multiple ways in which women are abused. These cannot in any way be said to belong to a "general" human context.

Women NGOs at the Beijing Summit identified twelve critical areas which, they claimed, have led to massive deprivation among women.[3] Many of the demands were for greater participation in the unjust system but some were applicable to both impoverished women as well as men.

Empowerment or Enslavement?

Many feminists argue that the establishment of women's rights will transform society, because women are inherently more just than men. This should be understood as an animating and enabling myth, rather than a literal truth. It energises women and enables them to struggle against the odds which have been stacked against them for millennia.

The Beijing Declaration states that "Women's empowerment and their full participation on the basis of equality in all spheres of society, including participation in the decision-making process and access to power, are fundamental for the achievement of equality, development and peace."[4] This, of course, plays directly into the hands of the unjust system and would lead to a more efficient, because apparently more impartial, administration of the abuses of human rights. Equal participation in a structurally unjust system or even a wholly matriarchal control, must leave most of the injustice intact.

"Empowerment" in such circumstances reduces women to exercising the same exploitative powers that men now possess. It makes them active participants serving the purposes of the system rather than the objectives of women. It effectively constrains them from demanding more fundamental changes, and is, of course, of a piece with the incorporation into industrial society of other groups who were earlier alienated from, or outside of it. In the end nothing is changed, except that dissenting voices are more readily silenced. A few women may benefit from the better application of individual rights in the system but often at the cost of other women's and men's rights. If women rise within the system they must hurt others.

Empowerment is also to be used as a means of transferring blame for environmental damage from Western hyperconsumers to impoverished women: "Equitable social development that recognizes empowering the poor, particularly women living in poverty, to utilize environmental resources sustainably is a necessary foundation for sustainable development."[5]

The problem is complicated by the fact that most traditional societies were and still are terribly unjust, though some small tribal and matriarchal communities were relatively more equitable in their treatment of women. However, women could probably obtain quicker justice by fighting for their rights within small communities, where the factors requiring change and the people in control are more manageable, than in large populations as a whole. This has been observed in Adivasi communities, where women have obtained justice fairly easily when they organise themselves to fight against forms of oppression operating at the community level. For instance, they obtained equal rights with men on the village council. Such rights can hardly be obtained by fiats from Central Governments or Beijing Declarations.

Women and Work

The involvement of women in paid labour is a complicated issue. For one thing, participation in paid employment actually gives women and men a sense that they are contributing to the wealth of society, whereas in so many other areas of life, in domestic labour, in parenting, in social commitment, they appear to have no purpose at all, but to form a reservoir of "demand" for the constantly proliferating goods and services spewed forth by a bottomless market. This could be why there is such a strong sense of being imprisoned among many women who are compelled to remain alone with children, without social or human resources to spread the burden, without a rich texture of social and affective life to sustain them. To work in such a context becomes a safeguard of sanity, rather than some hankering after luxury goods.

Where traditional community life has been destroyed by "development" causing supportive networks to disappear, women often want to work outside their home to escape isolation and consequent depression. This is partly due to the negation of women's—and men's—contribution to home and family by a society which values only remunerated work because it bestows purchasing power.

Demands by some feminists for equal opportunities in employment in industry and commerce are increasingly success-ful, with women now in high positions, both in government and in business. Unfortunately, such women have shown little, if any, tendency to use their power and influence for the purpose of increasing justice, their behaviour not being noticeably better than that of men in similar positions. Outstanding examples range from Margaret Thatcher to Indira Gandhi, and include many represen-tatives of Western countries at the UN, in international financial organisations and in the boardrooms of transnational corpora-tions.

In fact, Western women politicians and industrialists seem to feel the need to be more aggressive in their dealings, particular with the Two Thirds World, as if they have to prove that they can drive harder bargains and be more exploitative and callous than men. The visits to India of high-ranking women in the Clinton administration, such as the Secretary for Energy and the Assistant Secretary of State, have had an overwhelmingly negative impact on the human rights situation. They have not only insisted on the opening up of the Indian economy to foreign luxury consumer products and to exploitative US multinationals, but backed up their demands with the liberal use of threats.

But then these women may have reached their positions precisely because they have cultivated qualities—aggressive behaviour and ability to dominate—required by both women and men who wish to "succeed" in the present unjust system and have left behind the gentler and more intuitive sides of both genders. This shows, once again, the need to work outside the Western system if women are to attain true justice. Of course, other parts of the feminist movement recognise the need for a change in the economic and social paradigm, before such rights can become effective.

The Marketing of Motherhood

Article 25 (2) is an instance where "rights" have been co-opted by Western economic interests. It promotes the institutionalisation of motherhood and childhood rather than the rights of mothers and children. Numerous expensive techniques can then be promoted under the guise of satisfying women's rights.

Women have lost control of the birth process itself. Childbirth has been made painful, mentally and physically, by removing it from the private, caring family environment to the cold, compassionless atmosphere of a hospital. Power has been transferred from the local community to the state and from the traditional midwife and women birth and postpartum attendants to high-technology male specialists. Jean Robert has called this the masculinisation of midwifery into obstetrics.[6]

There is, however, a determined move by women to return to home births, for medical as well as emotional reasons. The risk of postoperative infection is much less if relatively simple precautions are taken, and the total "package" offered by the local midwife is often preferred.

New technologies for birth management also contribute to the increased abuse of women. Amniocentesis and ultrasound imaging were developed to detect foetal abnormalities. But the techniques are widely used instead for determining the sex of the foetus, while the right to abortion is used to kill the foetus if it is female. This technological intervention has led in some regions of India to a male-female imbalance in the population: a ratio of 1000 males to about 930 females. Although banned by law, the practice still thrives, particularly where social pressures cause many women themselves to prefer sons to daughters.[7]

Lakshmi Lingam says that "sex-determination tests are seen as providing a 'reproductive choice'—a choice to decide to have a boy or a girl! This is in line with the choice of commodities, consumer products and now the choice of the 'right' baby."[8]

Numerous techniques have been promoted presumably to help infertile women to have children. In-vitro fertilisation techniques involving the woman's own eggs or eggs from an aborted foetus and their subsequent implantation, have been developed and are widely claimed to be solutions to the problems of infertility. Much time and money is spent on developing these complicated and expensive techniques, while the causes and prevention of infertility have been relatively neglected. Such a situation arises perhaps because scientists benefit most from working with highly interventionist techniques. Such technologies require the use of women's bodies as experimental laboratories by medical engineers.

Artificial insemination using the sperm of unknown donors raises important ethical questions which are often brushed aside as irrelevant by the technologists involved, even though they may seriously violate the rights of the child. Children born out of such methods are often psychologically bewildered by the fact that their parents were so unconcerned about knowledge of the identity of their partner and of the children they would produce. It is considered "natural" that the rights of individual adults take priority over those of children.

The use of egg cells from aborted foetuses in infertility treatment raises even more serious moral issues. The aborted foetus is the biological mother of the resulting child. The effects upon the child of discovering that she exists only because her grandmother chose to kill her mother so she could be born are abuses beyond calculation.[9]

The encouragement given to barren women in the West to exercise their right to have children is in sharp contrast with the emphasis on propaganda in the Two Thirds World aimed at influencing women to exercise their right to limit their families. The right of access to infertility services, being prohibitively expensive, is unavailable despite the low status assigned to married women who do not have children in many societies. This anomaly becomes explicable when one considers that an average child in the West consumes several times the resources used by its Two Thirds World counterpart. Concern for human rights is yet again secondary to the concern for economic profit.

CHAPTER 11

The Family

M en and women of full age, without any limitation due to race,
nationality or religion, have the right to marry and found a family.
*They are entitled to equal rights as to marriage, during marriage and at
its dissolution."*

*"Marriage shall be entered into only with the free and full consent of the
intending spouses."*

*"The family is the natural and fundamental group unit of society and is
entitled to protection by society and the State."* (UDHR, Articles 16 [1],
[2], [3])

Although at first glance these articles sound eminently reasonable, they serve to impose the universalised values of the West on
varied and diverse cultures. Here again, it is the individual rights
with their bias towards the market economy which are favoured,
even though marriage itself implies a reciprocal and voluntary
surrender of individual rights while taking on additional responsibilities towards the spouse and children.

There is no definition of the family in the UDHR article, but
it is evident that the nuclear family, consisting of parents and their
children alone, is seen as the sole basis for society. This is, naturally,
a reflection of the dominant Western paradigm. Even though the
nuclear family has shown itself to be a volatile and unstable
institution, this does not deter the framing of such articles based on
the assumption of Western universality.

It altogether neglects the extended family, in which each
member in more than two generations has a multitude of useful
roles to play. The extended family, as the nuclear family, may well

be unjust, with women often treated badly. The former, however, can offer several advantages, particularly to women who wish to or are compelled to work. It appears to be a better base from which to effect radical change than the nuclear family.

In most extended families, the aged are looked after with affection as a right for having brought up their children, as well as for their ability to teach, advise and hand down their wisdom and culture. Extra burdens on extended families are often shared by relatives, neighbours and the local community as a whole. Remnants of the rural supportive networks still exist and successfully operate in cities like Mumbai which have expanded around a multitude of village communities.

The extended family is polycentric, so that relationships, human emotions and passions do not work themselves out in the claustrophobic intensity of one woman and one man locked in perpetual tension. The existence of siblings, aunts and uncles, and grandparents, diffuses conflict, assuages hurt and mutes what otherwise become irreconcilable resentments and even hatreds. The nuclear family is too enclosed a space for relationships to be able to breathe, and this is why it, too, is in crisis. More ample structures of kinship, neighbourhood and being together are required for human survival.

In the West, the family has been pressed into the service of a growing and ever more florid individualism within a market economy which reflects and serves it. The market economy requires the destruction of the extended family in order to make people more dependent on commercialised extensive and expensive services which extended families provide free. The elderly have value by Western economic norms only when they can be exploited as consumers.

In any case, the estrangement between the generations in the West has now become a far deeper form of alienation. The old, like the young, have also been depowered, their wisdom degraded, their experience useless in a world in which the past has been definitively superseded. The young often disregard their grandparents, or regard them simply as a source of presents and money. In response, the elderly often have recourse to such consolations as they may seize from the pleasure-domes of consumerism, the melancholy fun of bingo, holidays abroad, and of course, endless hours alone in front of the TV set.

The less affluent have to make do with the consumption of
alcohol, tobacco and TV serials (all equally addictive), the advertising which necessarily accompanies the latter ensuring mutual
support. This process rapidly recycles any welfare provided by the
state. The consumption of these legal addictive "drugs" helps to
divert them from thinking about, criticising and even escaping
from the system.

The Right to Work Versus Children's Rights

In India, both partners can work outside the home only if they
employ someone to look after the children. Since the employee can
be paid only a small fraction of what is earned by both, injustice
prevails.

In the West in many families both parents feel compelled to
work because their role in society has been diminished to that of
consumer, though several other factors also exist. The rise in
material expectations results in seeming economic necessity, with
"abject" poverty being typified, perhaps, by such signs as the lack
of a washing machine, refrigerator or, especially pitiable, TV.

Such norms may be contemptible, but they are real: people
live within the society which shelters them. Hence again, the need
to present them with sources of satisfying fulfillment outside the
Western system.

The rights of both parents to be employed outside the home
may conflict with the rights of children to proper parental care. It
is true that parenting has been diminished by the coming into
existence of hosts of specialists, professionals, advisers, counsellors,
as well as by the provisioning of children's needs by the market,
whether in toys, clothes, goods, entertainment, food, in which the
role of parents is reduced to that of mere cash-dispensers.

Payment for surrogate child-care with baby-sitters or in
creches and day care centres are a poor substitute for a healthy
home life, where ideally, the family shares its vision, hopes, values,
experience, joys and sorrows in a secure environment. It may not
be simple greed, but the structure of the market and its cumber-
some control of answering need, that drives both into a search for
labour, partly to satisfy their own defunctioning in all other areas
of experience.

Impoverished parents in the Two Thirds World, also, have no choice but to work, since one person's earnings are usually insufficient to provide even basic support for the family. Their children of necessity either accompany them to work, or are left with elder siblings at home.

Offices and factories are more unjust than traditional home industries, with the whole family working together. Such industries seem to be the only type which can provide employment for all men and women, as well as reducing the need for nonrenewable energy to sustainable levels. The adults could then also reclaim their traditional roles of transmitters of knowledge and providers of health care, making working at home fully satisfying.

Whatever the motives of parents who both work, whether in the West or the Two-Thirds World, the conflict between the rights of parents to work and the rights of their children to their care is a direct result of a clash between human rights and the inhuman rights of an uncaring economic system.

While children are often denied the parental attention that is their due, they are later encouraged to claim the right to independence, seeking accommodation away from their parents. This illusion of freedom dislodges them from their roots, making them mobile for shuffling around jobs. Indeed, the word "flexibility" is much heard in the West now. This means remaining infinitely available, acquiring "transferable" skills, avoiding rootedness, commitment and stability, so that they may respond to the latest whim of the market, the next windblown craze that will briefly call upon their energies for some short-lived labour that will suck them briefly into the system, only to expel them again as soon as there is no longer any "market" for what they have to offer. Extended families as well as the nuclear families are affected by this trend, as they are fragmented for the sake of the market place.

The claim to promote the rights of the family while simultaneously emphasising the supremacy of individual rights increases conflicts within families, often leading to extremes of violence. Furthermore, reluctance to "violate the privacy of the family" has perverse consequences when forcible confinement, domestic violence, child abuse, and torture take place within it.

The right to found a family is itself being violated as the varieties and quantities of chemicals that cause sterility increase rapidly in the environment. This right is being further eroded by testing to determine whether parents carry genes which could produce defective children. How extensive the defects must be before the parents are prohibited from having children has not been declared. One wonders whether, for instance, Stephen Hawking, would have been permitted to be born if genetic testing for Lou Gehrig's disease had been widespread before his birth.

With the disintegration of, first the village community, then the extended family, and now the nuclear family, individuals become ripe for thought control. Human beings need support when they have problems but all their traditional sustaining systems have been or are being destroyed. The gap is being readily filled by religious cults which claim to provide total support and security in exchange for the individual's free will and usually her or his wealth. Enormous numbers joining Christian cults, the Islamic fundamentalists, the religious communities in India and the Aum Shinri Kyo in Japan, reveal an unfulfilled need.

Divorce and Children

The right to dissolution of marriage is not seen as appropriate by many cultures because of the conflict it introduces with the rights of any children of the marriage. In the West, the accent on the individual's rights, with easy divorce laws enabling unions to be dissolved for minor reasons, makes marriage itself fragile. Many marriages today are being reduced to economic contracts, with legal arrangements mainly concerning distribution of property on dissolution signed even before ceremonies take place. This pre-marital emphasis on individual material rights not only brings marriage into the market place, but suggests that the relationship may be starting wrong. On the other hand, the absence of the possibility to dissolve marriage condemns many women, men, and also children, to lives of torment by violent and abusive parents

The rate of divorce is rapidly rising in the West, whether due to an increase in women demanding their individual rights, unrealistic expectations brought about by media and advertising, intolerable stress from unemployment or the threat of loss of employment, or simply the loneliness of couples devoid of wider affective, social and spiritual supports. More than half of new marriages in the West will end in divorce or separation. Each of these broken marriages causes perhaps irreparable damage to the children affected. It is also true that millions of children are damaged by unhappy parents staying together "for the sake of the children". Relationships that are fissured and fractured from within also take their toll on children. To assume that "broken marriages" are necessarily causal in the impairment of the chances of children takes too little account of the ruined relationships in which so many children are compelled to seek a safe passage to adulthood, but which may not have shown up in the statistics as formal breakdown.

Children of divorce are much more likely to drop out of school, to have premarital sex and to become pregnant outside marriage than those in intact families. Young adults, of 18-22 years, from divorced families are twice as likely to have poor relationships with parents and show high levels of emotional distress as children in unbroken families. Divorce contributes to as many as three out of four teenage suicides. Parents' remarriage does not protect their children against behavioral and other problems.[1]

A happy, stable family is important for the healthy development of children, there being considerable evidence of children's mental disorders resulting from divorce and single parenting. The affection and security associated with the family are the best available predictors of good health. Children who receive consistent love and attention are bigger, brighter, more resistant and more resilient, and, as a result, they live longer.[2]

CHAPTER 12

The Population "Problem"

Traditionally, for a small community, survival as a group took priority over the rights of its individual members, male or female, adult or child. Since no single person could survive without the community's support, a reduction in individual rights was a small price to pay in exchange. The survival of the community took the form of encouraging women to have children when populations were low due to war, famines or epidemics, or promoting birth control, abortion and infanticide, all of which were commonly practised in practically every part of the world, when numbers were seen to be rising too fast.

The West has now turned these local rights into a global "population problem", allegedly caused by the irresponsible multiplication of illiterate people in the Two Thirds World. The "problem" has been effectively used as an instrument for enhancing Western control. In this process, women have often been co-opted to serve Western purposes through the misuse of the issue of women's reproductive rights. A brief look at the history of the "problem" would be therefore instructive.

Western "charitable" institutions and rich individuals were pioneers in this field. The Ford Foundation tried to introduce population control in India as early as 1951 but was repulsed by Nehru who saw it as an intrusion in a sensitive area.[1] In 1952, the US-based Population Council was set up at the instance of John D Rockefeller III.[2] The International Planned Parenthood Federation (IPPF) was promoted by Margaret Sanger, who considered herself a pioneer in birth control. The pharmaceutical industry saw these moves as an opportunity to greatly increase its sales of a whole range of contraceptive devices and drugs.

However, the targets had first to be "educated" to believe that to control one's fertility was an inalienable human right. The natural right of parents to regulate their families in line with the needs of the local community had to be replaced with the civic right to reduce the number of their children subject to the demands of the West.

One of the important steps in inducing people to believe in the need to control the populations of the impoverished was taken by Hugh Moore, a businessman who had made a fortune selling disposable paper cups. In 1960, Moore launched the World Population Emergency Campaign, with the distribution of a pamphlet carrying the scary title, *The Population Bomb*. The campaign was run by the President of the World Bank, a cotton magnate and former US Under-Secretary of State, a former Secretary of the Treasury under Roosevelt, an army general, and a member of the Rockefeller family.[3] Their slogan claimed that the richest people in the world were being pillaged by the poor.

The connection between population control in the Two Thirds World and the interests of the West have been stated openly elsewhere too. Dr R T Ravenholt, the director of US AID's population control activities, proposed a programme known as "Advanced Fertility Management", whose objective was to sterilise a quarter of all Two Thirds World women within a period of nine years. He said in 1977: "The self-interest thing is a compelling element. If population proceeds unchecked it will cause such terrible economic conditions abroad that revolution will ensue, and revolutions are scarcely ever beneficial to the interests of the United States."[4]

Population control was and is promoted by the West, not so that diminishing resources can be more equitably distributed, but in an attempt to retain the world's remaining reserves to allay their own insatiable wants. With their own country resources having long been exhausted or being expended rapidly, and with exploitable colonies having been lost, other sources of supply become essential to sustain their hyperconsumption.

In order to ensure that the resources they covet are not consumed by the present owners, the latter's numbers need to be kept down. In a similar fashion, the hyperconsumers within the Two Thirds World impose family planning on the impoverished among their own people, so that more of the resources will be left for themselves. And so the world's hyperconsumers, having appropriated most of the world's wealth, now announce that those who are outside this select group should refrain from reproducing.

To achieve this end, populations of the Two Thirds World are accused of being the main cause of environmental degradation. The United Nations Fund for Population Activities (UNFPA) maintains that the "bottom billion"—the very poorest people in developing countries—"often impose greater environmental injury than the other 3 billion of their fellow citizens put together."[5] This is sheer nonsense.

The truth is that the affluent 20 per cent of the world's population consumes 80 per cent of the world's resources. Environmental degradation is the creation of the hyperconsumers, not of those practising voluntary or forced frugality. The environmental impact of 2.6 million newborn Americans each year far exceeds that of the 34 million newborn Indians and Chinese.[6]

Based on per capita consumption of energy alone, the effect on the environment of a citizen in the United States is around forty times that of a citizen of India.[7] Put another way, the consumption-equalised population of the US is 10 billion, forty times its actual 250 million population. It is the West which needs population—or rather—consumption control. But the satisfaction of the cravings of one person is more important to the US economy than the right to life of forty children in the Two Thirds World.

The promotion of population control for preserving resources for its rich advocates is, however, becoming too embarrassing. Promoters, therefore, now claim that control is required to prevent expanding populations from reducing their own national consumption to below subsistence levels. People, they considerately argue, have a right to a better life, and those who have too many children deny their compatriots their rights. It is also claimed that any attempts to further justice through a more equitable distribution of wealth would be vitiated by growing populations.

Perhaps it could be true that at some stage such a situation might arise, but the present system makes sure that injustice continues to thrive, since there is no sign of even a feeble attempt at a more equitable distribution of wealth. The claim that with equitable distribution there will be insufficient food for all is false because much agricultural land is wasted on nonessential cash crops or converted to non-agricultural use. Further, edible produce is itself diverted from human consumption to industrial use or animal feed.[8]

The West predicts that rising expectations are likely to ensure that the people of the Two Thirds World will also consume as much as those in the West. This is physically impossible because of resource limitations. In any case, it could only come about through the imposition of Western materialistic culture, with the resulting increase in appetites for consumer products. The West needs to sell its products to the middle and upper classes of the Two Thirds World to keep its economy expanding. The people who are expendable are the "poor" who are not potential hyperconsumers. This set of human beings—significantly, the only set which does not violate the rights of others—is targeted for elimination by birth control.

The reemergence of Malthusian doctrines which claim that "at nature's banquet no place is set for the poor" conceals the fact that the means to check effectively such growth are well known. They are well known because they were employed first in the West. The acquisition of a measure of social security is the surest way of limiting family size. Only when people are confident that one or two of their children are likely to survive into adulthood will they cease to have too many. When the family remains the only form of social security, and where infant mortality is high, or until recently was high, the only resource of the poor against worsening destitution is to maintain a family numerous enough to look after them in sickness and old age.

So, if such a simple answer is historically plain, and easily achievable, why has it not been attained? Could it be because such a desirable goal would require a radical redistribution of the world's finite resources to the advantage of the poor? Whatever designs the global system may have, the voluntary surrender of wealth by the rich is not one of them. Quite the contrary. In the past forty years, the proportion of the income of the world that has accrued to the richest 20 per cent of people compared to the poorest 20 per cent has doubled.

This then is the reason why the "population problem" has gained such prominence. It is quite simply a substitute for social justice. It blames the poor for their poverty and releases the rich from any responsibility for a state of affairs which could be quite easily remedied.

Moreover, the West actively contributes to the insecurity of the poor. The impoverishing effects of the SAPs works in a contrary manner: by reducing incomes it forces couples to have more children merely to earn enough for family survival.

Reproductive Rights of Women

Some women argue that economic and political rights, important as they are, have little meaning for women without the freedom to control their reproductive capacity, one of the most fundamental freedoms for women. Their full reproductive rights include the right to liberty and security of person, an absolute right to bodily integrity and the freedom to decide on matters of sexuality and child-bearing with no interference from their partners, family, health care professionals, religious groups, the state, or any other person or institution. Coercion is defined to include forced abortion, sterilisation, contraceptive use, the denial of safe abortion, and more subtle activities such as psychological pressure and incentives that compromise voluntary choice.[9]

Several of these concerns are certainly valid, but there is no doubt that those promoting population control have seized the issue of women's reproductive rights for their own purposes. The basic motives for population control are nowadays camouflaged by claims that women have to be given a chance to access the method of contraception of their choice, that there is an "unmet need" which family planners and pharmaceutical industries are merely fulfilling.

At the first World Population Conference, held in Bucharest in 1974, more than 130 countries agreed that: "All couples and individuals have the basic right to decide freely and responsibly the number and spacing of their children and to have the information, education and means to do so." This has been regularly repeated at ten year intervals, in the Mexico City World Population Conference in 1984, and in 1994 at the International Conference on Population and Development in Cairo. At the 1995 Social Summit, the NGO statement was limited to "Women must be guaranteed sexual and reproductive choice and health."[10]

Many of the problems concerning women's rights arise from the conflict between their rights as individuals and the rights of the family and community to which they belong. In Western perception today, the individual's rights take precedence over those of the community, local or global. It is assumed that the survival of the community will be ensured by technological control over nature, relieving individuals of any responsibility whatsoever towards achieving that end. Individuals are, therefore, free to pursue their own comforts and pleasures.

It is this individualism which is also responsible for most people's indifference to the severe environmental problems of today.

The claim that abortion is part of a woman's fundamental right to control her own fertility accents the right of the woman as an individual, but violates the unborn child's right to life. Just because a foetus is powerless is no argument for giving the mother overriding rights. While infanticide is usually abhorred, the killing of unborn children at whatever state of development is popularly recommended. However, the point at which life begins is still a matter for debate.

The rights of individual women to have or not to have children need, therefore, to be defined within the limits to population that community survival requires. This would be a voluntary submission, each woman realising her responsibility to the community. This is, however, complicated when the need arises to determine the exact community to which women are responsible.

In small tribal societies, where population numbers are dwindling rapidly, women may accept that community rights predominate. But do women have a duty to the nation and to society at large, particularly when that society is so unjust?

The unjust society claims that a woman in the Two Thirds World has a duty to practice birth control because the nation's population as a whole is rising. This ignores two important considerations: the rights of threatened indigenes within a country and the fact that population pressure in most of the Two Thirds World is exacerbated by the impoverishment of large numbers of people.

The West presents the choice as between having few children who grow up healthy and live an affluent life or having many children resulting in famines and utter poverty later. But it is the unjust society that first impoverishes people, forcing them to have many children in the hope that some would survive into adulthood to support them in their old age, in the absence of state provision.

It is assumed that the goal of the state is to lower rates of population growth, rather than to work towards a just society, enabling individuals greater freedom to determine their own fertility.

When women maintain that they own their bodies and have total rights over what they do with them, they could be treating their bodies as mere property, which taken literally, could introduce other inferiorising complications. As Farida Akhter puts it: "Implicitly we are demanding that women should own individually the reproductive factory she is carrying within her own body....It is important that we start to see that the reproduction of the human species is primarily a social activity which is realised through individuals, but it is never an individual affair."[11]

Lakshmi Lingam adds: "The slogans 'choice' and 'control over our bodies' used in the Western feminist movement (to denote access to safe contraception, the right to say 'yes' or 'no' to sex, etc) are also used by agencies hiring fertile women's wombs. These slogans are interpreted as the control of (the) body as a piece of property, the parts of which can be hired, leased, sold, donated and so on."[12]

With the market economy ruling, a few women have already begun to rent out their wombs. In Canada, surrogate mother arrangements are now being set up through several fertility clinics in Toronto. The going rent is US$15,000 for the mother and US$20,000 for the lawyers who draw up the contract. The practice has been defended on the ground that the exercise is not designed to make money but is meant to be a service to the infertile, even though the lawyers claim a larger share of the price.[13] Human ova are also available on the market, with agencies paying up to $1,500 for a single batch.[14]

Birth Control: Who Gains?

To promote population control, "charitable" foundations gave generous donations to Two Thirds World countries, while several governments, including that of the US, disbursed "aid", most of which returned to the West for the purchase of IUDs and chemical contraceptives (often out-of-date stocks) and the salaries of teams of "expert" advisors who demonstrated the use—or misuse—of these devices. Population control today has become a multimillion dollar business, furthering the transfer of wealth from the poor to the major pharmaceutical companies, with natural methods of birth control actively discouraged as unreliable.

The Western pharmaceutical industry manufactures a variety of contraceptive drugs and devices, using women as guinea-pigs for testing them. Women, mainly but not only in the Two Thirds World, are treated as cheap and plentiful experimental animals.

For example, vaginal rings to deliver steroids were tested in Brazil, Chile, Columbia, the Dominican Republic, India, Mexico, South Korea and other countries. In trials, some of them broke, caused lacerations and delivered unacceptably high levels of steroids.[15]

Norplant was developed by the Population Council, New York, and is manufactured only by Leiras Pharmaceuticals in Finland. It is a package of six hormonal capsules implanted under the skin of a woman's arm. The Norplant trials in India were conducted by the Indian Council of Medical Research and the Human Reproduction Research Centre. These institutions did not give the participating women sufficient details about Norplant or even tell them that the whole exercise was a trial. Many of the women were poor, and hence vulnerable to pressure from the experimenters. A study charged that the selection and information process adopted "takes away the control women have over their fertility without their realising it."[16] Serious side-effects of Norplant use in the UK are now coming to light.

Another contraceptive being promoted is a chemical called quinacrine, which comes in the form of pellets inserted into the Fallopian tubes to block them. Quinacrine is known to cause pain when it leaks into the peritoneal cavity. It can also excite the central nervous system if it enters the bloodstream in large amounts, resulting in transient psychosis.[17] It is difficult to insert the pellets, and pregnancy rates are high with its use. Testing was abandoned in Europe before 1984. Quinacrine is still being promoted in India.

In an apparent violation of Indian laws, the Population Council (PC) conducted a study of a contraceptive method in Chennai (formerly Madras) without getting the required permission from the authorities concerned. The PC distributed "wideseal diaphragms", marketed by an American company. The PC project director, John W Townsend, refused to publicise the project report, which according to informed sources, recommended to the government that the diaphragm can be included in the family planning programme as women's response to the method was "encouraging."[18]

The Western pharmaceutical lobby's control of the World Bank's population programmes is quite open. Recently, the World Bank reneged on its support for marketing Centochroman, a non-oesteroidal, weekly oral contraceptive pill developed in India. This drug has undergone twenty years of study and clinical trials, and has been in use in India for almost four years.

Under the India Population Project-7, the marketing costs of contraceptives including Centochroman were to be reimbursed by the World Bank. Close to Rs 170 million have been spent on selling and distributing this contraceptive but the World Bank has not reimbursed even a rupee for three years now. It is clear that the lobby pushing foreign contraceptives has a hand in scuttling the Indian pill.[19]

Contraception and the Rebirth of Fascism

Initially, birth control was promoted to eugenically "improve" the population in the West itself—with programmes mainly directed at the local impoverished—indistinguishable from Hitler's own intentions which were aimed at "purifying" the Aryan race. The IPPF, for instance, asserted without any scientific basis: "Nor need we question that a husband and wife living in squalor and ignorance who already have a number of children not being reared properly, might well be considered unfit to have additional children."[20]

In 1962, a meeting at the Ciba Foundation in London decided that the "general quality of the world's population is not very high."[21] Francis Crick, co-discoverer of the structure of DNA, even formulated a plan to put sterilising chemicals in the drinking water supply which would affect the whole population of a particular region. But he would then give selected individuals—according to his criteria of what human beings should be like—a chemical to reverse its effect.[22]

Another scientist, John Platt, Professor of Biophysics at the University of Michigan, considered mixing a contraceptive chemical in ordinary table salt used in India.[23] Fortunately, no such contraceptive has as yet been discovered.

Today, in China, marriages between couples likely to pass on genetic deficiencies preventing "the victim from living independently" are banned. Pregnant women will be required to undergo testing and advised to abort embryos with serious abnormalities. Chinese officials admit that the law is aimed at "improving the quality of the newborn population."[24]

Birth control has been used directly for ethnic control, an abuse of Article 16 (1) on race. In the US in the 1980s, 43 per cent of the women sterilised in federally funded population programmes were black. Moreover, more than 25 per cent of native American women were sterilised.[25] The survival of many American and other indigenous peoples is now being put increasingly at risk, often by their permanent sterilisation which irrevocably denies them their rights, with no redress if for any reason their existing children die.

Doctors injecting Depo-Provera into mothers after birth in London hospitals were doing it almost exclusively to Asian women, without their consent.[26] This ability to abuse other people's rights without their knowledge is apparently the principal advantage of injectable contraceptives.[27]

Genetic engineering coupled with in-vitro fertility techniques has made it easier to attempt eugenics. It would be interesting to observe what model would be taken for such experiments in eugenics. If the selected human beings are anything like their existing counterparts in the contemporary West, then the result of any such programmes is likely to hasten yet further the terminal pollution and degradation of the planet.

Indirect Population Control

There are numerous other indirect effects which tend to reduce populations, all a consequence of the West's industrial and economic policies.

Modern societies practise mass infanticide by malnutrition and by introducing toxic pollutants into the environment. The export of toxic products and the relocation of industries which produce toxic effluents, are both a form of population control, specifically targeted at the Two Thirds World. Such practices have been made easier by the WTO rules.

Populations were and still are reduced by the transport of diseases from the West, now perhaps inadvertently. In earlier times, the mere entry of Europeans carrying with them their large portfolio of pathogens, to which the indigenous communities were not immune, increased local death rates. Today, AIDS poses a new threat to great swathes of the population—usually the most economically active—in many countries of the world. Quick modern transport and sex tourism are major factors contributing to its rapid spread. Much of this is due to the promotion of sexual freedom as the individual's right.

Earlier, the Europeans claimed in regard to the Native American populations, that "taking all things into consideration, the disappearance of the race is scarcely subject for much regret. They are dying out in a quick, easy way, and are being supplanted by a superior race."[28]

Perhaps it is the turn of the "superior race" to die out, since their populations are seen as declining. The birth rate in much of Europe is now at the mere replacement level, lower in some countries, in spite of cash incentives provided to those who can bear children.[29]

The drop in birthrates has been partly associated with pure selfishness, resulting from the insistence on the rights of individuals with no concern for duties to the community as a whole. Married couples prefer to spend more of their incomes on material superfluities rather than on bringing up children who would interfere with their "enjoyment" of life. Such is the natural decline of a degenerate, affluent society.

It was recently reported in the UK that over 20 per cent of young white women, some only nineteen years old, have been voluntarily and permanently sterilised because they fear that children would disrupt their career and life-style. As many as one-fifth of the women born since the sixties may never bear children, according to a forecast by the Family Policy Studies Centre in London.[30]

What is more, the begetting of children is now highly commodified, so that it is quite common to hear Western people solemnly assert that they cannot afford to have another child, as though to fulfil their biological function were a superior form of consumer good. Calculations have been made as to the cost of raising children. The assessments vary, anything from $100,000 upwards; but all agree that children are an expensive item of consumption.

THE POPULATION PROBLEM   169

There are, of course, serious consequences to such forms of elective abstinence. For one thing, there is now widespread anxiety in both Europe and Japan that future generations will be unable, and probably unwilling, to shoulder the burden of caring for the growing elderly population. Indeed, the generation gap—that carefully crafted concept elaborated by those who identified teen-agers as a potentially lucrative market in the 1950s—now threatens to become something of a chasm. The young are unlikely to be merciful to the elderly whom they will regard as a hindrance and as rivals over dwindling resources, to which their own youth and energies place prior claim. Apprehension has been expressed over the growing number of attacks upon the elderly, muggings, break-ins, harassment and even killings, by the young, some of them even children. This is no momentary aberration, but prefigures wider social dislocations likely to appear as populations fail to replenish themselves, and as those who have already consumed tomorrow's substance are called to account by their uncomprehending succes-sors. Here, within the heart of Western society are human rights abuses practised by one generation against another, where conti-nuity is broken, the transmission of values destroyed, the sense of a shared predicament ruined.

There are also rational incentives not to reproduce, and people in the West now regularly say that they do not envy the young their life, they would not wish to be young now. This is maybe a recognition that the damage already inflicted upon the resource-base of the earth, and possibly even the gene-pool of humanity, is irreversibly destructive. The environmental situation looks so hopeless that people in the West frequently state they have no wish to have children who will further burden the resource base or who will be burdened by the, perhaps impossible, tasks of solving the problems this generation has created and is still industriously formulating. Earlier, the danger was seen as arising from nuclear catastrophes, then as particular environmental cri-ses; today it is the general resource consumption and accompa-nying pollution which gives rise to feelings of hopelessness. The system cannot reduce or completely do away with these reasons for race suicide, since such action would reduce economic growth, held to be more inviolable than mere human survival.

Several of the chemicals which have contaminated the envi-ronment in the past 50 years mimic the female hormone, oestrogen.

A widespread decline in human fertility in the West has been attributed to such chemicals. However, the people of the West consider these chemicals so essential for their comfortable lifestyle that many do not want them to be eliminated.

These chemicals, remarkably resistant to biodegradation, are now widely present in food-chains and have accumulated in human bodies. Among them are commonly used organochlorine pesticides and herbicides such as DDT, aldrin, dieldrin, endosulfan and atrazine. Other pollutants which cause similar effects are polycyclic aromatic hydrocarbons (PAHs) emitted by vehicles and waste incinerators; polychlorinated biphenyls (PCBs) used in plastics and for electrical insulation; and benzene, a common pollutant emitted by cars. Still others include phthalates which are added to plastics to make them more flexible and are used as ingredients in paints, inks and adhesives; and the breakdown products of surfactants in industrial detergents.[31, 32]

While the quantities of each of these in the environment could be extremely small, the combined effects of a multitude of different chemicals could still be damaging. Many of these chemicals, discharged as wastes, end up in water sources. A wide range of synthetic oestrogens once used to fatten livestock are now present in water supplies. Most of them have so thoroughly impregnated the global habitat, they cannot be removed.

The incidence of disorders in the development of the male reproductive tract has more than doubled in the past fifty years while sperm counts have declined by about half, states an article in *The Lancet*. The study argues that the increasing incidence of reproductive abnormalities in normal adult males could be related to increased oestrogen exposure *in utero*, since humans now live in a virtual sea of oestrogens. A single exposure of a mother to extremely small quantities of the chlorinated hydrocarbon, TCDD (dioxin), has no effect on the mother but reduces the sperm count in her children. The chemical has been proved to cause testicular abnormalities in experimental and wild animals.[33]

Similar sexual abnormalities have occurred in the sons of women exposed during pregnancy to diethylstilbestrol (DES). DES and other synthetic oestrogens, manufactured to be orally active and resistant to degradation, were used widely for about thirty years. It was only in the 1970s, that abnormalities were noticed in children born to DES-treated women.[33] Till then they

were not recognised as a risk, demonstrating the long length of
time often required for substances being routinely introduced into
the environment to reveal latent harmful effects, and the ineffec-
tiveness of the industry's testing procedures.

Breast cancer is also being closely related to exposure to
oestrogens. Death rates from breast cancer should have fallen over
the past years with increased screening, improvements in treat-
ments, and billions of dollars spent on research. But breast cancer
is now the leading cause of death in women aged 35-54, with its
incidence having risen steadily over the past few decades.[34] This
specific cancer kills nearly 50,000 women each year in the US
alone.[31] Women with high concentrations of chlorine-based chemicals in their blood and fat have been found to have breast cancer
risks four to ten times higher than women with low concentrations.[35] Breast cancer in the mother has also been linked with
significant risks of testicular cancer in male offspring.[33]

Exposure to ionizing radiation from nuclear explosions,
excess medical irradiation and leaks from nuclear power stations
also seem to contribute to the incidence of breast cancer.[34]

Natural oestrogens are found in plants, but these are of a
slightly different chemical type. They actually lower the risks to
women of developing breast cancer.[36]

Other cancers and health problems are caused by the thousands of untested toxic chemicals in use today. A report released
by the US Environmental Working Group and Physicians for
Social Responsibility states that more than 14 million people in the
US routinely drink water contaminated with carcinogenic herbicides. The herbicides have been linked with developmental abnormalities, birth defects and genetic mutations.[37]

Dioxins cause several types of cancer, disrupt orderly growth
of organs in embryos, irreversibly impair their functioning, and
even kill them. They also reduce fertility, cause abnormalities in or
reduce the size of male sexual organs, cause the immune system to
be overactive in some cases and to be suppressed in others. Dioxin
compounds may increase risk of diabetes and endometriosis in
women. In the US, people receive almost 90 per cent of dioxin from
milk and other dairy products and beef, pork and chicken that are
contaminated primarily by dioxin compounds settling out of the
air from the incineration of waste chlorinated materials.[38]

If the right to health took precedence over profits, with all this evidence mounting up, the chemical industry and the regulatory bodies around the world should have got together to phase out these chemicals. Instead, they avoid taking any action, asking for proof of human harm. But this can only be obtained after humans are already harmed, after rights to health and life are violated.

This is precisely what has occurred in the case of the Mad Cow Disease in Britain. Initially, the scientists said that there was no danger in feeding cows with the remains of sheep suffering from scrapie as the disease—they asserted—could not cross species barriers. But it did, with cows contracting Bovine Spongiform Encephalopathy (BSE), the equivalent of scrappie in cattle. Then the experts said that it could not affect humans who ate beef and other products of cows suffering from BSE. And it probably did, with a sudden increase in young people getting Creuzfeldt-Jakob Disease (CJD), the human equivalent of scrappie and BSE. The scientists have been proved wrong again.

The Mad Cow Disease scare has revealed the potential dangers of the present system. Some scientists, those dependent on politicians and industry, normally draw conclusions from available evidence that suit the objectives of the system. While the majority of scientists say that global warming could be disastrous, the system-dependent ones say that either there will be no warming at all or that life on earth will adapt to higher temperatures. Other troubling phenomena which are treated in a similarly cavalier way are the ozone hole and the toxic pollutants in the environment. If the same scientists are again proved wrong, it may not be just a few thousand who will die but millions. This is likely since most of the effects appear years or decades after the chemicals are introduced into the environment, and many of them cannot be removed once introduced. So nothing will be done until it is too late.

Any high consumption society has to extinguish itself unless it reduces its consumption in good time. It can sustain its unsustainability a little longer by exploiting the resources and pollution sinks of other societies. This is what the West is presently doing. There would be little objection, from those who have suffered and still suffer from the West's policies, to the affluent extinguishing themselves: the danger is that they may take the global population with them, committing the ultimate abuse of human rights—the extermination of the human race.

CHAPTER 13

The Rights of Indigenous Peoples

According to the UN working definition, indigenous peoples are "composed of the existing descendants of the peoples who inhabited the present territory of a country wholly or partially at the time when persons of a different culture or ethnic origin arrived there from other parts of the world, overcame them and by conquest, settlement or other means reduced them to a non-dominant or colonial situation."[1]

Indigenous peoples are not specifically mentioned in the UN UDHR, though they are included in the catchall "everyone". However, their rights, since they are not explicitly articulated, have often been grossly violated, the most commonly abused being their right to stay in territories which they have inhabited for generations. They are still being displaced from their homelands by hordes of invading industrial mega-projects.

Indian indigenes (Adivasis) are totally dependent for survival on their forests which provide their basic needs: food, herbal medicines, fuel, fodder, timber and a variety of other products. The Adivasis also have spiritual links with the land which has nourished them for centuries, and bonds with the trees and animals with which they coexist sustainably. Exclusion from their forests is an abuse of Article 9 of the UDHR: "No one shall be subjected to...exile." The right expressed in Article 13: "Everyone has the right to freedom of movement and residence within the borders of each state", logically includes the right to remain where one's ancestors have been staying for generations.

Enclosing their forests, whether for commercial exploitation, national parks, wildlife reserves, mega-projects like mines and dams, or whatever, breaks their life-sustaining links and is a denial of their right to life. Such displacement has an adverse impact on individuals as well as on the group, due to loss of education, health, dignity, and spiritual satisfaction. The right to food includes the right to wild foods and the fuel with which to cook them, both from the commons.

Much tribal knowledge is site-specific. Adivasis, therefore, have a right to their particular forests. Forcible removal, even to another forested area, means a loss of diligently acquired knowledge and violates their right to utilise and transmit this valuable education. Those transferred have to learn, all over again, the location of each of the hundreds of species of those plants which they were accustomed to use—if such varieties exist in the land allotted to them as compensation.

Exile produces direct as well as indirect harmful effects on their health. There are two plant species, now rare, that the Adivasis north of Mumbai consider precious. They insist that if they do not consume these at least once a year, their health will suffer. It is quite possible that these species do have potent preventive or curative properties, but even if they did not, the psychological effect of being deprived of them could be disastrous. Species such as these are also being lost because of clear-felling of natural forests and their replacement by plantation monocultures.

Adivasis in this same area believe that if they do not perform a religious ceremony in their fields using a particular herb at the beginning of the rainy season every year, their crops will suffer. Whether this is superstition or whether the plant used has definite crop-enhancing properties is again immaterial.

For the Adivasi who is moved to a deforested region which does not have these plants, no monetary compensation, irrigated farm plot or job in an industry can compensate for the loss. It is no wonder that so many of them pine and die of despair.

On the other hand, from the point of view of Adivasis who live "outside" the Western system, several of the Articles in the UN UDHR are positively harmful. The right to education, usually considered as a right to formal education only, has played a major role in the destruction of traditional self-reliant and sustainable knowledge systems and their associated methods of transmission. The right to health, limited as it is in practice to the promotion of the allopathic system, not only does not support their own knowledge of herbal medicines but explicitly disparages it. The right to work offered is the right to earn cash to purchase items produced by the mainstream, a right which is superfluous for those who find all their sustenance in a forest. The term "standard of living", used in Article 25, refers, by implication, to the monetised economy and even a high level of material affluence. But in traditional societies, many of the basic necessities were and still are obtained free or through barter, with little need felt for nonessential products.

It is seen here again why the West has found it necessary to separate the right to education, health and so on from the right to life. To feed the appetite for profits, education has to promote hyperconsumption and support for the unjust system, not the transmission of knowledge for a sustainable, minimal consumption life. Similarly, health care primarily promotes the drug industry, with improvement in health considered secondary.

The West continues to destroy indigenous cultures by disparaging indigenous values and ways of life and by the promotion of its own culture as supreme, particularly through the electronic media. In addition, the government and many activists make strenuous efforts to integrate the Adivasis within the Westernised mainstream. This results in varying degrees of destruction of their ethnic and cultural characteristics which determine their distinct identity, engendering considerable stress as they begin to question their own beliefs and practices. Stress can be a formidable factor in the determination of the will to live—or not to live. The loss of culture is a slow but exceedingly cruel process of genocide.

In the State of Mato Grosso do Sul in Brazil, members of a tribe of Indians called the Kaiowa, being driven to despair by the destruction of their culture, are committing suicide. In one reservation, home to 7,200 Kaiowa, more than a hundred young people have hung or poisoned themselves since the late 1980s. Only a few years ago they thought of themselves as descendants of the sun—before, in the words of one of their leaders, "the forest was cut, the birds flew away, the fish died."[2]

In the Andaman and Nicobar Islands in the Indian ocean, the indigenes are on the brink of extinction. The process began with the intrusion of the British who introduced them to tobacco, opium and alcohol, in an attempt to induce them to work at the destruction of their own forests for British benefit.[3] Numbering over 600 in the early 1900s, there now are just about 100 Onges alive. They are under the protection of the government, getting free rations, but this itself has eroded their will to hunt and fish and to live.[4] Just recently, a herb that they use has been found to be effective against malaria. Its imminent commercialisation will almost certainly deprive them of this medicine for their own use.[5]

The extent to which cultural damage is being done to ethnic groups can be gauged by its effect on languages. Of the around 5,100 languages still spoken, all but about a hundred may perish within a generation in the West's drive to promote a profitable monoculture.[6] Thousands of cultures and ways of survival in the world that were developed are being assigned to the landfills of history.

Of course not all the Adivasis wish to remain outside the mainstream, and insisting that they confine themselves to their own culture also violates their rights. But the mainstream culture has to ensure that it presents a true picture of itself, its unsustain-ability, its inherent violations of human rights and other warts, malignant tumours and all, so that the Adivasis can make an informed choice.

Mumbai is a unique city for it has a large national park within its urban boundaries. Within the park's boundaries live a few thousand Adivasis who claim that their ancestors have been in the area for generations. These Adivasis are daily exposed to the snares and temptations of the most Westernised city in India. Yet they prefer to stay in their small huts in the forest in spite of being offered, by the Forest Department, free accommodation in modern apartments, with formal schooling, medical care and a job thrown in.

The West has suddenly discovered the value of alien cultures, not their values of justice and sustainability, but the commercial value of the knowledge they possess. Western science had claimed that it had little to learn from tribes since their knowledge was pure, unadulterated superstition. However, arrogant Western attempts to dominate the whole of nature have resulted in obvious environmental disasters with even worse catastrophes predicted for the future. Desperate efforts are now being made to gather the knowledge of peoples who have lived in harmony with nature, but so much damage has been done in the past and by the continuing intrusion of Western values, that only a small fraction of the researched and tested knowledge of millennia survives.

The commercialisation of indigenous knowledge damages the culture that values it, that innovates technologies adapted to changing problems and that transmits such bodies of knowledge from generation to generation. Traditional knowledge is normally disseminated free for anyone to use. If commercialised, innovators would tend to conceal their work until they were assured of financial recompense. Some say that the innovators have a right to be paid in cash for their efforts, but this is a typical Western individualistic right.[7]

Article 21 (1) of the UN UDHR: "Everyone has the right to take part in the government of his country, directly or through freely chosen representatives", is limited to representative democracy alone, with other, often more just and equitable systems being considered inferior to it.

In surviving traditional, nondemocratic systems, not limited to Adivasis alone but in many small settlements, members of the community—sometimes a council of elders, often the males only, occasionally all the adults—get together to discuss their problems. Decisions are usually arrived at by consensus, though they are often influenced by the words of one "wise" person. Such practices may not be perfect, particularly when women are excluded from the decision-making process, but they form a better foundation to build upon than an easily corruptible representative democratic system.

In such community systems, each individual has rights as well as duties. Duties ensure that the survival of the community takes precedence over the rights of individuals, but the community is not the functional equivalent of the State, which is manipulated by an elite minority to its own advantage.

The rights and duties of Adivasis are embedded in their culture and implementation of these comes naturally. Such discipline has been passed on from generation to generation but new situations which require their alteration or adaptation are usually handled with ease by the community. Consensual processes may not be operable in larger societies, but then large nations may be inherently unjust.

Duties are usually enforced by penalties varying from fines

to excommunication, literally the cutting off of all communication, usually for a short period. Such punishment is much more effective than going through the mainstream legal system, in which the "crimes" may not even be recognised or the punishment does not fit the crime.

Some of the restrictions put by communities seem to be backward from the Western individual's point of view. On one occasion an Adivasi grew vegetables in his field which he had fenced, irrigating them with water from a small nearby stream. His fence was broken down and his crops destroyed by the community. By enclosing his field he had broken the rule that all village land was to be considered free community grazing land after the main crop was harvested. In using more water than the others, he was being unjust, since all the villagers would not be able to follow his example, the quantity of water available from the stream being limited. The Adivasis try to be strictly equitable, but the farmer who fenced his field was considered "progressive" by mainstream standards since he had enriched himself, regardless of the cost to the community. He could even have appealed to the mainstream legal system if he had wished to continue in his selfish course.

Where such equitable control is not in force, as in many parts of the country, selfish farmers and industrialists have overdrawn ground water, water tables have dropped drastically, sea water has flowed into the aquifers, and water is no longer easily available.

The genocide of indigenous peoples continues to this day, directly or indirectly, in many parts of the world. Their extermination in the US is fostered by their confinement in "reserves" or by absorption into the mainstream, by deliberate neglect and by their despair at seeing themselves as second rate citizens or permanent prisoners in their own country.

Half of all Native Americans live on reservations, which are often pockets of deep poverty and social suffering, subtly or directly deprived of rights to occupy their ancestral lands and to retain their cultural characteristics and ways of life. Their right to life is denied by their unsanitary and overcrowded housing conditions which contribute to high death rates from tuberculosis and dysentery, which are, respectively, nearly six times and twice that of the nation as a whole. Their infant mortality rate is higher than the national figure, and their average age at death is much lower than the rest of the population. While free to move out of the poverty and frustration of life on the reservation, migration to the cities makes their situation worse, since they possess neither the occupational skills nor the cultural background necessary to sustain themselves. Such inhuman conditions naturally result in a high percentage of family disintegration, alcoholism, and suicide.[8]

These acts are genocidal within the UN definition, as quoted earlier. [See chapter 1] This, perhaps, explains why the US ratified this Convention only in 1988, after forty years of inaction, and that too conditionally.[9] The narrow interpretation of the term "genocide", however, ensures that the US gets away with mass murder, though Article IV of this Convention states that such crimes are punishable whether committed by "constitutionally responsible rulers, public officials, or private individuals."

It was only after much protest that the UN finally set up a Working Group on Indigenous Peoples. The Working Group had five "experts", none of whom belonged to an indigenous group. The group produced the 1993 Draft Declaration on the Rights of Indigenous Peoples, which is an attempt by the West to legalise its occupation of vast territories, whilst leaving indigenous peoples with nominal and often unimplementable rights.[10]

Article 21 of the Draft Declaration states: "Indigenous peoples have the right to maintain and develop their political, economic and social systems, to be secure in the enjoyment of their own means of subsistence and development, and to engage freely in all their traditional and other economic activities. Indigenous peoples who have been deprived of their means of subsistence and development are entitled to just and fair compensation."[10] In effect, this ensures that indigenous peoples can be deprived of their "means of subsistence and development" and are merely entitled to monetary compensation. They can then be "secure in the enjoyment" of the paltry remnants of land and natural resources, if any.

Article 27 observes that "Indigenous peoples have the right to the restitution of the lands, territories and resources which they have traditionally owned or otherwise occupied or used, and which have been confiscated, occupied, used or damaged without their free and informed consent. Where this is not possible, they have the right to just and fair compensation. Unless otherwise freely agreed upon by the peoples concerned, compensation shall take the form of lands, territories and resources equal in quality, size and legal status."[10] There is no evidence that the Europeans occupying invaded lands intend to implement this article, since it will require their return to Europe. This Article entirely absolves those who conquered and subjugated indigenous peoples and serves merely to legalise appalling crimes.

Further occupation is also thoughtfully provided for in Articles 10 and 36: "Indigenous peoples shall not be forcibly removed from their lands or territories. No relocation shall take place without the free and informed consent of the indigenous peoples concerned and after agreement on just and fair compensation and, where possible, with the option of return."[11]

"Indigenous peoples have the right to the recognition, observance and enforcement of treaties, agreements and other constructive arrangements concluded with States or their successors, according to their original spirit and intent, and to have States honour and respect such treaties, agreements and other constructive arrangements."[12] All the treaties made with the indigenes of America were, however, obtained by the use of force. The honouring of such treaties implies that the invaders had a right to occupy indigenous lands.

"Indigenous peoples have the right of self-determination. By virtue of that right they freely determine their political status and freely pursue their economic, social and cultural development."[13] This concession is absurd at a time when all but a few indigenous peoples are subject to aliens occupying their homelands.

"Indigenous peoples have the right to participate fully, if they so choose, at all levels of decision-making in matters which may affect their rights, lives and destinies through representatives chosen by themselves in accordance with their own procedures, as well as to maintain and develop their own indigenous decision-making institutions."[14] Participation in the mainstream's institutions often ensures that basic opposition is greatly weakened and that the indigenes are effectively absorbed.

"Indigenous peoples have the right to establish their own media in their own languages. They also have the right to equal access to all forms of non-indigenous media. States shall take effective measures to ensure that State-owned media duly reflect indigenous cultural diversity."[15] Here the UN magnanimously awards indigenous peoples, who rarely have the wherewithal for bare survival, the right to establish their own high-cost, high-tech media. While the immediate State-owned media may make provision for equal access, though even this is very rare, the international communications invasion through the satellites does not provide opportunities for the propagation of any indigenous people's culture.

"Indigenous peoples have the right to maintain and strengthen their distinctive spiritual and material relationship with the lands, territories, waters and coastal seas and other resources which they have traditionally owned or otherwise occupied or used, and to uphold their responsibilities to future generations in this regard."[16] The ancestral rights of the indigenous peoples to control over their lands and other resources are being viciously destroyed for Western hamburgers, toilet paper and toilet paperbacks. It is the Western predators who need to be reminded about the rights of the indigenes.

"They have the right to special measures to control, develop and protect their sciences, technologies and cultural manifestations, including human and other genetic resources, seeds, medicines, knowledge of the properties of fauna and flora, oral traditions, literatures, designs and visual and performing arts."[17] The exercise of such rights often involves the commercialising of these activities and the co-option of indigenous peoples into the mainstream.

Nearly all of the forty-five Articles listed are similarly designed to reinforce the existing unjust relationship between the occupiers and the conquered peoples. It was natural that indigenous peoples objected to such impositions. In the "Statement of the Indigenous Peoples' Preparatory Meeting" in July 1994 in Geneva, they declared: "We would like to acknowledge that the Draft Declaration, in its present form, does include some positive principles that respond to the real conditions facing indigenous peoples. However, we continue to have strong concerns about other principles that do not fully accommodate the collective and individual rights and interests of indigenous peoples."

They were particularly concerned about the lack of provision for the implementation of their rights to self-determination and their inherent rights to lands, territories and resources. This concern was emphatically expressed: "Throughout our fight against a legacy of external control, indigenous peoples have recognized that this standard-setting process does not belong to us. We know and understand that the Draft Declaration is not our document."[18]

Article 1 of the UN UDHR states unequivocally that all human beings are born equal in rights, so it follows that the rights applying to those designated as indigenous peoples should apply to, for instance, ex-colonial peoples. If indigenous peoples have the right to compensation [UNWGIP: Article 10][11] then colonial peoples have an equal right. The imposition by the West of its culture on other nations would also be a violation of these rights. This shows, once again, how injustice has been concealed within the UN UDHR.

CHAPTER 14

The Rights and Duties of Individuals

The western development of the notion of human rights has been closely connected with the emergence of individualism, defined as a political and social philosophy that places high value on the freedom of the individual and generally accentuates the self-directed, self-contained and comparatively unrestrained individual or ego.[1] The term "human rights" itself implies that the individual takes priority over the community, many human rights problems arising from this particular ideology, as has been pointed out in earlier chapters.

Individualism is based on the belief that personal pleasure is the only good and personal pain the only evil. The unlimited pursuit of pleasure, usually confused with happiness, is considered the ultimate right of every person, thus transmuting selfishness into a universal virtue.

Individualism is essential for the success of the system's need for economic growth, since nothing is supposed to interfere with individuals "fulfilling" themselves, social values being considered secondary to the creation and satisfaction of wants. There is therefore no restriction on the consumption of luxuries even if it means the inexorable denial of the rights of others.

Individuals, in practice, have complete liberty to act as they wish, provided they do not encroach too violently on their neighbours' similar rights. But it is impossible for a Westernised person not to encroach on the rights of others, whether near or far, since practically every activity within the Western system produces greenhouse gases and other types of global pollution. Infringement also occurs by their excessive use of nonrenewable resources. Moreover, such rights cannot be universally implemented, because, for instance, a person using too much fossil fuel exhausts it more rapidly and prevents others from using it in even minimal quantities. The rights of all others, in particular of remote communities or future generations, are flagrantly violated by such actions. It is this hyperconsumption that is today the source of widespread human rights abuse by individuals but adding up to enormous global violations.

Western economics claims "consumer sovereignty" as a fundamental "ethical" right: "What I want, I have a right to get." The criteria people normally use when attempting to satisfy their wants are: "Do I like it?", "Can I afford it?" This implies that the money at the disposal of an individual has been justly earned and that no one has been impoverished or hurt by its acquisition. It further conveys that the purchase contemplated has in no way harmed or exploited those who produce it or the environment. In other words, money cannot be tainted and money itself overrides all other ethical considerations. The whole system is supported by the collusive ignorance in which consumers are maintained of the social and environmental injustice done by the acquisition of "just rewards", and all they can buy.

The extreme lengths to which individualism is taken in the West, for example, is seen when the US insists that its citizens have the right to the ease and comfort to which they are addicted, even though providing these makes it the largest global producer of carbon dioxide and other greenhouse gases. The "rights" to individual comfort are considered superior to the right to life of "others", even though the attainment of that comfort is responsible for rising sea levels which could drown or displace millions of Bangladeshis, Maldivians and other coastal low-lying communities. A few of the "privileged" create the cruel unfairness that the system compulsorily imposes on the mass of their fellow human beings.

The sombre side of the doctrine of individualism is that those disadvantaged by the same system must also take personal responsibility for their own misfortune, poverty or suffering. The West has accumulated such unparalleled wealth that the affluent can claim that only individuals who are flawed in some way could possibly fail to do the same. The system promotes itself as the most perfect form of human society achievable, given the fallen state of humanity. It is only one step from this to assert that all the problems of so prodigious a system must stem from the failings of human beings. Individuals can then be made to bear the burden of pain inflicted by social and economic wrongs as though these were their own self-inflicted tragedies. Unfortunately, the people of the West have been so profoundly saturated with the values of their system that they no longer see any divergence between their own being and the necessities of that system.

A strange kind of doctrine it is that passes on to atomised and dispersed individuals the responsibility for social and economic ills. This reveals a less benign intent towards the individual than is usually understood by the belief in individualism. The latter, it is clear, is primarily the justification through which the strong legitimise their oppression of the weak. All the rhetoric about enterprise, freedom, hard work, merit, rewards, go-getters, the pursuit of excellence, and so on serves a less openly avowed purpose, which is the perpetuation of poverty and suffering required for the acquisition of affluence by a select few.

The system, for instance, cannot provide enough jobs for all who need them, even with a large proportion of the work force earning an insufficient income. It then blames the unemployed or partly employed for being lazy, for not feeding their families or maintaining their health. The Westernised community has, in effect, shrugged off its responsibilities on to the individuals who clamour for their rights. To compound the insult, the victims of this system are portrayed as its saboteurs, willfully undermining national prosperity.

The question of duties comes up only in Articles 29 and 30 of the Declaration: "Everyone has duties to the community in which alone the free and full development of his personality is possible." "In the exercise of his rights and freedoms, everyone shall be subject only to such limitations as are determined by law solely for the purpose of securing due recognition and respect for the rights and freedoms of others and of meeting the just requirements of morality, public order and the general welfare in a democratic society." "Nothing in this Declaration may be interpreted as implying for any State, group or person any right to engage in any activity or to perform any act aimed at the destruction of any of the rights and freedoms set forth herein."

Since all people within the Western system violently infringe on the rights of others, the purpose of including these articles appears to be merely cosmetic. Further, with the "requirements of morality" often seen as being outside "the law", there are no legal regulations governing most of the abuses of the rights of others. The inclusion of the words, "public order and the general welfare" permits any of the assured rights to be abused with complete impunity.

Each right should have been specifically coupled with corresponding duties to the community, local as well as global. By not specifying these in the UDHR, individuals claim unbounded liberty to do whatever they please even when this violates the rights of others. In such a situation, the most powerful—those with the least concern for morality—"win". Individualism has bred a mentally and morally disadvantaged human subspecies who suffer from a lack of even a vestigial conscience or sense of social responsibility.

Duties, taken in the context of the community, require that each individual must guarantee the same rights for every other individual, even if it means a sacrifice of her or his own rights. Insisting on one's rights can often be harmful to the community as a whole. Justice in society depends wholly on the extent of selflessness of people in that society, people who make a substantial commitment to living together in a community. The community as a whole has reciprocal duties to the individuals it comprises, enshrined as their rights.

The human rights of individuals, therefore, can never be absolute: they must be subservient to the interests of the local community, rarely, however, to that of the "national interest", the nation being usually too large and heterogenous a collection of people to allow consensual decisions. Not only that, in most non-Western communities, the individual does not possess an inherently conflictual relationship with his community. It is through the community that the individual realizes his self as acknowledged in Article 29.

CHAPTER 15

Conclusion

With such symbiotic connections between the Western system and human rights violations, attempts to eliminate its
inherent abuse will always be frustrated. Striving to correct the
situation by making minor "improvements" in the application of
various stated "rights" may even serve to deny other people their
rights.

Corrections that can be made in the Western system from
within, by forcing its institutions—from the UN to local governments—to adhere to the rights listed in UN declarations are of their
very nature limited, since the rights themselves have been made
sufficiently malleable to be circumvented in practice. This is not, of
course to deny the Western formulation, but to reveal its main
purpose.

Human rights activists often say that their priority is to
correct the present violent abuse of the rights of individuals, not to
spend time on more fundamental changes whose implementation
is uncertain. But this is not an either-or situation; both need to be
tackled simultaneously.

While the movement towards the universal right to life and
social justice has to begin with resistance to the Western system as
a whole, the promotion of full human rights can only be possible
in systems operating "outside" the Western enclosures. It has,
therefore, become imperative to look beyond the West, and learn
from or develop more essentially civilised models. Human rights
needs to be based on the inclusive right to life and universal social
justice.

The inclusive right to life incorporates all the other sub-rights
listed individually in the UN UDHR. The inclusive right to life

requires the implementation of the rights of all human beings—indigenous peoples and others, of women, men and children. It requires their right to food, clothing, relevant education, health, shelter, freedom, and all those other nonmaterial needs that contribute to a mentally fulfilling life—the right to dignity, love and affection, care and concern, the freedom to express creativity, preserve one's own culture, with all together contributing to making each person's life on earth worth living. In dealing with these, no "universal" lists can be made out, only general indications of directions given, since these may differ from group to group, from place to place, from culture to culture.

The inclusive right to life applies to all people now living and to future generations, that is, universal social justice. This imposes corresponding duties which may limit the rights of each person. For instance, it limits the consumption of material resources, particularly nonrenewable ones, to minimum levels only. Consumption over basic need requirements—hyperconsumption—is an abuse of other people's right to life. The failure to observe this rule constitutes one of the major, yet rarely mentioned, violations of human rights today. It is an abuse that is perpetrated by nearly all citizens in the West and those in the Two Thirds World who imitate their life-styles.

The practice of a simple life-style is thus imperative. The universal application of the right to life is only possible if all live on a modest, yet secure, level of consumption. The satisfaction of the material needs necessary for survival will itself result in the satisfaction of the nonmaterial ones, or make it easier to implement them. It is possible to have a high quality of life without ever-rising incomes, within the constraints of universal equity.

The need for a simple life-style also logically follows from a holistic vision of the integration of human beings in nature. It does not mean a religious asceticism for its own sake or the denial of pleasure. A simple life-style can provide a "joyful frugality" which the accumulation of goods and services clearly does not furnish.

The shift to societies which are basically committed to human rights is not going to be easy. It is no use saying, as do Western cynics, that we have to live in the real world, that there is no possibility of perfecting the world, that human nature will always remain as it has been, that because ideologies of transformation have always ended in disaster, it follows that no further transformations may be contemplated in the existing global arrangements. Simply because perfection is not attainable does not mean that radical shifts are not desirable or necessary; for without them, our chances of perishing are high; and this would be an abuse of human rights to eclipse all others.

One of the most effective means of attaching people to the existing system is the apocalyptic imagery of what would happen were they to forsake their high dependency culture. It is regarded as unthinkable that we should disengage from the present mechanisms for providing us with our daily bread, even if it is now brought to us, not courtesy of the butcher and baker, but by courtesy of some vast transnational company. We are terrorised into accepting everything that goes along with our fragile and insecure privilege. The images of what horrors await us, should we seek the delusion of alternatives are lurid and relentless: homeless bands of marauders would roam the desolate landscape of our unlighted cities and rusting cars, hunting for such food as they could find, pillaging whatever resources they can lay their hands on.

Many criticisms are thrown against those who, in spite of the so-called end of ideology, in spite of the conviction that all utopias and visions are dead, continue to advocate the necessity for true social justice and respect for a wider version of human rights than those currently on offer. One such claim is that criticisms are an attempt at "turning back the clock." Well, if the revival of modest and frugal ways of life is turning back the clock, at least it is an improvement on those, who, urging on an industrialisation without end, risk turning back the clock to the Book of Genesis when chaos covered the face of the earth.

Another attack is that the present system reflects the reality of human nature and that this nature cannot be changed. "Human nature", in this context invariably means greed, selfishness and individual self-aggrandisement.

But human nature is also characterised by self-sacrifice, concern for others, compassion and cooperation; otherwise the human race would have extinguished itself long ago. So why is only this one-sided version of human nature purveyed, when it comes to justifying a cold, cruel system? Could it be that what is being described is the nature of the system, and the behaviour of human beings when they must survive within it?

A common belief is that a few people cannot change the system—it is simply too vast and powerful and it has left its victims nearly powerless to make positive changes. Such a belief implies that human beings are inherently and irredeemably inhuman. However, many examples show that while a perfect human society may not be possible, systems that are more just than the Western one already exist among non-Western societies and even in small groups within the geographical boundaries of Western societies themselves.

Moreover, the shift to simple life-styles—reducing the purchase and use of non-necessities—will itself undermine the system. In a sense, the "magic of the marketplace", can be used not only by choosing what we buy, but by choosing what we don't buy. The system, no matter how tyrannical it becomes, cannot deprive citizens of the right not to buy. And since the source of its wealth and power is the manufacture and sale of its products, not buying is a potent means of hastening its downfall.

There are several other ways in which a shift to simpler life-styles may be brought about or forced on a reluctant population. If the Western system continues on its present unjust course it must ultimately collapse due to resource exhaustion or overpollution, with or without social breakdown resulting from increasing inequity. The system is self-destructive, though unfortunately it may continue to violate the rights of millions before it does disintegrate.

Such statements are dismissed as the ramblings of irrational, millennium cultists; of people who have been predicting doomsday for generations. But doomsday has not yet come and will never arrive since Western science and technology are religiously believed to be capable of indefinitely substituting resources and eliminating pollution. However, even though it appears to be permanently entrenched, the Western system is already showing a variety of signs of deterioration.

True, doomsday has not come for the rich and powerful, but it has already arrived for the individual and collective impoverished as a result of the increasing abuse of their rights. Their forests and other commons on which they survived have been enclosed for industrial exploitation. Their agricultural fields have been taken over by agro-industries as a necessary corollary to liberalisation. Infrastructure development, power stations, wide expressways and other allurements to foreign investment, and the TNCs' factories and other establishments themselves, take up still more land. The impoverished cannot get employment within the system, since even if they acquire the skills and the education levels demanded, there are just no jobs available, as industries downsize in order to be internationally competitive—another corollary of liberalisation. Since these persons do not have the cash to purchase Western industrial products, they are of no "value" to the system and can be allowed to perish by free market murder. The barbarians are within the gates.

Partial collapse is also occurring in the West itself. There is a growing underclass being generated by increasing unemployment due to redundant skills and irrelevant education, even as the costs of food, clothing, and transport rise. They are thus made dependent on state welfare which is being eroded as a result of government anxiety to keep "costs" competitive with those of other nations competing for the same limited markets. There is increasing alienation from the mainstream as falling expectations result from a lack of any visible sign of hope for a better future.

Family breakdown, neglect in old age, homelessness, increasing addiction to tobacco, alcohol, caffeine, TV and drugs (prescribed or illegal)—all present a wretched scenario. People are terrorised by vandalism, random attacks and crime. It is a world in which neighbours and kinsfolk have been replaced by a human demonology of fiends, monsters, child-molesters, rapists, weirdoes, crazies, muggers, thugs, junkies, addicts and winos—a litany of disgrace which is itself evidence of a violated humanity.

· However, the West cannot easily extricate itself from the tangled web of its own weaving. Any endeavours to reduce its widespread and inherent abuse must lead to a reduction in consumption, with economic recession following.

An example of how the excessive exploitation of people is itself driving them to realise that the Western system is harmful is the case of the Enron power project in Dabhol in Guhaghar district. [See Appendix II]

When the people of the affected villages learnt that their lands were to be acquired for the project, they immediately objected but without much effect. When the project's Environmental Impact Assessment was obtained and analysed by a group in Mumbai, the inhabitants of neighbouring villages, farmers and fisherfolk, realising the extent of the environmental damage that would result, joined the protests.

After the farmers of fourteen neighbouring villages, owning about 7,500 hectares, received notices announcing a measurement of their lands for ultimate acquisition, they too joined the protests.

Initially, the people said that they would not accept highly polluting chemical industries but would welcome industries such as electronics assembly or garment manufacture. But when they learnt that even electronics factories are highly polluting and that any industry takes up land, they refused to accept any industrialisation at all, saying that they were content with their agricultural crops and fruit orchards. And this realisation is spreading to other neighbouring areas too, with local opposition to any industry attempting to set up a plant in the region.

Many ancient systems, still practised by indigenous peoples who have been living simply for thousands of years, provide viable and more just model alternatives to the Western system. They can teach the wisdom of smallness, the value of communities which include individual autonomy with communal generosity and a nonviolent ecological perspective.

There are those who voluntarily practice or adopt a simple life-style, groups which have survived the onslaught of the high-consumption society and the new arrivals, such as people concerned about the environment, true practitioners of some religions such as Jainism, Buddhism, early Christianity and so on. There are those who believe in universal social justice, others who extend justice—if such a concept can be used—to animals and plants, that is, to all creation.

The question of renunciation always arises in such discussions. "You can't expect people to give up their cars, TVs, and other luxuries", is the usual way in which the all-knowing berate foolish idealists and visionaries whose dreams have not a hope of ever being implemented. It has to be said, however, that the rhetoric of renunciation is perhaps not the most constructive approach. Rather than saying: "You will have to give up this or that consumer artefact", the appeal might better be phrased by asking: "Would you not like to be free of fear, insecurity, the aggravations and aggressions of daily life, the crime, violence, the subjective feeling of impoverishment even among our version of plenty, the break-down in human relationships?" The question is one of emancipation rather than renunciation; and put this way it may begin to gain assent from more and more people. The fact that such a project of liberation is also required in the interests of both social justice and protection of the resource-base of the earth is another powerful incentive to positive, rather than negative, change.

A true flowering of humanity could occur only at a constant, modest, yet secure, level of consumption. It is possible to have better education, health, and quality of life without ever-rising incomes. Perhaps, rather than talking about "zero growth" or "negative growth-rates", which unnecessarily frightens people, the discussion might centre on "positive rates of reduction"; for that would suggest liberation from some of the burdensome, crippling, and indeed, suicidal consequences of present ways of living. Human resources will be revitalised by release from market dependency. Buying in everything both reduces human efforts and energies and absorbs higher levels of material resources. We are looking at a different mix between the two, so that only the very poor would experience an increase in material resources, while the well-to-do would rediscover a remobilising of their somnolent capacities for self-provisioning, for creating and mobilising their own capacities to answer many of the needs of themselves and their loved ones.

Of course, it is true that in no society will the darker side of humanity be banished. Cruelty, greed, egotism, vanity, dishonesty are surely human characteristics, and will not be wished away by fine sentiments and noble ideals. What we can say, however, is that simply because the global system finds these qualities useful for its self-justifying expansion through the world, does not mean that this must remain so for ever. Although we may not believe in the perfectability of humanity, we can perhaps say that we can imagine circumstances, contexts and social frameworks in which some of the positive aspects of humanity are permitted and encouraged to flower. Simply because there has been no Utopia, just because no Garden of Eden exists is no reason for abandoning the search for greater social justice, concern for those who suffer and above all, responsibility to future generations. Indeed, this remains the objective of all our strivings: not the search for wild impossible dreams, but for realising a vision that will at least give humankind a future in which to continue the search for a more just world.

The Universal Declaration of Human Rights

Whereas recognition of the inherent dignity and of the equal and inalienable rights of all members of the human family is the foundation of freedom, justice and peace in the world,

Whereas disregard and contempt for human rights have resulted in barbarous acts which have outraged the conscience of mankind, and the advent of a world in which human beings shall enjoy freedom of speech and belief and freedom from fear and want has been proclaimed as the highest aspiration of the common people,

Whereas it is essential, if man is not to be compelled to have recourse, as a last resort, to rebellion against tyranny and oppression, that human rights should be protected by the rule of law,

Whereas it is essential to promote the development of friendly relations between nations,

Whereas the peoples of the United Nations have in the Charter reaffirmed their faith in fundamental human rights, in the dignity and worth of the human person and in the equal rights of men and women and have determined to promote social progress and better standards of life in larger freedom,

Whereas Member States have pledged themselves to achieve, in cooperation with the United Nations, the promotion of universal respect for and observance of human rights and fundamental freedoms,

Whereas a common understanding of these rights and freedoms is of the greatest importance for the full realization of this pledge,

Now, therefore, the General Assembly proclaims this Universal Declaration of Human Rights as a common standard of achievement for all peoples and all nations, to the end that every individual and every organ of society, keeping this Declaration constantly in mind, shall strive by teaching and education to promote respect for these rights and freedoms and by progressive measures, national and international, to secure their universal and effective recognition and observance, both among the peoples of Member States themselves and among peoples of territories under their jurisdiction.

Art 1. All human beings are born free and equal in dignity and rights. They are endowed with reason and conscience and should act towards one another in a spirit of brotherhood.

Art 2. Everyone is entitled to all the rights and freedoms set forth in this Declaration, without distinction of any kind such as race, colour, sex, language, religion, political or other opinion, national or social origin, property, birth or other status. Furthermore, no distinction shall be made on the basis of the political, jurisdictional or international status of the country or territory to which a person belongs, whether it be independent, trust, non-self-governing or under any other limitation of sovereignty.

Art 3. Everyone has the right to life, liberty and security of person.

Art 4. No one shall be held in slavery or servitude; slavery and the slave trade shall be prohibited in all their forms.

Art 5. No one shall be subjected to torture or to cruel, inhuman or degrading treatment or punishment.

Art 6. Everyone has the right to recognition everywhere as a person before the law.

Art 7. All are equal before the law and are entitled without any discrimination to equal protection of the law. All are entitled to equal protection against any discrimination in violation of this Declaration and against any incitement to such discrimination.

Art 8. Everyone has the right to an effective remedy by the competent national tribunals for acts violating the fundamental rights granted him by the constitution or by law.

Art 9. No one shall be subjected to arbitrary arrest, detention or exile.

Art 10.   Everyone is entitled in full equality to a fair and public hearing by an independent and impartial tribunal, in the determination of his rights and obligations and of any criminal charge against him.

Art 11. (1) Everyone charged with a penal offence has the right to be presumed innocent until proved guilty according to law in a public trial at which he has had all the guarantees necessary for his defence.

Art 11. (2) No one shall be held guilty of any penal offence on account of any act or omission which did not constitute a penal offence, under national or international law, at the time when it was committed. Nor shall a heavier penalty be imposed than the one that was applicable at the time the penal offence was committed.

Art 12.   No one shall be subjected to arbitrary interference with his privacy, family, home or correspondence, nor to attacks upon his honour and reputation. Everyone has the right to the protection of the law against such interference or attacks.

Art 13. (1) Everyone has the right to freedom of movement and residence within the borders of each State.

Art 13. (2) Everyone has the right to leave any country, including his own, and to return to his country.

Art 14. (1) Everyone has the right to seek and to enjoy in other countries asylum from persecution.

Art 14. (2) This right may not be invoked in the case of prosecutions genuinely arising from nonpolitical crimes or from acts contrary to the purposes and principles of the United Nations.

Art 15. (1) Everyone has the right to a nationality.

Art 15. (2) No one shall be arbitrarily deprived of his nationality nor denied the right to change his nationality.

Art 16. (1) Men and women of full age, without any limitation due to race, nationality or religion, have the right to marry and to found a family. They are entitled to equal rights as to marriage, during marriage and at its dissolution.

Art 16. (2) Marriage shall be entered into only with the free and full consent of the intending spouses.

Art 16. (3) The family is the natural and fundamental group unit of society and is entitled to protection by society and the State.

Art 17. (1) Everyone has the right to own property alone as well as in association with others.

Art 17. (2) No one shall be arbitrarily deprived of his property.

Art 18.   Everyone has the right to freedom of thought, conscience and religion; this right includes freedom to change his religion or belief, and freedom, either alone or in community with others and in public or private, to manifest his religion or belief in teaching, practice, worship and observance.

Art 19.   Everyone has the right to freedom of opinion and expression; this right includes freedom to hold opinions without interference and to seek, receive and impart information and ideas through any media and regardless of frontiers.

Art 20. (1) Everyone has the right to freedom of peaceful assembly and association.

Art 20. (2) No one may be compelled to belong to an association.

Art 21. (1) Everyone has the right to take part in the government of his country, directly or through freely chosen representatives.

Art 21. (2) Everyone has the right of equal access to public service in his country.

Art 21. (3) The will of the people shall be the basis of the authority of government; this will shall be expressed in periodic and genuine elections which shall be by universal and equal suffrage and shall be held by secret vote or by equivalent free voting procedures.

Art 22.   Everyone, as a member of society, has the right to social security and is entitled to realization, through national effort and international cooperation and in accordance with the organization and resources of each State, of the economic, social and cultural rights indispensable for his dignity and the free development of his personality.

Art 23. (1) Everyone has the right to work, to free choice of employment, to just and favourable conditions of work and to protection against unemployment.

Art 23. (2) Everyone, without any discrimination, has the right to equal pay for equal work.

Art 23. (3) Everyone has the right to just and favourable remuneration ensuring for himself and his family an existence worthy of human dignity, and supplemented, if necessary, by other means of social protection.

Art 23. (4) Everyone has the right to form and to join trade unions for the protection of his interests.

Art 24.   Everyone has the right to rest and leisure, including reasonable limitation of working hours and periodic holidays with pay.

Art 25. (1) Everyone has the right to a standard of living adequate for the health and well-being of himself and of his family, including food, clothing, housing and medical care and necessary social services, and the right to security in the event of unemployment, sickness, disability, widowhood, old age or other lack of livelihood in circumstances beyond his control.

Art 25. (2) Motherhood and childhood are entitled to special care and assistance. All children, whether born in or out of wedlock, shall enjoy the same social protection.

Art 26. (1) Everyone has the right to education. Education shall be free, at least in the elementary and fundamental stages. Elementary education shall be compulsory. Technical and professional education shall be made generally available and higher education shall be equally accessible to all on the basis of merit.

Art 26. (2) Education shall be directed to the full development of the human personality and to the strengthening of respect for human rights and fundamental freedoms. It shall promote understanding, tolerance and friendship among all nations, racial or religious groups, and shall further the activities of the United Nations for the maintenance of peace.

Art 26. (3) Parents have a prior right to choose the kind of education that shall be given to their children.

Art 27. (1) Everyone has the right to freely participate in the cultural life of the community, to enjoy the arts and to share in scientific advancement and its benefits.

Art 27. (2) Everyone has the right to the protection of the moral and material interests resulting from any scientific, literary or artistic production of which he is the author.

Art 28. Everyone is entitled to a social and international order in which the rights and freedoms set forth in this Declaration can be fully realised.

Art 29. (1) Everyone has duties to the community in which alone the free and full development of his personality is possible.

Art 29. (2) In the exercise of his rights and freedoms, everyone shall be subject only to such limitations as are determined by law solely for the purpose of securing due recognition and respect for the rights and freedoms of others and of meeting the just requirements of morality, public order and the general welfare in a democratic society.

Art 29. (3) These rights and freedoms may in no case be exercised contrary to the purposes and principles of the United Nations.

Art 30. Nothing in this Declaration may be interpreted as implying for any State, group or person any right to engage in any activity or to perform any act aimed at the destruction of any of the rights and freedoms set forth herein.

Adopted by the United Nations General Assembly, December 10, 1948.

Human Rights Violations by Industrial Development

Western development, promoted as a human right can only be carried out through the flagrant abuse of more fundamental human rights. A look at the manner in which a specific industrial project is being imposed on a rural area in India reveals the enormous volume and variety of human rights abuse produced by such industrialisation.

The Actors

The physical invasion and occupation of non-European lands, which cannot be blatantly carried out now, has been replaced by seemingly benign economic occupation. This has been accomplished under the guise of the globalisation of trade, which is nothing but a demand by the West for the unfettered entry of TNCs into the Two Thirds World. The TNCs exchange our natural wealth for their modern "glass beads" in the process of the development of poverty.

Local, mainly urban, political elites have eagerly accepted the role assigned to them in internally promoting the Western culture of economic domination, being rewarded with a small share of the loot from the wars waged on their own people. Large dams, power stations and other industrial and agroindustrial projects are among the major items on their agenda.

The project examined here as a case study is a thermal power plant under construction about one hundred and fifty kilometres south of Mumbai, in the Ratnagiri district of the State of Maharashtra. The power plant is being built by a consortium of US transnationals: the Enron Development Corporation, the General

Electric Capital Corporation and Bechtel Enterprises Incorporated. They are officially designated the "Dabhol Power Company" (DPC) but are interchangeably called "Enron" since Enron
is the managing partner.

The history of these three TNCs reveals a questionable
technical competence and environmental record; their corruption
potential is equally alarming. From influencing governments, to
manipulating politicians, to corrupting industrialists, to bribing
bureaucrats, to irresponsibly polluting the environment, Enron,
Bechtel and GE have "the power to do it all", as Enron's brochure
proudly asserts.[1] Whether Enron and its partners have used this
power here, their actions could tell.

The transmission lines through which such economic and
political power flows start with the Western TNCs and their
governments, the IMF, WB and WTO, the Indian government and
its ministries of power and the environment, the State governments,
politicians and industrialists, down to local bureaucrats. All these
play active roles in the abuse of human rights.

The "Right" to Invade and Occupy

Western industrialisation is as demanding as the physical
colonisation of land since the original inhabitants of the region
need to be summarily evicted to make way for it. Given the
continuity of colonialism, though now in a different disguise, it is
not surprising that the reasons used by the Europeans to justify
their earlier invasions are remarkably similar to those employed
today in the industrial trespass and occupation of rural lands.

Ratnagiri district is one of the most fertile and agriculturally
productive areas in the State. It is blessed with plenty of rain,
numerous rivers and streams and an easily accessible underground
water table. It supports a wide range of crops, orchards, forests
and wildlife. It is from such an Eden that the inhabitants are being
driven out, despite their not having committed any particularly
original sin.

It is but natural that they do not wish to be enveloped and
smothered by the Western industrial model of development. The
system has, therefore, to be forcibly imposed on them, since the
development enthusiasts covet their assets, their land, water and
clean air.

The seventeenth century colonisers justified their invasions by claiming that England was "full" while the Americas were "empty". Here we have the parallel in the cities being "full"—the Maharashtra government has already banned the entry of new industries in and around Mumbai. Special incentives are offered to industries to move to "backward", "empty" rural agricultural areas. The Environmental Impact Assessment report (EIA) of the DPC, following similar lines, states that the "general area has a relatively low population density."[2]

A more subtle form of fullness is the over-pollution of the cities. In 1992, Lawrence Summers, chief economist with the World Bank, wrote a memo which declared: "Just between you and me, shouldn't the Bank be encouraging more migration of the dirty industries to the less developed countries?" Summers also introduced the novel notion of the "underpolluted" country. He argued that clean air is valuable not because it is healthy to breathe, but because of its potential use as a sink which can be dirtied with pollution.[3]

But Summers merely made international what Westernised industry had long been doing within countries: a rural unpolluted region is designated by remote politicians as an industrial zone, thus permitting industries to economically "use" its pollution potential.

The Uncivilised

Since it was morally difficult for Europeans to appropriate land from equals, the indigenous Americans the Europeans encountered had to be inferiorised. The British thus argued that the native Americans "are not industrious, neither have (they) art, science, skill or faculty to use either the land or the commodities of it..."[4]

The very idea that other nations need to "develop", with the categorisation of whole nations as "undeveloped", "underdeveloped" or "developing" is racist. The people are viewed as inferior and without the scientific and technological knowledge or management skills to process their own natural wealth. This prevents them from becoming civilised hyperconsumers of the earth's resources, and hence they have no "use value" for the system. They need the expertise of TNCs in order to "develop".

Robert N. Bakley, President of the DPC, claimed that "the Enron project had been conceived keeping the best interests of the people in mind."[5] An enraged villager retorted that what Bakley was trying to suggest was that the villagers are not intelligent enough to understand what was in their own interest. We in India, it now appears, need Americans to come and tell our self-suffi-cient, nature-conserving farmers, horticulturists and fisherfolk that a power plant with a total permanent employment capacity of 250 to 300 (the majority of whom will be white immigrant workers) is a better alternative for a population of ten thousand which largely enjoyed happy, healthy and sustainable life-styles till the arrival of the company.

In January 1995, Linda Powers, a vice present of Enron Development Corporation explained to a committee of the US House of Representatives, the deplorably primitive state in which Enron found Indian conditions. Indians, she claimed, did not know how to live and needed to be "educated." To this end, Powers stated, her "company spent an enormous amount of its own money —approximately $20 million—on this education and project development process alone, not including any project costs."[6] Leaving the overpowering arrogance aside, the magna-nimity in bearing the latest white (wo)man's burden is thrown into question since Enron has not produced any accounts for the claimed expenditure in spite of repeated promises to do so.

Local urban elites, on the other hand, scornfully categorize rural people as "backward", "uncivilised", "illiterate", "igno-rant", "unskilled" and "lazy", dependent on "traditional" technol-ogy, and living in the "bullock-cart era." Farmers and fisherfolk who do not possess the subservient mentality required to defer to urban-based expert opinions, are termed "incorrigible." Urban elites claim superiority over rural farmers and artisans because of their use of "modern" agricultural and industrial systems to provide a high-consumption life-style. This superiority, they claim, gives them the right to occupy rural territory in the name of "development."

The farmers, fisherfolk and artisans occupy space which— the invaders insist—they are not putting to productive industrial use.

Enron's EIA report states that the land to be acquired is "wasteland", "unused land", "not very productive..." The horticulture is said to be "poor." "The vegetation on the project site is scrubby and sparse because of the rocky soil..."²

None of this is true. One of the villages occupied by the project is Anjanvel. The land that the EIA classifies as waste land in this village has been built up by its people over the last two centuries. The ruler of the region issued the following assurance to the peasants of Anjanvel on 4 January 1775: "Those peasants who create new fields out of rocky lands, on which neither tree nor grass grows, by filling them up with earth brought from other places, or those who create new fields by breaking rocky hills and filling them up with earth shall have half of the new fields in *inam* (free from tax), while the other half shall be exempt from rent for twenty years, then only a light rent shall be levied for the next five years, and thereafter assessed according to the standard rule."⁷

Local farmers state that about 50 per cent of the land acquired for the DPC was under crop cultivation, 5 per cent under horticulture, 10 per cent kept for pasture and 35 per cent under private forests. They cultivated thirteen cereal, pulse and oilseed crops and seventeen species of fruit trees. The uncultivated pasture and forest lands provided wild foods, fuel, herbal medicines, fodder for draught animals, biomass for manure, and met many other essential needs. Seven species of large trees provided excellent timber for housing and for the construction of fishing boats. Trees also provided resins for waterproofing boats and dyes and tans for strengthening and rot-proofing natural fibre fish nets.

The land occupied by the project was so fertile that in 1966 the government of Maharashtra vigorously promoted agriculture, horticulture and forestry in the region. For about five years preceding the acquisition, all horticultural development in the region had been fully subsidised. This scheme was a great success, increasing horticultural output and quality.⁸

These accomplishments have now been reversed. Subsidies are being lavishly bestowed on those who will clear fell the orchards and forests. The forests are to be replaced by concrete jungles inhabited by industries which so poison the land that nothing can grow in it again; the present policy is leading to irreversible consequences.

Attempts to partially justify the active promotion of human rights abuse are made by transferring blame to the victims, just as the American Native was earlier held responsible for his own destruction, since he refused to "learn the arts of civilisation...he and his forest must perish together."[9] The EIA report claims that the farmers do not use irrigation and their crop outputs are low, implying that they are incapable of improving their agriculture. Although the first fall in productivity was brought about by the British with their high taxes and the enclosure of the pasture and forest commons, today the blame lies with the government for not providing them with irrigation. This it could easily have done, as their undertaking to supply the enormous water requirements of Enron from the Koyna waters demonstrates.

The EIA report faults the local inhabitants because they do not have modern sanitation facilities, do not use expensive allopathic equipment, or are not educated. Yet sewage disposal systems are to be provided in Enron's temporary and permanent housing colonies, but they will not be connected to the nearby villages. Dispensaries and schools are to be set up for the permanent employees, but none for the local people.

Forests and Wildlife

The EIA report claims: "The district of Ratnagiri has a very low forest cover. In the study area, there are no reserved or protected forests." Nor are there "any endangered species of flora and fauna in the study area."[2] However, a plan in the report itself shows "forests/thick vegetation" within a short distance of the project site. Where low forest cover does occur in parts of the district, it is due to earlier destruction for industrial use, particularly for charcoal production to fuel industries in Mumbai.

In addition, the land acquired for Enron was partly covered by natural forests maintained by farmers on their private land holdings, as part of an integrated village resource system. These had, at times, greater cover than that of official Reserved and Protected forests.

Such lands supported numerous species of mammals, birds, insects and other creatures, comprising a highly diversified ecosystem. Several protected species, plant and animal, grew in large numbers within and near the site. There were over thirty large banyan trees (*Ficus bengalensis*)—a protected and sacred species— within the area but the EIA report claims that there is only one tree.[2]

There were also rare and endangered species, as several studies of flora in the area show.

The EIA further claims that the "wandering cattle, monkeys and wild pigs are a nuisance to the mango gardeners."[2] What it fails to mention is that this is a direct consequence of the construction of the Koyna dam, at the eastern boundary of Ratnagiri district. When completed in the 1960s, numerous wild pigs, monkeys and other creatures were driven from their habitats by the filling of the reservoir. They crossed over into Ratnagiri district and have since then—and since then only—caused immense damage to crops and plantations. So much so that second (rabi) cropping, which was extensive earlier, became impossible because of the depredations by wild boars. It is not to be wondered at, therefore, that agriculture and horticulture are not as productive as they should be in such a fertile region. This large scale destruction and loss increased the emigration of people from the area to the cities. The EIA report presents all these direct consequences of earlier "development" as the original natural conditions of the area.

What the Koyna dam "development" initiated, the new industries will continue. The EIA report admits: "Wildlife in the area will move away due to habitat destruction and disturbances. These impacts are however, inevitable and minor."[2] The pigs and monkeys have once again been evicted, exerting further pressure on the remaining habitat with additional loss of food rights by the remaining people. For instance, the damage to mangoes by monkeys increased to almost 50 per cent of the crop, in the year following the acquisition. Claiming that such important impacts are minor and inevitable shows that the environmental consequences of the project are of minimal concern to Enron.

The Fishing Community

The project site is adjacent to the estuary of the Vashishti river and coastal sea areas which are, or rather were, highly productive fishing zones. The project will have an enormous negative impact on the fisherfolk in the area. The traditional fishing system, therefore, needed to be belittled, with the EIA report filled with pages of totally false reporting.

For instance, the EIA claims that "trawler fishing in open waters predominates...Open sea fishing provides a livelihood for a small majority of the population in the immediate vicinity of the project....Fishing in the Vashishti estuary only provides some subsistence to the fisherfolk during the monsoons when they cannot go out to the open sea."[2]

In estuarine fishing, small boats owned by individual fisherfolk are used. Each adjacent village has its own designated space within the estuary, and within this space each individual has a right to fish in an assigned tract. The process of fishing itself does not require much labour. After landing the catch, the excess over immediate home requirements is sold to non-fisher neighbours or bartered for grains and fuelwood. A few species are dried for home storage or sale. The fisherfolk also fish along the coast from September to May. Such fishing has been carried on sustainably for hundreds of years, providing employment to most of the villagers.

The waters of the river have, however, been increasingly poisoned over the last two decades by "development" of the Lote-Parshuram industrial estate, about fifty kilometres upstream. With a large number of chemical industries operating in the estate, huge quantities of untreated toxic wastes have been pumped directly into the river.

Fisherfolk report that catches have been continuously decreasing. While earlier there were over fifty individuals with small boats who obtained a decent living from the estuary, not even fifteen can be supported now. Formerly, the catch of one working person could feed two families, now that of four can barely feed one. While in the past they measured their catch in boatloads, now it is in just tens of kilograms. Several of the fisherfolk have been reduced to utter poverty.

Following this catastrophe, the government requested the local banks to give loans to the unemployed fisherfolk for purchasing trawlers to operate in the open sea. Only about fifteen of the richer villagers could take advantage of this offer because of the high initial deposits and security required by the banks. Most of those who can no longer fish on their own now work on these boats as meagrely paid labourers.

Over 700 large corporate-owned trawlers from around Mumbai also ply from June to September off the Ratnagiri coast. Their operators keep only the larger fish and discard the numerous small fish which the fisherfolk would have otherwise netted.

Further damage is done to the nets of these fisherfolk as the trawlers often plough through them without concern. Those fish that would have come into the estuary are also picked up by the trawlers. With all these attacks by "modern" trawlers and their methods of fishing, the local fishing industry has been brought to the brink of collapse.

The use of trawlers in the area is seen as progress, with the EIA report claiming that the "fishing economy in these villages has boomed only since the National Credit and Development Corporation started giving loans."[2] Only the commercial fishing economy has grown somewhat, but accompanied by a decrease in the small subsistence fishing. And this "progress" has increased income differences in the villages.

Whatever little fish is still caught in the estuary is highly contaminated, although the EIA report insists that "the estuary sediments in the general area are expected to be free from industrial pollutants."[2] While instruments may not detect the limited number of chemicals for which the sediments are tested, the results of pollution are visible for all to observe.

The fish are deformed and unpalatable, with a nauseous taste and smell, spoiling soon after being caught. The scales of some living fish fall off, the fins of others rot, some get paralysed, others die quickly and are often found floating belly-up in the estuary and along the coast. Those species that enter the estuary from the sea are quickly poisoned. Such contaminated fish cause serious health problems to those who consume them.

Mangroves still cover about twenty hectares on the near coastline. Four important species provide construction timber and firewood throughout the year. Crabs and some fish from the mangroves yield a considerable quantity of food. The mangrove and other tidal zones in the area form spawning grounds for a large number of fresh and salt water fish and crustaceans. The area covered by mangroves will be reduced by the project, and oil spills and toxic discharges will interfere with the breeding of fish and crustaceans.

Jetties for unloading equipment and fuel for the first phase of the project are being constructed in the estuary. The site chosen for these jetties is exactly where the most productive remaining fishing is being carried out now. A channel will have to be dredged continuously to accommodate the large cargo ships and tankers that will use it. Such dredging would seriously disturb organisms on the estuary bed.

The EIA report claims: "Although in perspective, the benefits accruing from the power project will far outweigh any losses from fisheries, every attempt will be made to protect the fisheries in Vashishti."[2] Benefits, if any, would accrue to people far away, while the costs have to be borne by the local people: the fisherfolk who will lose their livelihood and the consumers of fish who will have less protein or who will have to pay more for it.

Land Acquisition

Aware that the theoretical foundation for occupation does not rest on solid grounds, the industrial aliens provide a facade of legality before they invade rural lands.

The British enacted the Land Acquisition Act of 1894, which enabled them to take over private property for "public purposes". Although the term "public purpose" was sufficiently vague and elastic to cover most British requirements, the Maharashtra Government did not find it good enough for its objective of acquiring land for individual private industries. Accordingly, the Maharashtra Industrial Development Act, 1961, was promulgated, legalising the acquisition of land by the Maharashtra Industrial Development Corporation (MIDC), constituted to implement the Act. The public purpose clause was dropped, with acquisition now carried out in the name of "development", such "development" automatically assumed to be in the "national interest", which, of course, never includes the interests of the multitude of people harmed by acquisition. The rural populations most affected by such a law, were not consulted by the "democratically" elected legislature which enacted it. With liberalisation, the national interest has become the international interest of TNCs and foreign governments. This Act legalises the whole process of continuing physical colonisation.

The conditions for acquisition are completely arbitrary. The Act states, under the heading of Compulsory Acquisition: "If, at any time in the opinion of the State Government, any land is required for the purpose of development...the State Government may acquire such land by publishing in the Official Gazette a notice..."[10] There is no obligation to choose land that will affect the least number of people or which will do minimal damage to agriculture or the environment. Any land that industrialists covet can be acquired by the mere publication of a notice.

The Act continues: "After considering such cause, if any, shown by the owner of the land and by any other person interested therein and after giving such owner and person an opportunity of being heard the State Government may pass such orders as it deems fit."[10] All that is available to the evicted is "an opportunity of being heard", not necessarily answered. In the Dabhol case, the objections of the occupants were given in writing but no answers were received, written or oral.

The Act legitimates the use of force: "If any person refuses or fails to comply with an order made under section (5) [to surrender possession to the Government], the State Government may take possession of the land, and may for that purpose use such force as may be necessary."[10] The Act does not provide for any resettlement; it only ensures that forced displacement is legalised.

Knowing that people object strongly to such projects, the government conceals all pertinent information about it until the land acquisition notices are actually served on them. No informed consent is obtained or thought to be necessary by the authorities. Using this totally unjust law, more than 700 hectares of productive land have been acquired for the Enron project, with further acquisitions proposed for an airstrip, helipad, roads and other infrastructure.

The 1993 Resolution of the UN Commission on Human Rights, "Affirms that the practice of forced evictions constitutes a gross violation of human rights, in particular the right to adequate housing." The resolution, "Urges Governments to undertake immediate measures, at all levels, aimed at eliminating the practice of forced evictions." India is a member of this Commission, but the laws which legalise forced eviction continue to be applied.

While this UN Resolution appears revolutionary, there are several loopholes which vitiate it. The limit to "large-scale displacements"—which are not defined—implies that the displacement of individuals or small groups is not a "gross violation" of their rights. Further, by emphasising presumably urban housing, rural evictions from agricultural lands and forests are ignored, even though these may result in a total loss of livelihood.

The term "indigenous people", by UN definition, is limited to those who were displaced by invaders, and the descendants of those displaced. It is mainly in the territories occupied by migrant Europeans that a clear distinction can be made between indigenous people and other early inhabitants. While the rights of such indigenous peoples to their homelands is at least acknowledged today, other natives whose ancestors have also lived in their villages for hundreds or thousands of years cannot claim such rights. However, Article 1 of the UN UDHR states unequivocally that all human beings are born equal in rights, so it follows that the rights applying to those designated as indigenous peoples should apply to other long-resident natives. Among these are the right not to be forcibly removed from their lands (Article 10), and not to be forced to abandon their lands or means of subsistence (Article 11 [c]). This would protect people not coming under the strict definition of indigenous peoples from the incursions of the mainstream industrialists.

As these rights are not recognized, local people are, often with the use of force, thrown out of their ancestral lands. Such displacement involves a loss of livelihood, knowledge, health, dignity and other material and spiritual rights. Moreover, only the landholders are offered compensation, with all the others, including landless labourers, being left to fend for themselves. While megaprojects like large dams produce highly visible effects, small projects, mainly industries of the Western sort, when all added together, do much more damage.

The people displaced point out that they are socially, culturally and emotionally strongly bonded to their environment. Such attachment is not limited to tribals only, but to all people who have lived in a specific region for generations. With the loss of their land, goes the culture that maintained, added to and transmitted the knowledge of a self-reliant, sustainable system, from generation to generation. Such losses will be also borne by the descendants of the people for generations to come. These are all violations of the rights to culture, education, employment and health. Economic compensation for displacement from their lands or for the appropriation of their commons, assumes that every aspect of living, including mental anguish, can be monetised.

Enron got around the potential problem of resettlement with ingenuity, as some of the project-affected villagers explained: "The boundary of the land being acquired is so demarcated that residential clusters are excluded from acquisition. At some places land on three sides of a residential cluster is acquired." This tactic eliminated the need for resettlement but effectively isolated the villagers from their means of livelihood, thus forcing them to move out on their own.

The EIA report unconsciously admits that those to be dispossessed have rights as it laments that: "All these communities are well conversant with the monetary economy, are politically extremely conscious of their rights and socially well organised along caste lines." Therefore, this "displacement needs to be well planned."[?] Planned, only to ensure that people's rights are eventually overruled by Enron's political power. The statement about castes is totally false and uncalled for, unless, of course, it is intended to use, as the British did, the "divide and rule" formula.

The EIA report threatens: "As much as possible, involuntary resettlement will be avoided even though the Land Acquisition Act, 1894 and the Resettlement Act, 1989 of the Government of Maharashtra allow for involuntary resettlement." Possession of the land will be taken by the "use of such force as may be necessary." It has been reported that "if there is resistance from some farmers, the MIDC would use its powers to forcibly acquire the land..."[11]

In spite of all the blandishments and threats of the government and the DPC, few of the people were prepared to move out of their own free will. Only those who have permanently migrated to Mumbai or who have no clear title to the land have accepted the compensation doled out without any protest.

On 21 September 1995, government officials took possession of the land with the help of about 700 policemen. The people were told that if they did not accept the compensation being given, they would not get anything at all later. Policemen were stationed outside the homes of those known to be against the project while reporters and activists were prevented from entering the area.

Although the affected residents have not been driven out of their homes, they have been deprived of their sources of livelihood and are forced to migrate from the area. The displaced become people without a country, driven to the concentration slums of cities, adding to the corpus of disemployed. These new migrants cannot use their rich survival skills in cities where, in spite of their knowledge, when immersed in the Westernised urban culture, they will be treated as ignorant and have to learn how to live all over again. Such economic and mental impoverishment needs to be recognised as an abuse of the fundamental right to life.

Within a few days of Enron occupying the land, every valley was filled and every hill was laid low, every single tree, shrub and blade of grass was removed or buried and fertile soil was covered by layers of rock. Trees were felled even in the region where Enron had undertaken to keep a green belt. The EIA had claimed that the area was barren—when it was fully covered with plants. Now it is a desert.

A high barbed wire fence was erected all round with numerous armed guards as added protection. The fact that it needed such defences revealed that Enron was aware that it was not welcome to the people. Construction of the factory buildings and a jetty has been partly completed.

The land that is privatised for industry gives the owner the civil right to immediately "protect" it by high walls, barbed wire fences and armed guards, to exclude all but the new owners and their employees. Whereas the use of land for the good of the community as a whole was the first priority, now the right of individuals to own private property allows them to deprive neighbours of their natural rights and to exploit "their" property without considerations of justice or sustainability.

Democratic Disregard for People's Opinions

Those who object to being "developed" are seen as impertinent impediments to the spread of "development". The continuous encroachment by the State on people's inherent rights to autonomy to preserve their habitat and way of life merely produces an escalation in the use of force in the urban-rural war. The so-called democratic process fails miserably and, if the protests turn violent, the government acts as any other police state in suppressing the people by force. The State becomes, increasingly, a terrorist state.

The people attempted redress through legal channels. A writ petition filed in the Bombay High Court challenging the legality of the acts and the procedures for acquisition was summarily thrown out in July 1994.[12]

To suppress protest in the DPC project area, laws against assembly of more than five persons were freely used though they are against the "right to freedom of peaceful assembly and association". Further, about twenty years ago, the Supreme Court had ruled against the use of arbitrary power to ban public meetings, a ruling that is ignored with impunity.[13] Those still protesting or attempting to obstruct the construction work on the site were beaten up by the police and arrested.

The arrested were charged with bailable offences such as unlawful assembly, rioting, the use of criminal force to deter a public servant from discharging his duty and criminal intimidation. Later, the police released all the arrested and charged them immediately under sections which made it difficult for them to obtain bail. But instead of acting as a deterrent, the agitation spread, with fisherfolk—not directly aggrieved by land acquisition—joining in.

To control the situation, the district administration imposed prohibitory orders in the entire Guhagar taluka. The orders prohibit, among other things, the carrying of any implement (including agricultural tools in daily use) or weapon, the exhibition of figures or effigies, the public utterance of slogans, singing of songs and playing of music, the use of gestures or mimetic representations, and the preparation, exhibition or dissemination of pictures, symbols, placards, or any other object or thing which may in the opinion of such authority offend against decency or morality. It also prohibits any assembly or procession whenever and for so long as it (the authority) considers such prohibition to be necessary for the preservation of public order. Offenders can face imprisonment terms of up to one year and a fine.

To enforce the regulation, two platoons of the Special Reserve Police (SRP) were brought in. Such enterprises as the DPC can only come up and continue to exist with the aid of security guards, the police, perhaps even the army, and lots of guns, bullets and tear gas.

The Bharatiya Janata Party (BJP) had used the Enron deal as a major plank of its platform for the State Assembly elections held in February 1995, committing itself to closing down the project entirely. Gopinath Munde, who later became the deputy chief minister, said in a speech [translated from the Marathi]: "I have come here to promise you that I am not going to remain in the background of this fight against Enron but would be fighting along with you till the time Enron is removed from this land."

The BJP MLA from Guhagar, Vinay Natu, and several other BJP candidates were elected by a large majority, mainly on their strong anti-Enron stand. The party in conjunction with the Shiv-Sena party, also anti-Enron, won the elections.

But the State government reversed its stand after the elections. It permitted work to proceed at the site, with local bureaucrats and police giving all possible help to the company. Munde, when reminded about his promise, claimed it was only an election speech. All that the government undertook to do was to review the project in order to decide whether it was to proceed or not.

When the intention to review the project was made public, it hit panic buttons at the DPC. Rebecca Mark, the Enron CEO, descended on Mumbai, throwing arrogant tantrums around with abandon. Ms Mark openly threatened the government, exhibiting the conceit of TNCs in claiming their right to bully sovereign governments. Like Shylock, she repeatedly demanded her pound of flesh, claiming that if the project were cancelled, the Maharashtra Government would have to pay DPC a penalty of a hundred million dollars at least. She was oblivious to the fact that if the project had been accepted purely on its technical and economic merits there could be no objection to a review. The US Energy Secretary Hazel O'Leary had earlier twisted arms in Delhi to get the DPC to be given special concessions.

The Review Committee, appointed by the Government, appeared to be biased right from its inception. The affected villagers requested that all work at the project site be stopped, at least till the Committee announced its decision. Their grievance was that the speed of construction at the site was such that a mere two to three weeks would be enough for DPC to extensively damage the area, making regeneration difficult. Even those agricultural lands and plantations were being destroyed on which no project activity was planned in the near future. Properties which were not acquired but which bordered the site were also being illegally denuded and mined for construction material.

When one of the committee members mentioned resettlement, the villagers made it absolutely clear that they would accept nothing short of total withdrawal of the project from the Konkan region. Since no such assurance was given, and there was no indication at all that the government was with the villagers, the latter decided that they would carry on with nonviolent protests to get the work stopped.

To make matters worse, crime in the neighbourhood has increased after the work began. As predicted, with about 1500 workmen on the site, the local women and young girls were being increasingly harassed. One woman, peacefully passing through the site since a bypass road had not yet been constructed, was picked up in a mechanized shovel and dropped off only when villagers who heard her screams rushed to the site.

This incident led to immediate violence against the workers and their foreign supervisors. Several were mildly injured, and much of the equipment on the site was damaged. About 150 protesters were arrested on that day, more on the following days. Instead of being kept in local prisons, many of them were sent to a jail some three hundred kilometres away.

All work at the site had to be stopped and the place was completely deserted for a few days, except for the police and private security guards. In addition, the State government stationed about 150 men of the State Reserve Police on the site. Robert Bakley later claimed that the presence of State police was an indication of government support for the project but this speaks loudly of the government's support for its own people.

Some days later, three members of the Review Committee, including Gopinath Munde, visited the area, where they heard the villagers' complaints. One of the memoranda submitted by residents appealed to the Committee to kindly fire 2000 bullets in the hearts of the 2000 residents of their village, in case it decided in favour of Enron.

Immense pressures were brought to bear on the Maharashtra and Central governments by Enron, by the US government and even by the UK government, to allow the project to proceed. The US Energy Secretary publicly warned India that "failure to honour the agreements between the project partners and the various Indian governments will jeopardize not only the Dabhol project but also most, if not all, of the other private power projects being proposed for international financing."[10] The US ambassador to India, Frank Wisner, led a seven-member delegation to the BJP's leaders in an attempt to pressurize them not to cancel the Enron agreement.[14]

The British Chancellor of the Exchequer, Kenneth Clarke, leading a delegation to India, declared that "if there is a project that is signed up and the rules are changed, there is bound to be an enormous risk."[11] Such interference in the internal affairs of India are examples of democracy at work at the international level.

Similar contemptuous tactics have been used by Enron in their dealings with the government of Mozambique. Enron was keen on obtaining the contract for a $500 million gas project and pipeline from Mozambique to South Africa. For this, Enron's excellent connections with the US government came in useful. John Kachamila, Mozambique's minister of natural resources, described the methods used by the US embassy in Maputo: "There were outright threats to withhold development funds if we didn't sign, and sign soon. Their diplomats, especially Mike McKinley (deputy chief of the US embassy), pressured me to sign a deal that was not good for Mozambique....It was as if he was working for Enron." They threatened to cut $40 million in US AID for development projects in Mozambique. "If the Mozambicans think they can kill this deal and we will keep dumping money into this place, they should think again," one State Department official said. "We got calls from American senators threatening us with this and that if we didn't sign." Kachamila ultimately agreed to the deal, though he was able to obtain better terms for his country than those initially offered by Enron.[15] Till lately the CIA assisted Renamo— a terrorist force created and designed by the US and the apartheid regime in South Africa to destroy the Mozambican economy.

In the case of the DPC, the Maharashtra government gave in to the pressures to renegotiate and the project has now been allowed to proceed, the politicians being rightly accused of selling out to Enron.

But, more important, this confirms that democracy in practice is a mere farce. The people have no control over those whom they have elected, once the ballot is in the box. Further, unless the very concept of development is radically changed, whichever party gets elected, it will always be the industrial system that calls the tune. Alcide de Gasperi, the first post-war Italian president, acknowledged his government's dependence on what he called "the fourth party", the big industrialists and financiers, which forced him to adapt his policies to their needs rather than to the needs of the people.[16]

The right of the local people to decide what sort of development they want should be paramount, since ultimately they have to pay the costs. In addition to those directly affected by the project's proximity, many more will be affected to a smaller extent by the higher cost of electricity and by rising costs of industrial products produced by that electricity. Further, large numbers will be affected by the loss of their basic necessities, like cereals, pulses, fruit and vegetables which need to be exported to earn foreign exchange to allow the DPC and other TNCs to take their exorbitant profits out of the country.

It appears that no Western-type industrial project can be undertaken in countries with a high population density like India without encroaching on people's rights with the increasing use of force.

Rights to Employment

Numerous farmers, fisherfolk and landless people have been deprived of their right to employment by the Enron project. The DPC's Bakley, while not denying this, countered: "Local people now have priority over jobs at the project site. More than half of the work force of 1500 come from the affected villages.[5] But the work that is offered is only manual labour of the most monotonous and arduous sort, not to be compared with the work of self-sufficing agriculture and fishing. Moreover it is temporary, with later jobs only as domestic help to the immigrant US staff. The US Energy Secretary has admitted that employment will be mainly created in the US. The power stations being put up by US TNCs in India, she said, would "support" 34,000 jobs in the US.[17]

The DPC documents make ridiculous statements such as the following, as if this were a unique feature which gave the people of Guhagar a low status: "Due to lack of job opportunities in the area, many male members of the area work in distant cities (and even abroad) sending money home for their families." There is a lack of job opportunities in all parts of India and even in the US. The foreign technicians and management personnel of the DPC will also send money home.

The West is exporting its present unemployment, just as the English did a hundred years ago, and continues to do so along with other Westerners.

The EIA report claims that the Enron project would encourage growth of other industries in the area. "The growth would help the area's economy, create more employment opportunities and potentially reverse the outmigration trend."[2]

Enron and the industries to come, first increase "outmigration" by displacement, then claim that they will reduce it. However, most of those employed in such industries are "skilled" personnel and "professionals", brought in from Mumbai or other existing industrial centres. These newcomers add to the cultural disruption, crime and violence. Such mandatory consequences of urbanisation are not entered in the cost-benefit analysis balance sheets.

The "development" professionals and politicians are the main beneficiaries of such "progress". The extreme bias of those who promote such projects is unveiled here, in that only the "benefits" to industrialists and the Westernised economy are proclaimed, never the costs to the local people who are banished from their ancestral homelands with measly "compensation".

Environmental Rights

The Ministry of Environment and Forests (MOEF) requires that each project promoter submit an Environmental Impact Assessment (EIA) report. Enron submitted its Rapid EIA report to the MOEF in June 1993 and provisional clearance was granted on that basis. The EIA contains gross errors and omissions, intentional or otherwise, and makes several outrageous statements. Above all, it reveals how the rights to health through a clean environment are to be abused.

The erection of the power plant is totally dependent on the impoverishment of farmers, fisherfolk and artisans, yet the EIA claims that the project will benefit these unfortunates.

The report states: "The site and the area along the Vashishti river are expected to be classified as industrial area." Merely reclassifying a presently quiet and peaceful rural area into an industrial zone subjects the occupants to higher maximum allowable pollution levels, even though the people themselves do not contribute to the emissions. This is another compulsory adjunct of the development to which they have a "right".

The environmental "protection" standards merely institutionalise Lawrence Summers' economics of underpollution.

The EIA report takes pains to claim that the project site area is unpolluted, giving measurements made only when the wind direction was from the sea and not from the highly polluting Lote-Parshuram industrial area nearby.

The EIA report mentions that among the effluents which are to be monitored—presumably because they will be discharged—are the heavy metals mercury, iron, cadmium, chromium, lead, zinc, arsenic and copper.[2] Most of these accumulate in living organisms and cause serious health problems. Mercury was responsible for the Minamata disease in Japan, arsenic is a deadly poison and lead causes brain damage in children.

"Operators will be trained in plant safety and safety drills will be scheduled for plant personnel."[2] The examples of Bhopal, Chernobyl, Three Mile Island and Exxon Valdez show how effective such training is.

"The fallow and marginal agricultural land will become available to meet the demand for industrial, commercial and residential uses in the vicinity of the project....In the long term, many beneficial changes in land use and in the composition of the population will take place. Land prices will tend to increase, greater trade, transport and communication will take place."[2]

The "improvement in the composition of the population" emphasises once more the arrogant sense of superiority of urban elites. Farmers whose lands have been acquired do not benefit from future changes, particularly an increase in land prices, if benefit there be. The people to be displaced by Enron claim that the compensation promised does not take into account inflation, whereas prices of their agricultural produce would rise with inflation.

It will not be "fallow and marginal agricultural land", but fertile land which will be permanently destroyed. The ownership will change from that of small farmers to that of large industrialists and land speculators. The latter will probably use force to persuade unwilling farmers to part with their ancestral properties, as is being done in other places.

High prices will ensure that no small farmer will in the future be able to purchase land for agriculture. This has already occurred around the industrialised town of Ratnagiri. Such projects decrease agricultural output, not only because of direct occupation of land but also because the air, water and soil pollution will damage land and crops in a wide belt surrounding the factories. Even if in some areas the soils are not very fertile, they still produce some food; concrete jungles produce none.

Industrial rights now take precedence over the right to self-provisioning. While the government strictly prohibits Adivasis and other occupants of ancestral lands from using even a few wild animals and plants for food, the government itself carries out wholesale massacres of protected species in every industrial project it sets up.

The report repeatedly mentions the "management" of the environment, but it is not the environment that needs to be managed but the project which causes the damage.

Much industrial expansion is envisioned around the completed Enron project. The EIA report predicts that "the power production ... will enhance the economic and industrial growth of the region"; "ribbon development of commercial establishments, services and small industries as well as residential housing" will take place along the new roads to be constructed. The report coyly discloses: "Already one hears of plans to install a copper smelter, an oil refinery, a steel mill and chemical companies."[2]

When examining the environmental and social impacts of a large industrial project it is logical to include the impact of future "development" in the same region. However, the MOEF examines and clears each project individually, their sum and synergy deliberately ignored. The reports show that each of the numerous proposed projects requires the eviction of only a small number of local people, the acquisition of only a few hectares of agricultural lands, the clearance of small patches of forests, and the production of pollution below specified limits. Each project shows little damage to the ecosystems, thus making each enterprise appear socially and environmentally innocuous, allowing it to be expeditiously cleared. The process of creeping colonisation, the gradual extension of the industrial frontiers, thus carries on smoothly, environmental protection laws to the contrary. After a few of the "environmentally safe" projects start operating, the damage becomes easily visible, but additional projects can still be cleared to operate in the area.

Official environmental guidelines place limits of 500 tonnes/day on sulphur dioxide emissions in unpolluted industrial areas, falling to 100 tonnes per day in polluted areas, from single projects.

The total emissions of all industries expected to come up in the regions should be below the limits of 500 tonnes/day, otherwise such limits become meaningless. The DPC's own emissions are just at the limit of 100 tonnes/day.[2]

The EIA report claims that the "positive effect of improved communication and health services will lead to a decrease in death rates..."[2] There is no indication at all that there will be improved health services for the local people. It is far more likely that such a traumatic event will cause immense stress in the population which, together with the accompanying heavy pollution, will lead to increased disease and higher death rates, though this could benefit the commercial suppliers of health services.

The EIA report sees urbanisation of the area as a positive benefit to the local people though it admits that some problems accompany it. "Industrialisation, availability of power and good transport and communications are the three major factors of urbanisation and induce major land changes....In the general area, outside the permanent housing colony, the problems accompanying urbanisation, namely petty crimes, alcoholism, etc, may appear."[2]

"With substantial additional population gathering around the project area, bottlenecks due to demand exceeding supply are to be expected...with regard to water, housing, medical and educational facilities."[2] In standard economics theory, when demand exceeds supply, prices must rise. Not mentioned in such theory, however, is that a large layer of the population who are unable to pay such prices will be deprived of their essential needs.

An example of such "development" has taken place in Lote-Parshuram, which, the EIA report claims, "is already a well developed Maharashtra Industrial Development Corporation (MIDC) area."[2] "Well developed" for whom? Absolutely not for the people who were displaced. Certainly not for the remaining population who, having seen such "progress" in operation for the last twenty years, contested in court the expansion of the estate by another 500 hectares. Not for the surrounding farmers who have seen their water polluted, their soil degraded and their crops ruined by leaks of liquid wastes from storage tanks, pools and corroded pipelines, and by leaching from solid waste dumps. Not for those who have seen their rights to health and life affected by poisoned food who must now drink toxic water and breathe

polluted air. Not for those who fished in the Vashishti river right
down to the Dabhol estuary, who have seen the fish dying or spiced
by a cocktail of toxic chemicals. Not for the factory workers, either,
exposed to workplace toxins and accidents.

In August 1994, six workers died and thirty-five were admitted for treatment for toxic gas inhalation, when a reactor in a
pesticide factory exploded, the third major accident at this plant.
No action was taken when—before the tragedy—local residents
had made several complaints.

The chemical industries at Lote-Parshuram no doubt solemnly vowed, when applying for clearances, to treat their wastes
before discharge. Yet, neither the MIDC nor the Maharashtra
Pollution Control Board (MPCB) have taken any action to prevent
the highly polluting liquid wastes which those same industries are
discharging directly into the Vashishti river. The MPCB and the
factory inspectors department have an abysmally low reputation
because of their sheer negligence and impotency. Industrialists are
also expert at evading laws; many of them discharge their pollutants only at night. Such practices give many industries in India an
international comparative advantage, additional to those of cheaply
acquired land and the exploitable manual labour that those displaced by the same industries provide.

The Right to Information

The liberalisation process is designed to facilitate a transfer
of wealth from the considerably impoverished to the already rich.
This is such an unadulterated offensive matter that the truth, if it
cannot be hidden, requires to be covered with multiple lamina-
tions of lies. The new propaganda machines operate on the simple
assumption that if lies and half-truths are repeated often enough
people will firmly believe in them. This has to be accompanied by
strict censorship of any information opposing the process. Enron
has made full use of these principles in defending its indefensible
project.

In a war of words, TNCs and other big businesses have the
advantage that they can spend lavishly to present a false image. In
a large advertisement, the DPC declared: "Nothing was done
secretly. There was total transparency at every stage of the negotiations. There is no secret clause in the Power Purchase Agreement

(PPA)."[18] All this was said even while the DPC claimed that its EIA report and the PPA were confidential documents. The publication of details of the PPA made clear why the company and the government tried so desperately to conceal this contract. The contract protected the DPC from any risks while at the same time guaranteeing it excessive profits. The Dabhol project would impoverish the State of Maharashtra. It is difficult to believe that such profitable and one-sided terms were obtained without considerable twisting of arms and/or greasing of palms.

Referring to the Foreign Corrupt Practices Act, Sutton said "no short cuts had been taken in the Dabhol project", whose sponsors were three large American companies "with high ethical and moral standards."[19] Their known track record, however, shows that these companies have frequently taken short cuts and have been charged with and often convicted of a whole range of crimes, including some under the Act mentioned. Frauds were committed against the US Defence Department, and in Puerto Rico, in Israel, in the Philippines, and probably in many other countries. The offences, whether environmental or financial fraud, were repeated again and again, even after convictions, heavy fines and imprisonment of the officials involved. If such behaviour is so common in the US, where both the government and environmental groups are vigilant, one can scarcely expect them to become angels of mercy here.[20]

Falsehoods—under oath—have been liberally uttered in Indian courts and even in the US House of Representatives by Linda Powers. She claimed that Enron had already spent $20 million on "medical, educational, employment and other benefits."[6] At the time she gave that testimony, nothing at all had been spent on medical, educational and other benefits.

When articles in the press became too threatening to Enron, several reporters were requested by their editors to stop being critical of the project. When the stick would not work, carrots did. One prominent critic's husband was given an important job in the DPC, seducing her to write favourably on the project. While reports of agitation by the local people against the project were mentioned regularly in the local Marathi newspapers, stories in English papers in cities were limited or even totally absent.

Even in environmental matters, the liberalisation regime is vigorously protecting industry's right to violate rights. Rules that made important documents on new projects, such as project reports and environmental impact assessments mandatorily available to the public, have all been made discretionary to the MOEF, thus nullifying the right to information.

Justice K K Mathew has observed: "The people of this country have a right to know every public act, everything that is done in a public way, by their public functionaries....The right to know which is derived from the concept of freedom of speech, though not absolute, is a factor which should make one wary, when secrecy is claimed for transactions which can, at any rate, have no repercussion on the public security....Such secrecy can seldom be legitimately desired. It is generally desired for the purpose of parties and politics or personal self-interest or bureaucratic routine. The responsibility of officials to explain and to justify their acts is the chief safeguard against oppression and corruption."[21]

Developing Injustice

One of the most blatant abuses of human rights occurs in the growth in inequity which the setting up of new industries usually promote.

Huge quantities of fresh water will be required for construction and for domestic use by the project's staff. This is to be supplied from a reservoir, which at present sustains about 12,000 residents in its neighbourhood. The water fills their limited needs for a whole year when the monsoon is good but not when the rains are below normal or delayed. There is, therefore, no excess water in the reservoir to cater to the enormous quantities required by the project, so the present users are bound to suffer.

The EIA report admits that the presence of nearly 4000 construction labourers "has the potential to have a considerable socio-economic impact on surrounding villages whose population together is also about 4000."[2] The latter figure is incorrectly low, but the enormous increase in the population will substantially boost the local prices of food and other essentials.

"The initial construction activities and developments will make the area an attractive place for people to move in or return to the area."[2] Attractive for outsiders, but for the local people? "Because of an influx of construction workers, the current sex ratio will be changed. At present, the sex ratio is biased in favour of females."² The influx of 4000 males will cause immense gender-related problems, including harassment and rape.

"Health problems are also likely to be experienced in the area as a result of migrant labour being careless about personal hygiene and mosquito and fly-borne infections prevalent in the area..."² It is far more likely that the workers will bring in resistant strains or strains of a host of serious illnesses to which the local people are not immune. The situation will closely parallel the transfer of diseases by the Europeans into the territories they occupied and the resulting extermination of natives.

"The construction phase may also witness some social problems such as alcoholism, gambling, etc, typical of any development project site....The culture of the migrants may be alien to the local population. Therefore...clashes can be expected. This may lead to a feeling of insecurity among the local people."² Such cultural degradation is presented as a normal accompaniment of industrialisation, which it is.

A housing colony for "non-manual employees" is to be located on a forty hectare plot. "Once the project is commissioned 150 to 200 project personnel with their families will live in the project township. These will be a skilled and professional group of people with relatively high incomes."² The racism of TNCs is evident: they see nothing wrong in taking away all the land of the natives to provide "professionals", mainly foreigners, with 2000 square metres per family.

The EIA report claims that one of the benefits that the project will bestow on the people is that the professionals "will require additional people to provide them the necessary services."² Perhaps the local people have to be thankful that, while the Europeans turned the original American inhabitants into slaves or slaughtered them, here they will be merely "providing services" to the new invaders. This is how "development" trickles down.

The invading population, moreover, will be provided with facilities including "an elementary school, retail shops, civic facilities such as post office, fire station and health centre; and recreational facilities."²It is doubtful whether local villagers, who do not have such necessities now, would be allowed access to these facilities. Most likely the whole area will be enclosed within a modern "stockade", well insulated from the original inhabitants.

The Final Solution

Thomas Jefferson's prophecy of the US "traversing all the seas with the rich productions of their industry, engaged in commerce with nations who feel power and forget right", has come true.[22] Jefferson and others claimed that the Europeans were superior to all other "races" and this gave them the right to exterminate them. The elites apparently believe that to them "belong the destinies of the future", that they are "the noblest division of the human species."[23]

Might becomes right in the enforcement of the "involuntary resettlement" of those who would rest content with a simple happy life-style. The TNCs with much local assistance, attempt to exterminate the project-affected people by slow death through loss of livelihood leading to starvation.

Francis Parkman predicted that the American Natives "were destined to melt and vanish before the advancing waves of Anglo-American power."[24] So too, the rural subsistence farmer is destined to melt and vanish before the advancing surges of Westernised industrial and agricultural power.

Europeans claimed that they were not responsible for the deaths of millions of the Natives since the latter died of diseases inadvertently brought in by them. In a similar manner, the new industrialists and politicians claim they are not responsible for the millions who are dying because of the new pollution diseases, intrinsic by-products of industrialisation.

G Stanley Hall gloated that the "lower races" were being extirpated as "weeds in the human garden", an inevitable process since they were "primitive races" which were "either hopelessly decadent and moribund, or at best have demonstrated their inability to domesticate or civilise themselves."[25] Traditional farmers and fisherfolk are the industrial equivalent of "primitive races". Their ancient, but stable and sustainable systems, appear moribund compared to the frenetic pace at which "civilised" Westerners are destroying life on this planet. They can therefore be "extirpated as weeds" by those who employ their political might, without pity and sympathy, that being their main claim to be the fittest, the leading edge of human evolution.

Theodore Roosevelt pontificated that the extermination of the American Natives and the expropriation of their lands "was as

ultimately beneficial as it was inevitable. Such conquests are sure
to come when a masterful people...finds itself face to face with the
weaker and wholly alien race which holds a coveted prize in its
feeble grasp."[26] The coveted land is held in the feeble grasp of
farmers, who are treated as if they were "utterly shiftless" and
"worthless" by Western-oriented gentlemen. The latter believe
that the spread of Westernised industrialisation is inevitable and
immediately beneficial, taught so by the "masterful" Westerners to
the "weaker and wholly alien", "undeveloped" peoples of the Two
Thirds World.

In the current war, waged by the urban elites, the owners or
cultivators of land are treated as superfluous and expendable,
modern human sacrifices to the Western supreme god Mammon.
Farmers are today tolerated only because they still provide the
food, industrial raw materials and export earnings without which
the elite urbanite cannot live "the good life". But once manufacturing industry and industrialised agriculture release the urbanites
from such bondage, they will be able to import all their needs and
wants using the foreign exchange earned by industrial exports. At
least, so goes the theory.

It is not only the farmers who lose out but also the rest of the
country since the former producers of food now become consumers only and though it be ever so little, as the demand increases,
prices rise a bit. Enron will not produce food though it may claim
that its electricity could pump water for irrigation and so increase
productivity somewhere else. But with high prices of unsubsidised
electricity, farmers will not grow food, only the most expensive
cash crops, so the price of food must rise further.

Columbus, searching for signs of wealth, sent "two men
upcountry." He wrote: "They travelled for three days, and found
an infinite number of small villages and people without number,
but nothing of importance."[27] Today, the urban elites proclaim in
similar manner that the occupants of the lands they covet are
"nothing of importance."

The Melancholy Opponents

Andrew Jackson, in his second annual message to Congress,
observed that while some people tended to grow "melancholy"
over the Indians being driven by White Americans to their "tomb",

an understanding of "true philanthropy reconciles the mind to these vicissitudes as it does to the extinction of one generation to make room for another."[28]

Today's elites blame environmentalists and defenders of human rights for being unduly "melancholy" over the fate of the displaced. True capitalist ideology reconciles the mind to these "vicissitudes" of the victims who have to sacrifice all in the sacred interest of "development" and its eternally elusive trickle down benefits.

Conclusion

The Dabhol project is just one small example of Western "development". Such "development" enriches a few people as seen by the increasing affluence of the middle and upper classes, but this occurs only at the hidden cost of the denial of rights of millions of others.

A rapidly increasing number of people in India will have their rights violated by similar projects in the future. No rights to ancestral land, forest, farm or fishing-ground can ever be secure. No self-reliant, independent community of people can ever live in the certainty that they will be allowed undisturbed access to what they have regarded as their common sources of livelihood for centuries.

The industrialisation promoted by the likes of Enron is undertaken in the belief that "development" can proceed with the natural sustainable capital of soil, water, air, plants and animals, replaced by the artificial capital of Westernised industries inhabiting concrete jungles. Such a belief rests on the assumption that food and other basic necessities will be obtained from some other region, either where the "locals" unfortunately do not have the "advantages" of "development", or from foreign sources. But there is no guarantee that basic necessities will be available, particularly when they will need to be humbly sought from foreigners who have openly said that they will use food as a weapon.[29]

Agricultural economists reiterate that the per capita agricultural land holding is decreasing rapidly, yet the government is prepared to cover this productive soil with permanently sterile concrete. When realisation finally dawns that these policies are ruining the country, it may be too late to take corrective action and reverse the process. The "dead" buildings in the concrete jungles do not decay into chemicals that can be assimilated by plants, and cannot be composted, recycled or reused. They will occupy precious land for ever. It may not be possible, even after decades, for the soil to recover from pollutants, or for underground water sources to return to their pristine purity. The process has to be stopped now if the right to food is to be protected.

In attempts to do just this, writ petitions were filed in the Bombay High Court by the people locally affected by the project challenging the validity of the acquisition laws and by a consumer organisation protesting the high cost of electricity to be provided by the DPC, and by activists concerned with environmental and social justice issues. In addition, protests have been launched by trade unions and a number of other concerned organisations. Power engineers and economists have criticized the project because of its high capital and electricity costs. But modern democracy ignores all such people's protests; the cases have been summarily dismissed. The people of the area are left with no option but to nonviolently defend their land and homes from trespassing employees of the DPC.

The US invaded Haiti, giving as its compelling reason the abuse of human rights, including the lack of democracy, by the native regime. However, the subversion of a country's sovereignty by the US government and its TNCs in collusion with the WB, IMF and WTO, is not considered a desecration of democracy. The impoverishment of thousands of forcibly displaced persons, with their possible starvation and death, the poisoning of people, the dissemination of false information, are not considered abuses of the rights to life, health and education. It is not the petty dictators in Haiti and Iraq who are the main abusers of human rights but the West and the power elites here.

Notes and References

Chapter 1: A Brief History of Human Rights Violations

1. Sale, Kirkpatrick, *The Conquest of Paradise*, Hodder & Stoughton, London, 1990, p 32.
2. Ibid. p 245.
3. Ibid. p 249.
4. Nef, John U, "An Early Energy Crisis and its Consequences", *Scientific American*, November 1977, p 140.
5. Ponting, Clive, *A Green History of the World*, Sinclair Stevenson, Solihull, UK, 1991, p 130.
6. Crosby, Alfred W., *Ecological Imperialism: The Biological Expansion of Europe, 900-1900*, Cambridge Univ. Press, Canto edition, 1993, p 199.
7. Taliman, Valerie, "Waste Merchants Intentionally Poison Natives", *WISE*, 28 March 1993, p 10.
8. Stannard, David E, *American Holocaust: The Conquest of the New World*, Oxford University Press, New York, 1993, p 268.
9. Sale, op. cit. p 154.
10. More, Thomas, *Utopia*, 1516, Dent edition, p 70.
11. Jennings, Francis, *The Invasion of American Indians, Colonialism, and the Cant of Conquest*, Chapel Hill: Univ North Carolina Press, 1975, pp 82, 135-138, quoted in Stannard, op. cit. p 234.
12. Winthrop, John, "Reasons to be Considered, and Objections with Answers", quoted in Stannard, op. cit. p 235.
13. R.C., "Reasons and Considerations Touching Upon the Lawfulness of Removing Out of England into the Parts of America", quoted in Stannard, op. cit. p 235.
14. Williams, Roger, "A Key into the Language of America (1643)", quoted in Stannard, op. cit. p 236.
15. Locke, John, *Two Treatises of Government*, ed. Laslett, Peter, Cambridge University Press, 1960, quoted in Stannard, op. cit. p 234.
16. Belich, James, *The New Zealand Wars and the Victorian Interpretation of Racial Conflict*, Auckland University Press, 1986, p 299, quoted in Stannard, op. cit. p 244.

17. Hietala, "Manifest Design", quoted in Chomsky, Noam, *Year 501, The Conquest Continues*, South End Press, Boston, 1993, p 28.

18. Quoted in Takaki, Ronald T., *Iron Cages: Race and Culture in 19th Century America*, cf. Stannard, op. cit. p 240.

19. From "Inaugural Addresses of the Presidents of the United States", Washington, D C, Government Printing Office, 1965, p 13, quoted in Stannard, op. cit. p 240.

20. Chomsky, Noam, *Year 501: The Conquest Continues*, South End Press, Boston, 1993, p 22.

21. Quoted in Dyer, Thomas G, *Theodore Roosevelt and the Idea of Race*, Baton Rouge, Louisiana State University Press, 1980, cf. Stannard, op. cit. p 245.

22. Farrar, Frederick and H K Rusden, quoted in Evans, Raymond, et al, *Exclusion, Exploitation, and Extermination: Race Relations in Colonial Queensland*, cf. Stannard, op. cit. p 244.

23. Stannard, op. cit. p 255.

24. Sunderland, J T, *India In Bondage*, Publ R Chatterjee, Calcutta, 1929, p 132.

25. Ibid. p 67.

26. Purandare, B M, "Denotified Tribals The Worst Off", *The Times of India*, 19 May 1987.

27. Sunderland, op. cit. p 64.

28. Ibid. p 389.

29. Ibid. p 119.

30. Ibid. p 117.

31. Ibid. p 118.

32. Ibid. p 120.

33. Spear, Percival, *Oxford History of Modern India: 1740-1975*, Oxford University Press, Bombay, 1994, p 341.

34. Sunderland, op. cit. p 381.

35. Ibid. p 388.

36. Alvares, Claude, *Decolonising History: Technology and Culture in India, China and the West 1500 to the Present Day*, The Other India Press, Mapusa, Goa, 1997. p 159.

37. Chomsky, Noam, "Human Rights In The New World Order", Speech delivered at Liberty's Human Rights Convention, Friday 16th June 1995, p 3.

38. Sutherland, op. cit. p 34.

39. For a detailed discussion see Chapter 6: "The Fabric of Industrialism", in Pereira, Winin and Jeremy Seabrook, *Global Parasites*, Earthcare Books, Bombay, 1994.

40. *Encyclopaedia Britannica*, 1995, CD-ROM 2.

41. Seshagiri, N, *The Food Weapon*, National Book Trust, New Delhi, 1979, p 195.

42. *Encyclopaedia Britannica*, 15th Ed, 1985, Vol 21, pp 753, 799.

43. Chomsky, Noam, *Deterring Democracy*, Vintage Books, London, 1992, p 182.

44. Chomsky, 1993, op. cit. p 23.

45. *Encyclopaedia Britannica*, op. cit. Vol 21, p 797.

46. Black, Maggie, "The End Of Total War", *New Internationalist*, February 1992, p 20.

47. Subrahmanyam, K, "The Nazi Legacy: Auschwitz And Nuclear Hypocrisy", *The Times of India*, 31 January 1995.

48. Quoted in Dower, John W, *War Without Mercy: Race and Power in the Pacific War*, Pantheon Books, New York, 1986, p 64, cf. Stannard, op. cit. p 252.

49. Anon, "SS Member Was Also An 'Important American'", *The Asian Age*, 12 April 1995.

50. Kristof, Nicholas D, "Japan Hoped To Wage Biological Warfare On U.S. During World War II", *The Times of India*, 21 March 1995.

51. Waldron, Jeremy, ed., *Nonsense Upon Stilts: Bentham, Burke And Marx On The Rights Of Man*, Methuen, London, 1987, p 154.

52. *Encyclopaedia Britannica*, op. cit. Vol 29, p 142.

53. Muzaffar, Chandra, *Human Rights and the New World Order*, Just World Trust, Penang, 1993, p 15.

54. Ibid. p vi.

55. Natarajan, C R, "US Biased", *The Economic Times*, 23 February 1995.

56. Muzaffar, op. cit. p 21.

57. *Encyclopaedia Britannica*, op. cit. Vol 29, p 142.

58. *Encyclopaedia Britannica*, op. cit. Vol 29, p 143.

59. Muzaffar, op. cit. p 149.

60. Anon, "Censure The Censor", *The Times of India*, 17 November 1995.

Chapter 3: The Right to Life

1. Anon, "Right to Hold Gun a Passion in America, *The Times of India*, 27 March 1995.

2. Parekh, B, "Gandhi's Concept of Ahimsa", *Alternatives*, April 1988, p 195.

3. Muzaffar, Chandra, "Rethinking the Concept of Human Rights", *IDOC Internazionale*, 1993/4, p 8.

4. Williams, Raymond, *Culture and Society 1780-1950*, Penguin Books, Harmondsworth, UK, 1968, p 305.

5. See Chapter 6: "Interconnections of Violence", Pereira, Winin and Jeremy Seabrook, *Asking the Earth*, The Other India Press, Mapusa, Goa, India, 1992.

Chapter 4: Democratic Rights

1. Dharampal, "Europe And The Non-European World Since 1492-1991", *PPST Bulletin*, June 1992, p 8.

2.   Chomsky, Noam, "Human Rights In The New World Order", Speech delivered at Liberty's Human Rights Convention, Friday 16th June 1995, p 9.

3.   Majumdar, Asim, "U.S. Human Rights Postures: A Case of the Pot & the Kettle", *Amrita Bazar Patrika*, 29 December, 1993.

4.   Goddard, H H, *Psychology of the Normal and Subnormal*, Dodd, Mead & Co, 1919, p 237-246, quoted in Gould, Stephen J, *The Mismeasure of Man*, W W Norton, New York, 1981, p 161.

5.   Navarro, Vicente, "Dangerous To Your Health: Capitalism In Health Care", *Monthly Review Press*, New York, 1993, p 32.

6.   Chomsky, Noam, *Year 501: The Conquest Continues*, South End Press, Boston, 1993, p 38.

7.   Kramer, Michael, "Rescuing Boris", *Time International*, 15 July 1996, p 28.

8.   *Encyclopaedia Britannica*, 15th Ed, 1985, Vol 29, p 177.

9.   Anon, "US Banker Nominated WB Chief", *Indian Express*, 13 March 1995.

10.   Reiffers, Jean-Louis, et al, *Transnational Corporations And Endogenous Development*, UNESCO, 1982, p 96.

11.   "Bechtel Group, Inc.", *Hoover's Handbook of American Business*, USA, 1994.

12.   McCartney, Laton, *Friends in High Places: The Bechtel Story: the Most Secret Corporation and How It Engineered the World*, Simon and Schuster, New York, 1988, p 87.

13.   Hayes, Peter, et al, "Korea: A Nuclear Bonanza", *Multinational Monitor*, May 1984, p 17.

14.   Anon, "Kissinger Worth $30 m", *Financial Express*, 2 April 1992.

15.   Wolff, Simon, "How To Win Funds and Influence People", *New Scientist*, 1 February 1992, p 57.

16.   Chomsky, op. cit. ref 2, p 12.

17.   Pearce, Fred, "Britain's Abandoned Empire", *New Scientist*, 23 April 1994, p 26.

18.   Lobe, Jim, "Mauritius: A Case History Of US Press Ignorance", *Third World Network Features*, No 805, 1991.

19.   Anon, "UK Must Aid Democracy In HK: Patten", *The Economic Times*, 11 April 1993.

20.   Stephens, Philip, "Major Attacks China's Human Rights Record", *The Times of India*, 5 September 1991.

21.   Chomsky, op. cit. ref 6, p 31.

22.   Ibid. p 43.

23.   Morrison, David C, "Reagan's Secret Soldiers", *South*, October 1985, p 37.

24.   Gutman, W E, "Politics Of Assassination: The Bloody Legacy Of The U.S. Army School of the Americas", *Z Magazine*, September 1995, p 54.

25. Chomsky, op. cit. ref 6, p 190.
26. Ibid. p 36.
27. Herman, Edward S and Noam Chomsky, *Manufacturing Consent, The Political Economy Of Mass Media*, Pantheon Books, New York, 1988, p 71.
28. Ibid. p 72.
29. Russell, Grahame, *The Hand Behind the Guns*, Toward Freedom, UK, October 1995.
30. Chakravorti, Robi, "Free Press And Realpolitik", *Economic & Political Weekly*, 22 July 1995, p 1838.
31. Herman, op. cit. pp 73, 77.
32. Chomsky, op. cit. ref 6, p 28.
33. Ibid. p 30.
34. Ibid. p 29.
35. Weiner, Tim, "CIA Funded Guatemalan Military", *The Times of India*, 3 April 1995.
36. Anon, "11 Executed In Guatemala", *The Asian Age*, 12 October 1995.
37. *The US Invasion of Panama: The Truth Behind Operation 'Just Cause'*, The Independent Commission of Inquiry on the US Invasion of Panama, South End Press, Boston, 1991, quoted in "The Reasons Why", *New Internationalist*, October 1991, p 15.
38. Anon, "Panama Likes Democracy But Wants Something Else Too", *The Economist*, 2 February 1991, p 39.
39. Cockburn, Alexander and Andrew Cohen, "Explosive Mix", *New Internationalist*, October 1991, p 14.
40. Danner, Mark, *The Massacre at El Mozote*, Vintage Books, quoted in *The Economist*, 18 June 1994, p 97.
41. Herman, op. cit. p 29.
42. Ibid. pp 186, 192.
43. Ibid. p 178.
44. Ibid. p 203.
45. Anon, "War Stories", *New Internationalist*, February 1991, p 18.
46. Herman, op. cit. p 197.
47. Ibid. p 184.
48. Harris, Greg, NBC-TV, 27 October 1967, quoted in Herman, op. cit. p 203.
49. Herman, op. cit. p 205.
50. Lal, Sham, "Myths And Realities", *Mainstream*, 9 February 1991, p 7.
51. Kemf, Elizabeth, "Casualties Of Vietnam's recovery", *New Scientist*, 14 September 1991, p 40.
52. Herman, op. cit. p 242.
53. Ibid. p 240.
54. Ibid. p 33.
55. Brazier, Chris, "Changing Charity", *New Internationalist*, February 1992, p 4.

56. Anon, "Talks On East Timor Postponed", *The Asian Age*, 9 April 1995.
57. Noorani, A G, "Imperialist Intrigue And International Law", review of *The Kuwait Crisis: Basic Documents*, Grotius Publications, UK, *Economic & Political Weekly*, 15 June 1991, p 1458.
58. Bennis, Phyllis and Michel Moushabeck, ed., *Beyond the Storm: A Gulf Crisis Reader*, Canongate, Edinburgh, UK, 1992, pp 356, 358.
59. Chomsky, op. cit. ref 6, p 48.
60. Clark, Ramsey, et al, *War Crimes: A Report on United States War Crimes Against Iraq*, Maisonneuve Press, Washington D C, 1992, p 66.
61. Muzaffar, Chandra, *Human Rights and the New World Order*, Just World Trust, Penang, 1993, p 153.
62. Hedges, Chris, "Turkey To Keep Force Inside Iraq Indefinitely", *The Times of India*, 26 March 1995.
63. Pilger, John, "How the US Bought Itself Control of the Gulf War", *Third World Network Features*, No 956, 1992.
64. Clark, Ramsey, *The Fire This Time: U.S. War Crimes In The Gulf*, Thunder's Mouth Press, New York, 1992, p 153.
65. Ibid. p 170.
66. Smythe, Tony, "Gulf War A Disaster For All Concerned", *The Guardian Weekly*, 30 June 1991.
67. Anon, *New York Times*, 17 January 1991.
68. Anon, *Time*, 28 January 1991, quoted in de Alwis, Mala, "A Feminist Critique Of Gulf War", *Economic & Political Weekly*, 7 September 1991, p 2086.
69. de Alwis, Mala, "A Feminist Critique Of Gulf War", *Economic & Political Weekly*, 7 September 1991, p 2086.
70. Clark, Ramsey, op. cit. ref 63, p 94.
71. Shourie, Dharam, "U.S. Firm On Exercising Veto To Frustrate Lifting Of Embargo On Iraq", *The Times of India*, 8 March 1995.
72. Sivard, Ruth Leger, et al, *World Military And Social Expenditures 1993*, 15th ed, World Priorities, Washington D C, 1993, p 56.
73. Clark, Ramsey, op. cit. ref 63, p 109.

Chapter 5: The Right to Development

1. Chomsky, Noam, *Year 501: The Conquest Continues*, South End Press, Boston, 1993, p 38.
2. Ibid. p 35.
3. Human Rights: Vienna Declaration 25 June 1993, *PUCL Bulletin*, August 1993, p 27.
4. Majumdar, Asim, "PSEs: the Liberators' Milch Cows", *Amrita Bazar Patrika*, 28 March 1995.
5. Khor, Martin, "Structural Adjustment Degrades", *Our Planet*, No 7.1, 1995, p 20.
6. Sommer, Mark, "Free trade or fixed trade? Nafta in deep trouble", *The Asian Age*, 12 March 1996.

7. Silverstein, Ken and Alexander Cockburn, "Who Broke Mexico? The Killers And The Killing", *The Ecologist*, January/February 1995, p 2.
8. Muzaffar, Chandra, *Human Rights And The New World Order*, Just World Trust, Penang, 1993, p 167.
9. Oil and Gas Journal, 28 December 1992, quoted in Sastry, G R N, "Status and Future of Petrochemical Industry in Gulf Cooperation Council (GCC) States", *Chemical Weekly*, 28 February 1995, p 129.
10. De Meyer, Daniele, "Man's Quest For Development Leaves Mother Earth Threatened", *The Asian Age*, 15 October 1995.
11. Toynbee, Arnold, "Mankind and Mother Earth", page 6, quoted in O'Mahony, Patrick J, *The Fantasy of Human Rights*, Mayhew-McCrimmon, 1978, p 157.
12. Anon, "US-China Ties To Be Delinked For Human Rights: Christopher", *The Economic Times*, 22 December 1995.
13. Jain, Ajit, "Canada To Soften Stand On Human Rights Violations", *Indian Express*, 15 February 1995.
14. Sharma, L K, "New International Aid With Strings", *The Times of India*, 19 August 1991.
15. Sunderland, J T, *India in Bondage*, Publ R Chatterjee, Calcutta, 1929, p 24.
16. Anon, "Copenhagen Alternative Document: An NGO Statement", *Vikalp*, Vol 4.1, 1995, p 47.
17. *Social Summit: Report of the World Summit for Social Development* (Copenhagen 6-12 March 1995), UN, April 1995, Commitment 10 (c), p 33.
18. Ibid. paragraph 17, p 109.
19. Ibid. paragraph 14, p 6.
20. Ibid. paragraph 4, p 5.
21. Ibid. paragraph 1 (n), p 13.
22. Ibid. paragraph 6, p 5.
23. Ibid. paragraph 26 (k), p 10.
24. Ibid. Commitment 1 (e), p 12.
25. Ibid. Commitment 1 (k), p. 12.
26. Edit, "Matter Of Development", *The Economic Times*, 25 January 1995.
27. Anon, "U.S. Houses Largest Number Of Prisoners", *The Times of India*, 6 December 1995.
28. Chomsky, Noam, "Human Rights In The New World Order", Speech delivered at Liberty's Human Rights Convention, Friday 16th June 1995, p 12.
29. Bandarage, Asoka, "Population And Development: Towards A Social Justice Agenda", *Vikalp*, October 1994, p 11.
30. Rajghatta, Chidanand, "New Arms Twisting Policy To Be Instrument Of US Foreign Plan", *Indian Express*, 19 February 1995.
31. Sivard, Ruth Leger, et al, *World Military and Social Expenditures*, World Priorities, USA, 1993, p 5.

32. Chomsky, op. cit. ref 28, p 6.
33. Baxi, Upendra, "A Work In Progress?": United States' Report To UN Human Rights Committee", *Economic & Political Weekly*, 3 February 1996, p 283.
34. Seshagiri, N, *The Food Weapon*, National Book Trust, New Delhi, 1979, pp 191, 193.
35. Beedham, Brian, "Breaking Free: A Survey of Defence in the 21st Century", *The Economist*, 5 September 1992.
36. Morris, Janet and Chris Morris, *Nonlethality: A Global Strategy*, Massachusetts, 1994, p 3.
37. Ibid. p 10.
38. Ibid. p 6.
39. Dalyell, Tam, "A Strong Odour of Fish", *New Scientist*, 18 November 1995, p 74.
40. Parasuram, T V, "Clinton Ignores Human Rights, Alleges HRA", *The Economic Times*, 9 December 1995.
41. Chomsky, op. cit. ref 1, p 48.

Chapter 6: The Right to Food and Health

1. Keatinge, G F, "Agricultural Progress in Western India", *The Poona Agricultural College Magazine*, July 1913, p 3.
2. Seymour, Jane, "Hungry for a new revolution", *New Scientist*, 30 March 1996, p 32.
3. See chapter 4, "The Diversion of Food," in Pereira Winin, *Tending the Earth*, Earthcare Books, Mumbai, 1993.
4. Chowdhury, Zafrullah, *Politics of Essential Drugs*, Vistaar Publications, New Delhi, 1996, p 140.
5 Quoted in Berry, Wendell, *The Unsettling of America: Culture & Agriculture*, Sierra Club Books, San Francisco, 1986, p 8.
6. Seshagiri, N, *The Food Weapon*, National Book Trust, New Delhi, 1979, p 7.
7. Ibid. p 24.
8. McNeil, Maggie, "US To Use Muscle To Hike Food Sales", *The Times of India*, 15 April 1995.
9. Das, Monalisa, "What helps US wheat grower is good for S Indians!", *The Economic Times*, 20 February 1996.
10. Kakkar, Renu M R, "Will India Trip Over TRIPS?", *Indian Express*, 30 April 1991.
11. See Pereira, Winin, Chapter 4: "The Diversion of Food" in *Tending the Earth*, Earthcare Books, Bombay, 1993.
12. Chowdhury, op. cit. p 2.
13. Ibid. p 4.
14. Ibid. p 63.
15. Ibid. p 71.

16. Ibid. p 73.
17. Ibid. p 74.
18. Ibid. p 151.
19. Ibid. pp 154, 155.
20. Ibid. p 76.
21. Ibid. p 135.
22. Ibid. p 136.
23. Ibid. p 141.
24. Navarro, Vicente, *Dangerous To Your Health: Capitalism In Health Care*, Monthly Review Press, New York, 1993, p 16.
25. Edit, "Over The Odds", *The Times of India*, 28 February 1995.
26. Antia, N H, "Heal Thyself", *The Times of India*, 16 February 1995.
27. Ghoshal, Sumit and Quaied Najmi, "Kidney Racket Prompts Move To Screen Aliens", *Indian Express*, 26 February 1995.
28. Anon, "Mortality Rate Of US Blacks Is Highest", *Indian Express*, 12 February 1995.
29. Anon, "EC firms dump banned drugs in Third World", *Third World Resurgence*, January 1992, p 11.
30. Bal Arun and Anil Pilgaonkar, "Counterfact On Analgin", *Economic & Political Weekly*, 4 March 1989, p 445; and "Dangerous Drugs", *Economic & Political Weekly*, 21 November 1987, p 1979.
31. Chowdhury, op. cit. p 6.
32. Cassell, Gail, "From triumph to disaster", *Chemistry & Industry*, 3 July 1995, p 532.
33. Anon, "Madman's Mayhem", *The Times of India*, 20 March 1996.
34. Anon, "Patients, Doctors Face 'The Uncertainty Of Medicine'", *Financial Times*, 30 September 1995.
35. Friend, Tim, "95% Surgical Procedures Are Experimental", *Financial Times*, 30 September 1995.
36. Wilkie, Tom, *The Human Genome Project and its Implications*, reviewed by Caroline Richmond in *The Lancet*, 29 May 1993, p 1398.
37. Davidson, Stanley, *The Principles and Practice of Medicine*, The English Language Book Society and E & S Livingstone, UK, 7th edition, 1965, p 1406.
38. Navarro, op. cit. p 31.
39. Ibid. p 35.
40. Chowdhury, op. cit. p 7.
41. Navarro, op. cit. p 72.
42. Epstein, Edward Jay, "Peddling Delusions", *New Internationalist*, October 1991, p 16.
43. See Pereira, Winin and Jeremy Seabrook, *Global Parasites*, Earthcare books, Earthcare Books, Bombay, 1994, p 168 for further details.
44. Ransom, David, "The Needle & The Damage Done", *New Internationalist*, October 1991, p 4.
45. Anon, "Alcohol Abuse In America", *Financial Times*, 1 April 1995.

46. Anon, "Tobacco-Related Deaths On The Rise", *The Times of India*, 27 November 1995.

47. Epstein, Samuel S, "Profiting From Cancer: Vested Interests And The Cancer Epidemic", *The Ecologist*, September/October 1992, p 233.

48. Smith, Carl, "Countries Accept 'Dirty Dozen' Pesticides From U.S. Shippers Despite National Bans", *Global Pesticide Campaigner*, September 1995, p 3.

49. Newman, Penny, "Killing Legally with Toxic Waste: Women and the Environment in the United States", *Development Dialogue*, Vol 1-2, 1992, p 50.

50. Anon, "Riders on the genetic storm", *New Scientist*, 10 February 1996, p 3.

51. Anon, "US Dumps Wastes on Third World", *Indian Express*, 29 June 1990.

Chapter 7: The Rights to Education and Work

1. Macaulay, Thomas Babington, "Minute on Indian Educaton", 1835, quoted in Faure, Edgar, et al, *Learning To Be: The World of Education Today & Tomorrow*, Unesco, 1972, p 10.

2. Nyerere, Julius K, *Education of Self-Reliance*, Dar es Salaam, Ministry of Information and Tourism, 1967, quoted in Faure, et al, ibid.

3. Pereira, Winin, "An Analysis of School Textbooks", Maharashtra Prabodhan Seva Mandal, Bombay, 1986.

4. Pierre, Furter, *Les Modes de Transmission*, Institut d'Etudes de Development, Switzerland, 1976.

5. The School of Barbiana, *Letter to a Teacher*, Penguin, Harmondsworth, UK, 1970.

6. Galbraith, J.K., *The New Industrial State*, Houghton Mifflin, 1967, p 370, quoted in Navarro, Vicente, *Dangerous To Your Health: Capitalism In Health Care*, Monthly Review Press, New York, 1993, p 40.

7. Chomsky, Noam, *Year 501, The Conquest Continues*, South End Press, Boston, 1993, p 18.

8. Herman, Edward S and Noam Chomsky, *Manufacturing Consent, The Political Economy Of Mass Media*, Pantheon Books, New York, 1988, p 23.

9. *Encyclopaedia Britannica*, 15th Ed, 1985, Vol 29, p 150.

10. Korten, David, "How Corporations are Colonising Classrooms", *New Economics*, Winter 1995, p 4.

11. Anon, "Copenhagen Alternative Document: An NGO Statement", *Vikalp*, Vol 4.1, 1995, p 47.

12. Sharma, L K, "Copenhagen Summit To Focus On Jobs", *The Times of India*, 27 February 1995.

13. Cox, Jane, 1995, pers. comm.

14. Dembo, David and Ward Morehouse, *The Underbelly of the U.S. Economy; Joblessness and the Pauperization of Work in America*, A special report to the National Jobs for All Coalition, Council of International and Public Affairs, The Apex Press, New York, 1995.
15. Pereira, Winin and Jeremy Seabrook, *Global Parasites*, Earthcare Books, Bombay, 1994, Chapter 6.
16. Sebastian, P A, "Social Clause", *The Times of India*, 13 February 1995.
17. Brasuell, William, "Sins Of The Fathers", *The Economist*, 10 September 1994, p 6.

Chapter 8: Cultural and Communication Rights

1. Anon, "Languages are dying out, warn linguists", *The Times of India*, 2 April 1996.
2. Greer, Germaine, *Sex and Destiny: the Politics of Human Fertility*, Secker & Warburg, London, 1984, p 386.
3. Edwards, Rob, "Pyramids Broke the Backs of Workers", *New Scientist*, 20 January 1996, p 8.
4. Greer, op. cit. p 385.
5. For a discussion on traditional technological innovations see Pereira, Winin, "From Western Science to Liberation Technology", Earthcare Books, Bombay, 1993.
6. *Encyclopaedia Britannica*, 15th Ed, 1985, Vol 18, p 35, Vol 28 p 461.
7. Herman, Edward S and Noam Chomsky, *Manufacturing Consent, The Political Economy Of Mass Media*, Pantheon Books, New York, 1988, p 13.
8. See "Time Warps", *Anusandhan*, Bombay, 6 May 1986.
9. Herman, op. cit. p xiii.
10. "Advertising Enters A New Age", *Unilever Magazine*, 1991, No 79, p 4, emphasis added.
11. "Riviera To Top The Ratings", *Unilever Magazine* 1991, No 79, p 6.
12. Anon, "Cut", *New Internationalist*, October 1990, p 27.
13. Anon, "Brewing Trouble", *The Economist*, 26 May 1990, p 70.
14. Anon, "International Giants Lobby to Stall Local Ban on Tobacco Ads", *The Economic Times*, 10 November 1994.
15. "Philips Advertisement", *The Times of India*, 16 February 1995, p 16.
16. Letter dated 12 May 1995 from The Advertising Standards Council of India, Bombay to Sachetan (NGO).
17. Raote, Dilip, "The Queue As Democracy", *The Economic Times*, 27 February 1995.
18. Trux, Jon, "Desert Storm: A Space-Age War", *New Scientist*, 27 October 1991, p 30.
19. Sinha, Dipankar, "Information Game: Lesson From Gulf War", *Economic & Political Weekly*, 4 May 1991, p 1147.

20. Gottschalk, Marie, "Operation Desert Cloud: the Media and the Gulf War", *World Policy Journal*, Summer 1992, p 451.
21. Narain, Brij, "Danger From MNCs", *Economic & Political Weekly*, 7 September 1991, p 2070.
22. "The Economist", 24 August 1991, quoted in "P&G: Invading Citizens' Privacy", *The Times of India*, 3 October 1991, p 6.
23. Edit, "Spying Business", The Economic Times, 1 March 1995.
24. Chomsky, Noam, *Year 501, The Conquest Continues*, South End Press, Boston, 1993, p 53.

Chapter 9: The Rights of Children

1. Kirpekar, Subhash, "U.N. Move On Rights Of Child Adopted", *The Times of India*, 10 March 1995.
2. "Convention on the Rights Of Child and India", *Link*, 27 March 1994, p 14.
3. Greer, Germaine, *Sex and Destiny: The Politics of Human Fertility*, Secker & Warburg, London, 1984, p 293.
4. Anon, "Smoking Mothers Kill 6000 Babies In US Every Year", *Indian Express*, 13 April 1995.
5. Quoted in "Convention on the Rights of Child and India", *Link*, 27 March 1994, p 14.
6. Anon, "Mother's Milk Can Save A Million", *The Observer Of Business & Politics*, 9 March 1992, p 8.
7. Anon, "Case Against Nestle For Violating Law On Infant Food", *Indian Express*, 28 January 1995.
8. Edmonds, Patricia, "Society Closer To The Edge Than Anybody Ever Thought", *Financial Times*, 1 April 1995.
9. The World Human Rights Conference, Project No 6, June/July 1993, p 2.
10. Edit, "Juvenile Concerns", *The Economic Times*, 5 March 1995.
11. Kuczynski, Jurgen, *A Short History of Labour Conditions in Great Britain: 1750 to the Present Day*, Frederick Muller, London, 1947, p 24.
12. Seabrook, Jeremy, "Uses And Abuses Of Childhood", *The Other Side*, April 1994, p 20.
13. Anon, "US Signs UN Agreement On Children's Rights", *Indian Express*, 18 February 1995.

Chapter 10: The Rights of Women

1. "Human Rights: Vienna Declaration, 25 June 1993", *PUCL Bulletin*, August 1993, p 27, Paragraph 9.
2. "Beijing Declaration", 1995, Paragraph 9.
3. Krishnaraj, Maithreyi, "Beijing: In Retrospect", *Humanscape*, November 1995, p 5.
4. Beijing Declaration, Paragraph 13.

5. Beijing Declaration, Paragraph 36.
6. Robert, Jean, "Genesis and Development of a Scientific Fact: The Case of Energy", *WISE*, March 1995, p 16.
7. Kishwar, Madhu, "When Daughters Are Unwanted: Sex Determination Tests In India", *Manushi*, February 1995, p 15.
8. Lingam, Lakshmi, "Sex Detection Tests and Female Foeticide—Discrimination Before Birth", *Indian Journal of Social Work*, Vol. LII, No 1, January 1991, p 13, quoted in Reproductive Rights And More, Dr Lakshmi Lingam, *Radical Journal of Health*, June 1995, p 136.
9. Williams, Gareth, "Genetic Parenthood", *New Scientist*, 19 February 1994, p 50.

Chapter 11: The Family

1. Anon, "Saying 'No' to the Notion of No-Fault Divorce", *Financial Times*, 10 February 1996.
2. Sagan, Leonard A, "Family Ties, the Real Reason People Are Living Longer", *The Sciences*, March/April 1988, p 21.

Chapter 12: The Population "Problem"

1. Greer, Germaine, *Sex and Destiny: The Politics of Human Fertility*, Secker & Warburg, London, 1984, p 339.
2. Duden, Barbara, "Population", in *The Development Dictionary*, edited by Sachs, Wolfgang, Zed Books, London, 1992, p 150.
3. Greer, op. cit. p 321.
4. Ibid. p 295.
5. Hartmann, Betsy, "Consensus and Contradiction on the Road to Cairo", *Vikalp*, October 1994, p 5.
6. Berntsen, Thorbjorn, "Challenging Traditional Growth", *Our Planet*, 7 January 1995, p 11.
7. Davis, Ged R, "Energy for Planet Earth", *Scientific American*, September 1990, p 24.
8. See Pereira, Winin, *Tending the Earth*, Earthcare Books, Mumbai, 1993, Chapter 4.
9. Boland, Reed, et al, "Honoring Human Rights In Population Policies: From Declaration To Action", *Vikalp*, October 1994, p 23.
10. Anon, "Copenhagen Alternative Document: An NGO Statement", *Vikalp*, Vol 4.1, 1995, p 47.
11. Akhter, Farida, "Issues of Woman's Health and Reproductive Rights", Draft paper, undated, p 9, quoted in Lingam, Lakshmi, "Reproductive Rights And More", *Radical Journal of Health*, June 1995, p 136.
12. Lingam, Lakshmi, "Reproductive Rights And More", *Radical Journal of Health*, June 1995, p 136.
13. Medical Reform, Canada, Vol 14, No 5, December 1994, quoted in "Surrogate Mother Deals", *Consumer Currents*, February 1995, p 1.

14. Anon, "Controlling 'Human Hens'", *Down to Earth*, 15 December 1995, p 6.
15. Greer, op. cit. p 334.
16. Chaudhuri, Sriranjan, "Study Faults Norplant Trials", *The Times of India*, 16 March 1995.
17. Klitsch, Michael, "Sterilisation without Surgery", *International Family Planning Perspectives*, Vol 8, No 3, September 1982, p 102, quoted in Greer, op. cit. p 392.
18. Anon, "American NGO Flouts Indian Laws", *The Times of India*, 30 November 1995.
19. Rai, Usha, "World Bank Finds Centochroman Too Bitter A Pill", *Indian Express*, 14 February 1995.
20. Scheinfeld, Amram, *The New You and Heredity*, New York, 1956, p 543, quoted in Greer, op. cit. p 341.
21. Greer, op. cit. p 286.
22. Ibid. p 289.
23. Ibid. p 395.
24. Rufford, Nick, "China To Ban Birth Of Babies With Defects", *The Times of India*, 11 February 1995.
25. Greer, op. cit. p 280.
26. Ibid. p 43.
27. Ibid. p 383.
28. Belich, James, *The New Zealand Wars and the Victorian Interpretation of Racial Conflict*, Auckland Univ. Press, 1986, p 299, quoted in Stannard, David E, *American Holocaust: The Conquest of the New World*, Oxford University Press, New York, 1993, p 244.
29. Greer, op. cit. p 373.
30. Lightfoot, Liz and Stuart Wavell, "Tiny Tots Lose Their Charm For U.K. Women", *The Times of India*, 19 April 1995.
31. Wullen, Carrie, "Rachel's Children: Action For Cancer Prevention", *Global Pesticide Campaigner*, September 1994, p 16.
32. Gail, Vines, "Some Of Our Sperm Are Missing", *New Scientist* 26 August 1995, p 22.
33. Sharpe, Richard M and Niels E Skakkebaek, "Are Oestrogens Involved In Falling Sperm Counts and Disorders Of The Male Reproductive Tract?", *The Lancet*, 29 May 1993, p 1392.
34. Read, Cathy, "Breast Cancer Trials: A Chemical Smokescreen", *The Ecologist*, September/October 1993, p 162.
35. Anon, "Link To Breast Cancer", *Consumer Currents*, December 1993, p 9.
36. Davis, Devra Lee and H Leon Bradlow, "Can Environmental Estrogens Cause Breast Cancer?" *Scientific American*, October 1995, p 166.
37. News notes, "Study Reveals Widespread Herbicide Contamination Of US Drinking Water", *Global Pesticide Campaigner*, December 1994, p 22.

38. News notes, "U.S. EPA Draft Dioxin Reassessment Released", *Global Pesticide Campaigner*, December 1994, p 19.

Chapter 13: The Rights of Indigenous Peoples

1. Roy Burman, B K, "Indigenous and Tribal Peoples, Global Hegemonies and Government of India", *Mainstream*, 5 September 1992, p 31.
2. de Oliveira, Carilito, cited in Preston, Julia, "Despair of Brazilian Tribe Reflected in Suicides", *Washington Post*, 20 April 1991, quoted in Bruce, Rich, *Mortgaging the Earth: The World Bank, Environmental Impoverishment and the Crisis of Development*, Earthscan, London, 1994, p 316.
3. See Pereira, Winin and Jeremy Seabrook, *Global Parasites*, Earthcare Books, Mumbai, 1994, Chapter 7.
4. Whitaker, Romulus, "Onges", *Sanctuary*, 15 June 1995, p 73.
5. Acharaya, Samir, pers. comm., 1995.
6. Sachs, Wolfgang, "One World against Many Worlds", *New Internationalist*, June 1992, p 23 quoted in Rich, Bruce, *Mortgaging the Earth: The World Bank, Environmental Impoverishment and the Crisis of Development*, Earthscan, London, 1994, p 315.
7. See Pereira, Winin, "From Western Science To Liberation Technology", Earthcare Books, Bombay, 3rd edition, 1993.
8. *Encyclopaedia Britannica*, 15th Ed, 1985, Vol 29, p 177.
9. The UN Convention on the Prevention and Punishment of the Crime of Genocide, 1948.
10. United Nations Working Group On Indigenous Peoples (UNWGIP): Report of the 12th Session 25-29, July, 1994, Geneva.
11. Ibid. Article 10.
12. Ibid. Article 36.
13. Ibid. Article 3.
14. Ibid. Article 19.
15. Ibid. Article 17.
16. Ibid. Article 25.
17. Ibid. Article 29.
18. Ibid. Statement of the Indigenous Peoples' Preparatory Meeting, p 50.

Chapter 14: The Rights and Duties of Individuals

1. *Encyclopaedia Britannica*, 15th Ed, 1985, Vol 6, p 295.

Appendix 1: The Universal Declaration of Human Rights

Appendix II: Human Rights Violations by Industrial Development

(*Note: Much of the information on local conditions has been collected by Mangesh Chavan*)

1. "ENRON: The Power To Do It All", Enron's brochure, undated.
2. "Dabhol Power Project. Proposed 2000 MW Natural Gas Based Power Plant at Dabhol, Maharashtra State, India", Environmental Impact Assessment (Rapid Study Report), Associated Industrial Consultants (India) Private Limited, June 1993.
3. Anon, "Let Them Eat Pollution", *The Economist*, 8 February 1992, p 62.
4. RC, "Reasons and Considerations Touching Upon the Lawfulness of Removing Out of England into the Parts of America", 1832, quoted in Stannard, David E, *American Holocaust: The Conquest of the New World*, Oxford University Press, New York, 1992, p 235.
5. Anon, "Dabhol Sets The Record Straight On Environmental Issues", *The Asian Age*, 15 May 1995.
6. Testimony by Linda F Powers before the Committee on Appropriations, Subcommittee on Foreign Operations, US House of Representatives, 31 January 1995.
7. Vad, G C and D B Parasnis, ed., "Selections from the Satara Raja's and the Peshwa's Diaries", quoted in Fukazawa, Hiroshi, *The Medieval Deccan: Peasants, Social Systems and States, Sixteenth to Eighteenth Centuries*, Oxford University Press, New Delhi, 1991, p 188.
8. Writ Petition No 1694 of 1994, in the Bombay High Court, Chargaon Sangharsha Samiti & Others vs The State of Maharashtra & Others.
9. Parkman, Francis, *The Conspiracy of Pontiac and the Indian War after the Conquest of Canada*, Scribner, 1915, quoted in Stannard, David E, *American Holocaust: The Conquest Of The New World*, Oxford University Press, New York, 1992, p 245.
10. The Maharashtra Industrial Development Act, 1961, Government of Maharashtra, Bombay.
11. Date, Vidyadhar, "Enron project work to begin soon", *The Times of India*, 5 September 1994.
12. Writ Petition No 2735 of 1994, in the Bombay High Court, Ganapat Dhondu Bhuvad & Others vs State of Maharashtra & Others.
13. Noorani, A G, "Right To Assembly", *Economic & Political Weekly*, 1 July 1995, p 1549.
14. Hall, G Stanley, *Adolescence: its Psychology and Its Relations to Physiology, Anthropology, Sociology, Sex, Crime, Religion, and Education*, Vol 2, D Appleton and Co, N York, 1904, p 651, quoted in Stannard, David E, *American Holocaust: The Conquest Of The New World*, Oxford University Press, New York, 1992, p 245.
15. Fleming, John, "The Houston Chronicle, November 1, 1995 quoted in Trade Follows The Flag, Or Is It The Other Way Around?", *CounterPunch*, No 4.
16. Ginsborg, Paul, *A History of Contemporary Italy*, Penguin Books, Harmondsworth, UK, 1990, p 77.

17. Anon, "Labour Bias", *The Economic Times*, 27 December 1994.
18. Anon, "The Power Of Truth", *The Times of India*, 1 June 1995.
19. Kirpekar, Subhash, "No Objection To Review Of Enron Project", *The Times of India*, 14 April 1995.
20. Mokhiber, Ralph, *Corporate Crime and Violence: Big Business Power and the Abuse of Public Trust*, Sierra Club Books, San Francisco, 1988, Chapter 14.
21. Bhat, Shrikant, "The Right To Know", *Indian Express*, 12 April 1995.
22. Quoted in Takaki, Ronald T., *Iron Cages: Race and Culture in 19th Century America*, cf. Stannard, David E, *American Holocaust: The Conquest Of The New World*, Oxford University Press, New York, 1992, p 240.
23. Quoted in Evans, Raymond, et al, *Exclusion, Exploitation, and Extermination: Race Relations in Colonial Queensland*, cf. Stannard, David E, *American Holocaust: The Conquest of the New World*, Oxford University Press, New York, 1992, p 244.
24. Parkman, Francis, *The Conspiracy of Pontiac and the Indian War after the Conquest of Canada*, Scribner, 1915, cf. Stannard, David E, *American Holocaust: The Conquest of the New World*, Oxford University Press, New York, 1992, p 244.
25. Howells, William Dean, "A Sennight of the Centennial", *Atlantic Monthly*, July 1876, cf. Stannard, David E, *American Holocaust: The Conquest of the New World*, Oxford University Press, New York, 1992, p 245.
26. Quoted in Dyer, *Thomas G, Theodore Roosevelt and the Idea of Race*, 1980, cf. Stannard, David E, American Holocaust: *The Conquest of the New World*, Oxford University Press, New York, 1992, p 246.
27. Quoted in Morison, Samuel Eliot, ed., *Journals and Other Documents on the Life and Voyages of Christofer Columbus*, 1963, cf. Stannard, David E, *American Holocaust: The Conquest of the New World*, Oxford University Press, New York, 1992, p 63.
28. Quoted in Takaki, Ronald T, *Iron Cages: Race and Culture in 19th Century America*, 1979, cf. Stannard, David E, *American Holocaust: The Conquest of the New World*, Oxford University Press, New York, 1992, p 240.
29. A former US Secretary of Agriculture, Earl Butz, said "Food is a weapon", quoted in Berry, Wendell, *The Unsettling of America: Culture & Agriculture*, Sierra Club Books, San Francisco, 1986, p 8.

Index